FOUCAULT AND THE POLITICS OF RIGHTS

FOUCAULT

AND THE

POLITICS

OF RIGHTS

BEN GOLDER

STANFORD UNIVERSITY PRESS
STANFORD, CALIFORNIA

Stanford University Press
Stanford, California

Printed in the United States of America on acid-free, archival-quality paper

Library of Congress Cataloging-in-Publication Data

Golder, Ben, author.
 Foucault and the politics of rights / Ben Golder.
    pages cm
 Includes bibliographical references and index.
 ISBN 978-0-8047-8934-9 (cloth : alk. paper)--ISBN 978-0-8047-9649-1 (pbk. : alk. paper)
 1. Human rights--Philosophy. 2. Foucault, Michel, 1926-1984--Political and social views. I. Title.
 JC571G623 2015
 323.01--dc23

                         2015019552

 ISBN 978-0-8047-9651-4 (electronic)

Typeset by Bruce Lundquist in 10/14 Minion Pro

For Emily

CONTENTS

ACKNOWLEDGMENTS

Over the course of writing this book I have accrued a significant number of personal and institutional debts. The following thanks are an insufficient attempt to repay these debts, but I shall try anyway.

Work on the manuscript commenced in earnest while I was the recipient of a Law School Research Fellowship at the Faculty of Law, University of New South Wales (UNSW), and continued while I was on sabbatical in 2012, hosted first at the University of Technology, Sydney (UTS) Faculty of Law and then at the Center for the Study of Law & Society at Boalt Hall, UC Berkeley. I am deeply grateful for the hospitality and the institutional and intellectual support provided by my hosts at both these institutions. I am also very grateful to Chrissie, Robert, and Alister for housing, feeding, and looking after us all in California.

Parts of the manuscript were first presented as seminar papers at a number of universities and research institutes. I am grateful to the organizers of the relevant seminar series or workshop for the invitation to present this work, and to the audience on each occasion for their critical engagement with it. These institutions include: Birkbeck College School of Law, Julius Stone Institute (University of Sydney); Socio-Legal Research Centre (Griffith University); UNSW Law, Institute for International Law and the Humanities (University of Melbourne); UTS Faculty of Law, Centre for Post-Colonial and Globalisation Studies (University of South Australia); and the Legal Intersections Research Centre (University of Wollongong). Parts of the manuscript were also presented at meetings of the following conferences: the American Political Science Association (Seattle and Washington DC), the Foucault Circle (Alberta and Malmö), the Law and Society Association of Australia and New Zealand (Wellington), the Australian Society of Legal Philosophy (Melbourne), and the Australasian Society for Continental Philosophy (Brisbane).

Some of the ideas worked out in greater depth in the following pages, and often in very different directions, were first broached in the following publications: "Foucault and the Unfinished Human of Rights," *Law, Culture and the Humanities* 6, no. 3 (2010): 354–74; "Foucault's Critical (Yet Ambivalent) Affirmation: Three Figures of Rights," *Social & Legal Studies* 20, no. 3 (2011): 283–312; "Foucault, Rights, and Freedom," *International Journal for the Semiotics of Law* 26, no. 1 (2013): 5–21; and "What Is an Anti-Humanist Human Rights?," *Social Identities* 16, no. 5 (2010): 651–68.

Several friends and colleagues were very generous with their advice and support at the beginning of the project. These include Eve Darian-Smith, Stuart Elden, Peter Fitzpatrick, Colin Gordon, Bonnie Honig, Martin Krygier, Bronwen Morgan, Pat O'Malley, Austin Sarat, Miguel Vatter, and Karen Zivi. Some of these scholars and others had draft chapters inflicted upon them and cheerfully bore the imposition; these include Stuart Elden, Peter Fitzpatrick, Colin Gordon, Bonnie Honig, Martin Krygier, Jane McAdam, Daniel McLoughlin, Pat O'Malley, and Karen Zivi. I am particularly grateful to Marcelo Hoffman, Samuel Moyn, Paul Patton, and Jessica Whyte, each of whom read the draft manuscript in its entirety and made a range of criticisms and suggestions for improvement. I was blessed to have as peer reviewers Colin Koopman and Samuel Chambers, who read the manuscript on behalf of Stanford University Press. They have been, in print and in person, unfailingly incisive in their critiques and consistently generous in their suggestions for reading and revision. This book also bears the imprint of sustained conversations about not just Foucault but the politics of rights more broadly with three friends in particular. I have learned more from Daniel McLoughlin, Illan rua Wall, and Jessica Whyte than it is possible to explicitly record here, although the pages that follow do so implicitly, I believe. I have benefited in innumerable ways from the vibrant collegiality, intellectual culture, camaraderie, and good sense of my colleagues in the Gilbert + Tobin Centre of Public Law as well as UNSW Law more broadly. Among the contributions of many excellent colleagues, the sustaining friendship of Michael Handler since I started at UNSW Law deserves special mention—thanks for everything, Mike. Thank you, finally, to Emily-Jane Cohen at Stanford University Press for her support of the project and her excellent editorship, and to Dr. John Golder (Dad) for *his* excellent editing of the manuscript.

It is customary in these pages to thank one's immediate family for granting a reprieve from the routines of parental life, and for allowing an absent academic parent conveniently to remove him or herself to an attic in the home stretch. Certainly I need to thank Mum and Dad again for their love over the years (and for so reliably and beautifully caring for my children over the last six in particular). But in reality I cannot thank Phoebe and Leo for going away because, thankfully, they went nowhere. And let me go nowhere. While not versed in the finer points of Foucault (although like all children they are active and rambunctious rights claimants), Phoebe and Leo animate the pages that follow and give meaning to the work it represents. But when all is said and done, it is their mother for whom every word is written and who makes it all possible. Like the last one and the next, this book is dedicated to her with all my love and thanks.

FOUCAULT AND THE POLITICS OF RIGHTS

INTRODUCTION

I try to consider human rights in their historical reality while not admitting that there is a human nature.

Michel Foucault

The Impossible Object of a Foucauldian Politics of Rights?

The anthropologist Clifford Geertz's well-known review of Michel Foucault's *Discipline and Punish* in the *New York Review of Books* in 1978 opens with the following tart, yet characteristically acute, observation:

> Michel Foucault erupted onto the intellectual scene at the beginning of the Sixties with his *Folie et déraison*, an unconventional but still reasonably recognizable history of the Western experience of madness. He has become, in the years since, a kind of impossible object: a nonhistorical historian, an anti-humanistic human scientist, and a counter-structuralist structuralist.[1]

It could not have been apparent to Geertz in 1978, but today, with the benefit of hindsight, we might add to his list of putative paradoxes the even more surprising figure of Foucault the political defender of rights. Indeed, as many readers of Foucault have noticed in the thirty-seven years since Geertz's review, something quite remarkable happens in Foucault's work from the mid- to late 1970s onward. Having made up to that point in his career a series of powerful critiques of the philosophical presuppositions of rights, Foucault begins increasingly to make appeals to the discourse of rights. He does so in philosophical work that engages with rights as a subject of analysis, but also in more directly political texts such as his often co-signed or collaboratively authored activist statements, interviews, and journalistic interventions. What may account for this puzzling shift from an iconoclastic anti-humanism and imperviousness to rights talk to a seemingly liberal defense of the classical Enlightenment tradition (of the rights of prison inmates, sexual minorities, asylum seekers, and many more besides)—and this in such a staggeringly short period of time? What happens to Foucault in this interim? Does he recant and revise his former critical positions, acceding to a liberal politics of rights, or is there something else at work in the later body of work, in this curious Foucauldian *Spätstil*?

This is a book about Foucault and the politics of rights. As to the latter, we are frequently told in tones either celebratory or skeptical that we live today (and have for some time now) in the age of rights.[2] The phrase implies that rights function as the dominant contemporary political idiom—as something much like what Jean-Paul Sartre, speaking of Marxist communism in postwar France, once famously called "the unsurpassable horizon of our time."[3] All manner of claims for justice—social and transitional, individual and communal—are made in the name of rights, channeled through their particular juridico-institutional avenues, stamped with their moral imprimatur. One index of the success of this discourse of rights—best exemplified in today's ideologically hegemonic version of rights, namely, human rights—is the extent to which even those critical thinkers routinely suspicious of claims to universality, of liberal *doxa* concerning the subject of rights, and of the constraints of "juridifying" political claims through rights and law,[4] have nevertheless themselves come to accept rights as forming some part of a critical, radical, or left politics. Of course, such "acceptances" of rights are nuanced and often ambivalent encounters, and accordingly need to be understood both in terms of the historical location of the theorist as well as the political work that rights are said to perform in their theory. Nevertheless, the phenomenon of what Costas Douzinas has recently called "rights revisionism"[5] on the left is an observable and remarkable one in the thought of thinkers as diverse as Claude Lefort, Jean-François Lyotard, and Étienne Balibar in the 1980s and 1990s,[6] as well as in the more contemporary work of Jacques Rancière, Judith Butler, and Slavoj Žižek.[7] Rights emerge in these varied accounts not as an end in themselves but rather as a tactical means, as an opening to other forms of emancipation, rearticulation, and struggle—that is, as representing some form of political possibility, whereas hitherto they had merely represented a blockage, an obstacle, an ideological mystification, or an unhelpful displacement of political energies onto legal-formalist terrain.

Foucault, as we have observed, is a thinker who in his late work makes a surprising turn to rights. This book presents an account of that body of work and proposes a reading of it. But in addition to being a study in the philosopher's late political thought—which articulates a specifically Foucauldian politics of rights—it also uses the particular case of Foucault to reflect more broadly upon the phenomenon of "rights revisionism" just instanced—and thereby to begin to provide an assessment of the political possibilities (and limitations) of such a return to rights. The first task is interpretive, the second more diagnostic and reflective. The book has two aims therefore: I want first, by reconstructing from a number of Foucault's different writings, to explain exactly what I mean by the notion of a "Foucauldian politics of rights" in the late work and hence distinguish it from a range of other possible approaches to rights politics. I shall very shortly come to describe Foucault's own approach, but for now let me simply signal that the interpretation pursued in the following pages is one of a critical politics of rights: anti-foundationalist, non-anthropologically grounded, openly political, and tactically oriented toward intervening into existing formations of law, state, and power. In other words, I do not read Foucault's turn to rights as simply coincident with liberalism but rather as critically engaged with (and transformative of) it. Second, however, and simultaneous with the above task of explanation, I want to begin to analyze both the possibilities opened up and the limits encountered by such a politics. As a result, this book is simultaneously expository and analytical—I am concerned to construct a plausible interpretation of Foucault's theorization and deployment of rights in the late work but, at the same time, to submit this very understanding of Foucault's politics of rights to critique as the argument develops. The first task raises interpretive questions—just what is a Foucauldian politics of rights and how can it be understood in light of his work as a whole?—while the second broaches a range of wider but also more directly political questions. If, as I shall argue, Foucault can be understood to be making critical and tactical interventions into rights discourse, then what precisely is the value of such an engagement? How might such a politics navigate the dangers of co-optation by the hegemonic force of rights? What is gained and/or lost in the political encounter with rights, and do we thereby relinquish the possibility of thinking a political alternative to rights? In thinking rights differently and critically, do the possibilities of alternative organizations and figurations of the political become fainter? Here my reading of Foucault will also be a historical, symptomatic one, in which Foucault's critical yet ambivalent engagement with rights will be seen to index wider changes in the culture of rights criticism—changes which continue to structure and animate many contemporary approaches today.

There are at least two ways to grasp Foucault's importance to, and distinctiveness within, this broader tendency within political theory toward critically re-engaging with rights. The first of these approaches is simply to read Foucault alongside a range of other theorists who deploy rights in a similar way. This body of work includes thinkers influenced by Foucault or who reacted to him, as well as thinkers from different or theoretically opposed schools of thought whose thought parallels, complements, or challenges Foucault on rights. Accordingly, in the chapters that follow, I read Foucault alongside (and sometimes against) important figures in contemporary philosophy and political theory such as Wendy Brown, Judith Butler, and Jacques Rancière, as well as work within and indebted to the Marxist tradition and recent contributions within the field of critical legal theory that take up the work of Foucault's contemporary, the radical lawyer Jacques Vergès. My intention is to situate Foucault within a political theoretical tradition that critically engages with and deploys rights, showing how his thought impacts upon and is impacted by others thinking along similar yet sometimes opposed lines. This is obviously one way to avoid the mistake of treating Foucault in conceptual isolation from other innovators on the political terrain of rights and, in the process, to tell a richer story both about Foucault and his relation to this broader critical tendency of which he is a part.

But the second way is not so much, or at least not primarily, conceptual as it is historical. This second approach is reflected in a burgeoning body of literature—in history, obviously, but also in law and political theory—that addresses itself to the question of the origins of contemporary human rights discourse. This scholarship intersects both methodologically and substantively with the account of Foucault that I provide in this book. The methodological question revolves around the political value and effect of genealogy as a mode of historical inquiry. Writing in 2012, the historian of human rights Samuel Moyn observed that "the historiography of human rights is currently in great ferment. Scarcely a decade ago, the field did not exist."[8] That it exists today cannot be credited solely to Moyn, of course, but that it has grown exponentially (especially since the publication of his book *The Last Utopia: Human Rights in History* in 2010) probably can. As Philip Alston recently put it (in the context of a critique of Moyn's work), "there is a struggle for the soul of the human rights movement, and it is being waged in large part through the proxy of genealogy."[9] Moyn's provocative book catalyzed that genealogical struggle, fomenting political and philosophical disagreement about the ends of human rights in and on the terrain of history. Briefly, *The Last Utopia* proposes a bold, revisionist understanding of the origin of contemporary human rights discourse that, instead of connecting it (as did previous historical accounts) to ancient sources in Western civilization (Micheline Ishay), the French Revolution and the American Declaration of Independence (Lynn Hunt), or the Holocaust (Michael Ignatieff), locates it much more recently and contingently in the late 1970s as a response to the failure of the dream of revolution.[10] That Moyn and others have troubled the triumphalist and teleological certitude of orthodox accounts of human rights, and have spurred rival and competing attempts to renarrate the origins of human rights, speaks to the productivity of genealogy as a critical tool. Yet more important than the methodological stakes of these histories (to this book, at any rate) is the substantive historical context that they provide. On Moyn's reading, human rights emerge in the vacuum left by the collapse of faith in the dream of revolution in the West. Human rights come to prominence as a form of moralistic anti-politics precisely in reaction to the "demise of the revolutionary privilege,"[11] and in the late 1970s there takes place a transfer of utopian energies and investments from revolution to compliance with international human rights law. The present book is not a work of history, but it is nevertheless important to locate Foucault historically. Rather obviously, his critical innovations with rights take place at the same time as the historical shift that Moyn describes is unfolding. Can Foucault's engagements with rights accordingly be read through the lens of a failed revolutionary utopia and a return to liberalism, or does he try to navigate a critical space between liberalism and revolution? If so, what are the nuances and ambivalences of Foucault's position and how can his experimental and evolving politics of rights be understood in relation to his present—and ultimately, to ours?

But this is already to get a little ahead of myself, for these are questions that will emerge as my account of Foucault's politics of rights develops throughout the book (and that will culminate in its final chapter). How, then, do I understand Foucault's approach to the question of rights? To foreshadow the argument of the coming chapters, let me say that I echo Foucault's own words and call it a *critical counter-conduct* of rights.[12] In my view, it is indisputable that Foucault engages much more (and much more seriously) with rights discourse in the period after the mid-1970s than in the preceding years. However, this engagement, *pace* many of Foucault's readers, can neither be easily reduced to a straightforward acceptance of individualist liberal rights discourse nor to an endorsement of the regnant pieties of contemporary human rights talk. (Or, at any rate, it cannot be so reduced without losing sight of a significant part of what Foucault was hoping to achieve.) In my view, Foucault seeks instrumentally to deploy rights in the service of particular political struggles in the years following the mid-1970s, but in so doing he has in mind a more critical and contestatory agenda—an agenda transformative both of power relations and of the relations to self that they engender and rely upon—than is encompassed either by liberalism or by orthodox mainstream human rights thinking. On my reading, there is indeed a shift in his late work concerning rights, but it does not amount to a radical break with, and rejection of, his previous methods and concerns. Rather, Foucault now better perceives the ways in which rights can function to contest and remake relations of power—but without ever losing sight of their (often paradoxical) limitations. His is a critical, but often quite ambivalent, appropriation of rights discourse. Rights emerge in Foucault's (later) account as potentially useful, tactical instruments in political struggle, as political tools immanent and not exterior to the field of political combat. (That is, as we shall shortly see, precisely as amenable to forms of counter-conduct in the language of the late work.)

Many readers of Foucault maintain that he makes a return to rights in the late work that is indicative of a shift in his political stance toward liberalism (a kind of détente or rapprochement). I disagree with both these positions. First, and bearing in mind the earlier work, Foucault's late engagement with rights cannot exactly be called a form of return or of "rights revisionism," as he does not express a clear (and hence revisable) view on rights prior to this point. Rights simply do not figure prominently enough in his earlier work for us to be able to make such a claim. What he does express is a critique of the philosophical presuppositions of liberal rights discourse—which has led many to style him as a rights critic, or cynic, by which is usually meant one who rejects rights out of hand. My account stresses both a continuity and a development; in the late work, Foucault maintains his earlier critiques but now tries to show how rights as political instruments can be understood differently and can in this light form part of critical political struggles. From this it follows that his late articulation of rights surely does not betoken some shift to liberalism, if what is meant by this is an embrace of the sovereign subject and an individualist ontology. Rather, he consistently refutes these intellectual positions. But we have to be careful here to do justice to Foucault's position, for to deny that he adopts or comes closer to adopting a "liberal" position in this philosophical or ideological sense is not to rule out any critical engagement with, or adaptation of, the historical and contemporary resources of liberalism. Liberalism, Foucault insists in his 1979 Collège de France lecture course, "The Birth of Biopolitics," is not—or is not only—an ideology or a theory about the relation between the individual and the state or civil society. It is also, and more importantly, a set of practices and a way of governing and of conducting the relations between individuals, civil society, and the state. For Foucault, that is, liberalism primarily represents a form of governmentality and not a theory of the subject.[13] Rights are a key political technology within the repertoire of liberal practices of rule, and so just as he proposes to reunderstand and reappropriate elements of rights discourse, this also means that he enters onto the terrain of liberalism and works within and against its practices. Such a position reflects my understanding both of Foucault's concept of critique and of his methodological orientation toward practice. Foucault was indeed a critic of the liberal tradition (and consistently of its core philosophical tenets) well into the late work, but his critique is neither equivalent to rejection nor exclusive of adaptation or subversive borrowings from that tradition.

But perhaps it would be sensible to begin by taking a few steps back, in order to explain why the idea of Foucault as a rights theorist, or further, as a political advocate of rights, might strike many, if not most, of his readers today as a somewhat counterintuitive idea. After all, wasn't the philosopher a radical critic of rights, a poststructuralist undoer of the sovereign subject, indeed, even—*horribile dictu*—a denier of law's emancipatory possibilities? What is it that makes a specifically Foucauldian politics of rights seem so unlikely—or even, in Clifford Geertz's terms, "impossible"?

The beginnings of an answer to this initial question can be found in the scholarship for which Foucault continues to be best known in the humanities and social sciences, namely, his mid-1970s work on the political technologies of modernity.[14] Foucault's Nietzschean genealogies of the power to punish (in the book *Discipline and Punish*, for example), his brief but posthumously influential sketches of biopolitics (in the first volume of the *History of Sexuality* and in his 1976 Collège de France lectures), and his more detailed (and similarly influential) histories of changing forms of late modern and contemporary governmental reason and practice (in his 1978 and 1979 Collège lectures on governmentality)[15] represent the body of work—Foucault's genealogies and "power analytics"[16]—that for the majority of his readers is the most explicitly political. It is in this political corpus that Foucault treats questions of power— famously conceived as neither a thing nor a capacity but rather, after Nietzsche, as a complex, contingent, and fluctuating relation between forces. This body of work on power, much commented upon and critiqued in the post-Foucauldian literature, is distinguished by several methodological and substantive features, many of which I propose to discuss in the coming chapters. For the moment, however, let me simply note two that best clarify the reasons why the notion of Foucault as a theorist (or more peculiarly, as a proponent or advocate) of rights politics is so unlikely. The first is his critique of foundationalist understandings of subjectivity, and the second is his critique of traditional conceptions of sovereign power. Each of these critiques engages key components of an orthodox liberal account of rights. It is my contention that, in order to make a proper evaluation of Foucault's late deployment of rights, it is necessary to understand his theoretical objections to the orthodox liberal discourse of rights. Let me introduce these critiques briefly, starting with the question of the subject.

In short, Foucault's work of this period (indeed, both his earlier and later work) decenters the privileged position of the sovereign subject as a knowing and acting agent. As is now very well known, his 1970s work on rationalities and technologies of power (discipline, biopolitics, apparatuses of security) consistently maintains that subjects do not pre-exist the world, but rather are fashioned within it; subjects are "created," "fabricated,"[17] constituted by formations of power and regimes of truth. Any number of Foucault's statements in this period could attest to this, but perhaps the most often cited come from a series of admonitory "methodological precautions" given during his 1976 lecture course at the Collège de France, titled "'Society Must Be Defended.'" There he cautions against understanding "the individual as a sort of elementary nucleus, a primitive atom or some multiple, inert matter to which power is applied, or which is struck by a power that subordinates or destroys individuals." For Foucault, the subject is not "elementary"; it has no special, ontological status prior to its emergence in relations of power. There is no essence to the subject. Power in this view does not repress or disallow a pre-existing subjective essence; rather, it is that which itself enables the subject to appear, permitting "bodies, gestures, discourses, and desires to be identified and constituted as something individual" in the first place.[18]

Foucault's sustained critique of subjectivity—a critique consistently maintained, and yet modulated and variously articulated throughout his work—is a much-rehearsed (and -caricatured) topic in the critical literature, where may be found any number of solemn pronouncements on the dire ethical and political ramifications of such a pernicious doctrine that the subject is made and not given. For such readers, Foucault evacuates the position of the subject and into the resulting normative void slides every possibility of ethical responsibility, self-reflection, agency, engagement, critique, resistance, or progressive social and political change.[19] The overheated charges of nihilism, paralysis, and quietism leveled at much French poststructuralist philosophy and social theory (especially Foucault's) from the 1960s onward are doubtless familiar enough today to need no further elaboration here, but I shall touch upon Foucault's critique of subjectivity in later chapters and there look to problematize some of these statements. For now, it suffices to note that Foucault's position on the subject commits him to rejecting any universal constant in human affairs ("All my analyses are against the idea of universal necessities in human existence," he insists)[20] and to denying that the subject can be simplistically and unproblematically opposed to relations of power that challenge it from the outside, as it were. Rather, for Foucault, subjects and power relations are imbricated and co-constitutive.

We can immediately see that from the perspective of liberal political theory and its traditional understanding of the grounds and functions of modern rights discourse, these two tenets are deeply problematic. As regards the first of these, philosopher Paul Patton writes succinctly:

> Foucault is well known for his reluctance to rely upon any . . . universalist concept of human nature or human essence. By contrast, the predominant approach to the nature of rights in contemporary moral and political philosophy supposes that these inhere in individuals by virtue of some universal "rights bearing" feature of human nature, such as sentience, rationality, interests or the capacity to form and pursue projects.[21]

We might add to Patton's list that in the case of human rights today it is the supposed mere fact of our being human,[22] and not the manifestation of a given feature or capacity, that qualifies us as rights holders. However, as regards the second Foucauldian tenet, namely, that subjects cannot be ontologically separated from or straightforwardly opposed to relations of power from which they need protection or sheltering, we can see immediately that this also challenges a core understanding of liberal political thinking about rights. From this latter perspective, rights are supposed to reflect and protect the originary freedom of the subject (as against other subjects and the community at large). In her essay "Law, Boundaries, and the Bounded Self," for example, legal theorist Jennifer Nedelsky meditates at length upon the imaginative properties of the idea of the boundary "as a central metaphor in the legal rhetoric of freedom." She writes: "Everyone is familiar with, or at least would immediately recognize as intelligible, the image of rights as boundaries defining the sphere within which human autonomy (or freedom or privacy) resides. Certainly within Anglo-American legal theory that image is routine."[23] Nedelsky is surely right: the texts of law and liberal political theory are undoubtedly suffused with spatial metaphors (such as spheres, boundaries, zones, and limits) and the ontologically bounded subject they imply and re-perform. Moreover, these texts themselves function rhetorically through the very mobilization of such metaphors. Whereas in much liberal political thought, then, the subject of rights is presupposed as ontologically prior to and separate from the relations of power that compose the society in which that subject finds herself (and rights accordingly emerge as beneficial juridical tools to facilitate and mediate that separation, to protect or carve out a zone of liberty, privacy, and so forth), Foucault's position on the production of the subject in and through relations of power fundamentally challenges this core conception of orthodox liberal rights theory. We can thus appreciate how Foucault's critique of subjectivity undoes any easy justificatory resort to the familiar "grounds" of rights. Indeed, it goes further in reversing the assumptions embedded in the radical separatism (of the subject from surrounding power relations) characteristic of liberal rights discourse. Instead, Foucault points to both the connectedness and constructedness of subjects in and through rights. This might seem an unpropitious start to the task of trying to conceive of Foucault as a rights theorist or advocate, but it will be recalled that a moment ago I introduced a second (and related) objection—or rather, a second theoretical challenge—that Foucault issues to conventional liberal rights discourse. Foucault, that is, provides us not only with a critique of the subject but with a critique of sovereign power.

Foucault's analysis and critique of sovereign power is a topic to which I shall turn at length in Chapter 1. For now, I simply want to touch upon several aspects of this work that pose cognate problems to those raised by the critique of subjectivity just discussed—that is, potential stumbling blocks to conceiving of Foucault as a rights theorist. To start with, Foucault's critique of sovereign power—work largely conducted in the 1970s, the "middle phase" of his career—takes issue with the model of sovereignty for understanding how power functions in modern society. This problematization of sovereignty as an organizing principle for the analysis of power relations, and its ultimate inadequacy to the task of comprehending the actual movements of power in the modern world, is frequently expressed in what are now very well known and oft-cited decapitatory metaphors. "In political thought and analysis," Foucault remarks famously in the first volume of the *History of Sexuality*, "we still have not cut off the head of the king."[24] Again, in a 1977 interview titled "Truth and Power," he urges: "We need to cut off the King's head: in political theory that has still to be done."[25] What he means by inciting this act of analytic regicide is that the theoretical model of the sovereign who speaks the law and whose imperative commands are issued to his subjects in a restraining, negative, repressive, and top-down manner—imperatives obeying the juridical, sanctioning form of "a law which says no"[26]—fails to capture the actual dimensions of the modern exercise of power.

For Foucault, the discourse of sovereignty and the understanding of power it relies upon (and reproduces) first emerge in the historical context of the Middle Ages and are connected to the shape and function of monarchical institutions at that time. Indeed, according to him, the monarchy originally "made itself acceptable by allocating itself a juridical and negative function," mediating between warring feudal parties by deploying the threat of juridical sanctions so as to "put an end to war, violence and pillage."[27] This particular "system of representation of power" then gets redeployed and extended in the "subsequent era" by the "classical theoreticians of right"[28]—social contract thinkers of the seventeenth century such as Thomas Hobbes and John Locke, and then Jean-Jacques Rousseau in the eighteenth century—who come to understand power in terms of a discourse of sovereign legitimacy. When is the exercise of sovereign power justified and legitimate? When must the subject obey? The figure of the sovereign and his legitimate rights (and, conversely, the subject's rights vis-à-vis the sovereign) provided the model for answering these questions. That is, for Foucault, these "great edifices of juridical thought and . . . knowledge" (Hobbes's *Leviathan*, Locke's *Second Treatise*) functioned at one and the same time both to justify the existence of sovereign power and to police its limits:

> Either it had to be demonstrated that royal power . . . was perfectly in keeping with a basic right; or it had to be demonstrated that the power of the sovereign had to be limited, that it had to submit to certain rules, and that, if that power were to retain its legitimacy, it had to be exercised within certain limits.[29]

In Foucault's view, "from the Middle Ages onward, the essential role of the theory of right has been to establish the legitimacy of power."[30] As he sees it, from the Middle Ages through the classical era of social contract thinking to the modern state, political theory has "never ceased to be obsessed with the person of the sovereign"[31] and in so doing has simply supplied itself with a succession of inapt sovereign avatars (King, Leviathan, State) that fail to apprehend the actual exercise of power. As he puts it in "Truth and Power," "to pose the problem in terms of the State means to continue posing it in terms of sovereign and sovereignty."[32] But—and this is crucial for Foucault—these theoretical models fail to grasp the way in which power actually functions in modernity. In texts from the mid-1970s onward, especially *Discipline and Punish* and the first volume of the *History of Sexuality*, Foucault provides a contrary account of the way in which modern power functions—namely, through juridically unauthorized and asymmetrical relations of discipline and biopolitics that subsist alongside or underneath the majestic spectacle of the sovereign discourse of right. As he famously says of discipline, "the real, corporal disciplines constituted the foundation of the formal, juridical liberties. . . . The 'Enlightenment,' which discovered the liberties, also invented the disciplines."[33]

In conclusion, Foucault's thinking seems to undermine a resort to rights. Surely, a common argument would have it, for a politics of rights to be effective one must begin by assuming a stable and delimitable "ground"—an ascertainable subject of rights, an intentional, autonomous, and willing political actor in whose name rights are claimed and protected. "A long and distinguished tradition of modern, normative social criticism and historical interpretation," writes social theorist Nancy Fraser, "has developed around the humanist notions of autonomy, reciprocity, mutual recognition, dignity and human rights . . . [which] derives its normative force from . . . a metaphysics [of subjectivity]."[34] And yet, as we have just seen, Foucault begins precisely by seeking to displace and to trouble such assumptions about subjectivity: subjects (of rights) are neither prior to nor severable from surrounding networks of power but are indeed the very "effects" of them. Ultimately, for Fraser (and many others), this means that in rejecting these hallowed humanist premises Foucault dangerously leaves himself with "no foundation for critique."[35] To complicate matters further, Foucault's critique of sovereign power and his alternative conception of power as alternately disciplinary and biopolitical refuse the very concept of rights as a way of codifying or understanding power. If the discourse of rights cannot comprehend the operative movements of discipline, or of biopolitics— worse, if rights are in fact masking these very movements, or are in some way complicit with them—then of what use is a politics of rights in combating or reframing these relations? Can rights, as is claimed, even be said to mitigate the effect of power relations or protect the subject from them? We have returned, it seems, to Geertz's initial and unpromising summary verdict of impossibility. With what sense can Foucault himself plausibly talk of rights, or we today talk of a "Foucauldian politics of rights"? Very little, it would seem. As Joan Reynolds observes, expressing a widely held view, "To think of Foucault as a champion of human rights [and, we might add, rights more broadly] seems fraught with contradiction, if not downright perverse."[36]

Foucault's Curious Deployments of Rights

Of course, as seasoned readers of Foucault will already know, "contradiction" and "perversity" are the kinds of judgments that have routinely been made either of Foucault's political theorizations per se or of his concrete interventions into particular political questions and controversies of the day. Moreover, it is very often the case that Foucault's well-known theoretical positions on discourse, power, and the subject are themselves thought to render difficult—indeed, perhaps even contradictory or perverse—the kinds of political commitment and activity in which he nevertheless frequently engages. Often Foucault's particular political interventions are read as symptomatic of a disavowed normativity that he fails to confront or thematize in his theoretical work. This is the thesis of Foucault's "cryptonormativity" pursued by Jürgen Habermas, for example, who asserts that Foucault operates according to a hidden normative agenda. Alternatively, Foucault's interventions are read as revealing a split between the order of philosophy and that of politics, between his theory and his practice, between his words and his deeds.[37] This is definitely the case with the reception and understanding of Foucault's own late deployment of rights.

Against the background of these concerns, and in the light of his twin criticisms of the metaphysics of subjectivity and of the model of sovereignty over a number of years, Foucault begins to resort increasingly to the discourse of rights in his political, journalistic, and philosophical work of the mid- to late 1970s and into the early 1980s, before his death in 1984. This is no doubt a relatively short period of time, but this particular aspect of Foucault's work is nonetheless noticeable, remarkable, and illustrative of important dimensions of his broader approach to theorizing power and practicing politics.

Many commentators on Foucault's late deployment of rights discourse have located a retrospective "origin" for his "turn" to rights discourse buried in his closing comments to the second lecture of his 1976 Collège de France lectures.[38] There, having just made the argument—in line with his critique of sovereignty outlined above—that because "right, the famous old formal, bourgeois right . . . is in reality the right of sovereignty" and that "having recourse to sovereignty against discipline will not enable us to limit the effects of disciplinary power," he goes on to suggest that

> if we are to struggle against disciplines, or rather against disciplinary power, in our search for a nondisciplinary power, we should not be turning to the old right of sovereignty; we should be looking for a new right that is both antidisciplinary and emancipated from the principle of sovereignty.[39]

So, against the "old right of sovereignty" Foucault proposes a "new right" that would respond both to the problems of discipline and sovereignty itself. (More precisely, it would be opposed to the former and untethered from the latter.) It is noticeable that, in the years following this theoretical challenge—a challenge that, like many others issued in the forum of the Collège lectures, is never explicitly taken up again as such—Foucault begins to mobilize the discourse of rights and to make more concrete appeals to rights in his own work.[40] Can we read these subsequent discussions of rights as attempts to answer the question he had set himself in "'Society Must Be Defended'"? Perhaps. Foucault's discontinuous intellectual trajectory—his unexplained silences, changes of direction, changes of method—seems to militate against, or at any rate complicate, such a reading. Nevertheless, what is clear is that references to rights in his work after this point not only proliferate but also take on greater theoretical importance. Many of these references appear in interviews and in public political statements, but rights are also discussed in the context of his Collège lectures and in his philosophical work at this time. They concern appeals both to rights currently recognized and (more frequently, as we shall see) to rights not envisioned, accepted, or enforced at the time. They encompass procedural rights (that is, guaranteeing certain procedural protections) as well as substantive rights (to the enjoyment of certain things or ways of life). They feature rights traditionally enforced by, and held against, the state, and also those which recall or envision a theatre beyond the state. They concern rights attaching to individuals but also various rights grounded upon, claimed in the name of, and exercised in and by different kinds of collectives. And finally, they concern rights pertaining to political issues with which Foucault had previously engaged on a theoretical or an activist level (prisons and sexuality, for instance), but also to new and evolving contexts with which he had not hitherto centrally concerned himself (asylum, international humanitarianism, international solidarity). All in all, a very wide spectrum of different rights—let us briefly examine some of them.

In a lecture given in March 1976 at a University of Montreal conference on the rights of prison inmates, for example, Foucault observed critically of the prison that its "internal rules . . . are always absolutely contrary to the fundamental laws that in the rest of society guarantee the rights of man," and that this spatio-political arrangement thus constituted "a fearsome exception to right and to the law."[41] Indeed, elsewhere he had called for "immediate measures . . . [to] eliminate all abuses of rights in the way the law is applied" within the prison.[42] These interventions are in a political field with which Foucault's contemporary theoretical and activist work (*Discipline and Punish* and via the Groupe d'Information sur les Prisons [GIP]) is very clearly associated. But the philosopher's interventions into and deployment of rights discourse in this period go far beyond the question of intolerable conditions in French prisons. In December 1977, for example, in a statement published in *Le nouvel observateur*, "Letter to Certain Leaders of the Left," Foucault criticizes the Socialist Party (then in opposition) over their failure to respond urgently both to the deportation of Klaus Croissant, a lawyer for the Baader-Meinhof German terrorist group seeking political asylum in France, and to the government of the day's charging of two French women with themselves having "harboured" Croissant. In the course of this brief discussion Foucault not only invokes the right of asylum, but also criticizes the tendency of the contemporary "security pact" (between state and citizen) to produce "dangerous extensions of power and distortions in the area of recognized rights."[43] Again in *Le nouvel observateur*, this time in April 1979, Foucault writes an "Open Letter to Mehdi Bazargan," the then Iranian prime minister (who had been installed as the first prime minister after the revolution by Ayatollah Khomeini). Here Foucault publicly recalls private conversations with Bazargan (while he was chairman of the Association for the Defense of Human Rights in Iran, prior to the revolution), in which the latter had argued that a future Islamic republic would guarantee human rights. Now, in the context of postrevolutionary human rights abuses and political show trials, Foucault asserts the importance in the judicial system of affording the accused "every means of defence and every possible right."[44] Furthermore, in an interview published in English as "The Risks of Security," and in other fora, he advocated a "right to suicide."[45]

But perhaps the best-known example of Foucault's appeals to rights discourse is his invocation of the concept of the "rights of the governed" in the context of international affairs, refugees, and humanitarianism. From the late 1970s he had been politically involved in the question of Vietnamese refugees. In 1981 he attended a United Nations conference on piracy in Geneva. A brief statement he made to the conference, described by one of his biographers as "a sort of charter of human rights,"[46] was translated into English and published under the title "Confronting Governments: Human Rights." In this text, which makes no explicit reference to "human rights" as such, but rather mobilizes the concept of the "rights of the governed," Foucault refers to the rights of an international citizenry and the effective establishment of a "new right—that of private individuals to effectively intervene in the sphere of international policy and strategy."[47] Numerous other examples could be adduced at this stage, from Foucault's defense of rights pertaining to sexuality and to "relational rights" through to his support for the Polish Solidarity movement along human rights lines,[48] but I think it is probably clear from the foregoing that he is beginning at this time to affirm the political importance of rights in a way that seems, to put it mildly, somewhat at variance with the critiques—both of subjectivity and of sovereign power—that I outlined earlier. Thomas Keenan, in an insightful reading of Foucault's particular predicament, articulates these concerns. His comments are helpful to set out at length at this point, as they crystallize the set of concerns that I have been addressing:

> Is not Michel Foucault the most committed opponent of the discourse of rights, the operator of the theoretical guillotine that decapitates not only the king as political power principle but the individual, the human, and the humanism of human rights as well? Was not man's face erased from the sand at the edge of the sea in the final words of *Les mots et les choses*? Doesn't "right" belong precisely to the juridical vocabulary of power as sovereignty out of which Foucault tried to twist? Did not "power-knowledge" replace "right"? Doesn't "right" presuppose as the object of its legitimation or the target of its claims exactly the conception of power as negative, repressive, interdictive, against which Foucault tried to rethink power as positive, provocative, and productive (of exactly the subject, indeed, that would claim its rights and thus secure that play of power)? Did not Foucault contend that right in the West is the King's right and demand with distinctive epigrammatic economy that we "cut off the King's head"?[49]

There is an obvious conundrum, then: how interpret this late body of work, and how (if at all) relate it to Foucault's earlier critical investigations into discourse, power, and the subject? It is one of the purposes of this book to propose a particular answer to these questions, but before proceeding further I want to discuss some of the common readings of Foucault's "turn" to rights in the literature, a number of which have already been touched upon. This will prove helpful not only because I intend to situate my own answer in response to them (and in some places adopt and extend their insights), but also because unearthing and critiquing some of their presuppositions (about Foucault's work more broadly, and about the nature of critique and of politics) will allow me to clarify both the stakes and the contours of my own reading.

So, an initial response already foreshadowed above is to insist upon the normative incoherence of Foucault's advocacy of rights. Indeed, strictly speaking, the charge of normative incoherence—or normative "confusion,"[50] as Nancy Fraser puts it—affects Foucault's philosophy and politics more broadly (not simply those later sorties conducted in the language and idiom of rights talk). For his critics in this camp, any attempt by Foucault at critique, resistance, or political engagement is necessarily disabled by the lack of normative grounds. For Habermas, Foucault's critique of modern power is nothing more than the "arbitrary *partisanship* of a criticism that cannot account for its own normative foundations."[51] For Fraser, while Foucault's methodological "bracketing" of both epistemological and normative questions concerning the operation of modern power produces empirical insights of considerable merit, nevertheless his "work ends up, in effect, inviting [normative] questions that it is structurally unequipped to answer."[52] For her,

> Foucault calls in no uncertain terms for resistance to domination. But why? Why is struggle preferable to submission? Why ought domination to be resisted? Only with the introduction of normative notions of some kind could Foucault begin to answer such questions. . . . Clearly, what Foucault needs, and needs desperately, are normative criteria for distinguishing acceptable from unacceptable forms of power.[53]

For readers of Foucault in this vein, his critique of modern forms of power, alongside his critique of the standard humanistic resources with which one might furnish oneself in order to support such a critique (emancipation, liberation, enlightenment, the subject), leaves his political critiques and interventions without any underlying basis to recommend them. Why, so goes this reading, should we accept any of the claims of right that Foucault makes—on behalf of prisoners, sexual minorities, "the governed"? From this perspective Foucault's appeals to rights are incoherent and, hence, normatively unappealing to his audience.

A related way in which Foucault has been interpreted, and his appeals to rights summarily disposed of, is by pointing to a gap between his political activism and his philosophical work: between, as I put it above, Foucault's deeds and his words. Writing specifically of rights, Foucault's philosophical contemporary, Jacques Derrida, expresses this distinction in terms of a separation between the ethico-political and the philosophical. For him, attendant upon this distinction is an inescapable "difficulty . . . in making an ethico-political gesture (supporting the resistance of the Prague philosophers, who demand respect for human rights and articulate that with a philosophy of the subject, the person, individual liberty, etc.) coincide with a philosophical labor governed by the necessity of deconstructing precisely such philosophemes."[54] How indeed does one articulate a philosophical critique of rights, sovereignty, and subjectivity with the political mobilization of these very same concepts? For many readers of Foucault's late work, this admittedly difficult attempt to make the two coincide on the political territory of rights is bound to fail. In *Decadence of the French Nietzsche*, James Brusseau glosses the charge in these simple terms: "Foucault inside the university rails against subjugation while, apparently incompatibly, outside the university makes an appeal for human rights."[55] For Brent Pickett, this appeal to rights (and on occasion human rights) is a sign of Foucault's underlying political pragmatism. Discussing the "Open Letter to Mehdi Bazargan" and Foucault's support for the Solidarity movement, he asserts that the inconsistency between philosophy and politics revealed in the late work is ultimately resolved in favor of a pragmatist (and a progressive and reformist) conception of politics in which "theoretical consistency takes a backseat to what is more likely to effect positive change."[56]

These first two interpretations of Foucault's engagements with rights— namely, that his appeals to rights are normatively unsupported and that they express a tension[57] (or worse, an irreconcilable conflict) between his philosophy and his political aspirations—fault Foucault for not fully articulating the basis of his rights politics. The third interpretive strand in the literature on Foucault and rights essentially marginalizes Foucault's later work on rights. For these readers, Foucault's critical genealogical accounts of discipline and related forms of modern power in the mid-1970s encapsulate his position on rights (to the exclusion of the later political deployments of rights that are my focus here). For Kirstie McClure, Foucault in this period of his work arrives at a set of fairly "dismal conclusions with regard to the potential of rights as a language of political contestation or resistance."[58] For Alan Hunt and Gary Wickham, in their *Foucault and Law: Towards a Sociology of Law as Governance*, Foucault's attitude to rights amounts (much less plausibly) to a pernicious and misguided form of rights skepticism that fails to accord "any potential political value to tactics that seek to invoke rights against the incursions of disciplinary power and to advance or expand new rights." Discussing Foucault's call for a "new right" at the conclusion of the second of the 1976 Collège de France lectures, they go on to observe that Foucault "says nothing about what this 'new form of right' might be . . . [and never] return[s] to explore this idea."[59] Likewise for Nancy Fraser, who opines that rights for Foucault have "no emancipatory potential whatsoever, [and hence are] . . . reducible without remainder to . . . [their sovereign] function."[60] From this third perspective, then, Foucault's attitude toward rights can be encapsulated simply as one of critique, where critique is understood to issue in a thoroughly negative or rejectionist stance toward its object.

Of course, the flipside of utter rejection is uncritical acceptance. Hence it should perhaps not surprise us to learn that a fourth and final strand[61] in the literature interprets Foucault's late "turn" to rights discourse as a deliberate revision of his earlier genealogical work of the 1970s in favor of a celebratory "return" to liberalism. Here Foucault's varied invocations and deployments of rights discourse are implausibly assembled under the sign of "liberalism" and read symptomatically as a political evacuation of the genealogical project. This interpretation is often made alongside, or is underwritten by, a reading of his late work on ethics and on technologies of the self as tacitly reintroducing some manner of pre-discursive, constituent or at any rate more strongly agentive "subject" into his analyses of power-knowledge.[62] I shall propose my own reading of Foucault's ethics in Chapter 2 and in so doing address the question of the subject. For the moment, however, we may simply observe that in such readings of Foucault he somehow "becomes cozy with a kind of liberal individualism"[63] and the late work as such constitutes a "capitulation in the face of the moral superiority of humanism."[64] This Foucault—a figure now barely recognizable as the iconoclastic author of *Discipline and Punish* and the first volume of the *History of Sexuality*—sues belatedly for admission to the liberal fold, reintroducing the elusive and talismanic subject and directing his chastened political interventions via the orthodox institutional channels of sovereignty and right. Characteristically, such readings are configured by the reconciliatory trope of an "embrace": late in life a mature and repentant Foucault finally comes to "embrace ideas he had labored to undermine: liberty, individualism, 'human rights,' and even the thinking subject"![65]

A Critical Counter-Conduct of Rights

We have just seen a series of different interpretations of this late body of work end up rendering Foucault's deployments of rights discourse normatively incoherent; severing them from his philosophical work; marginalizing them as an inconvenient (or forgotten) addendum to his more properly critical work of the mid-1970s; or indeed casting them as an embarrassing humanist volte-face and a return to liberal individualism. It is clear that there is some manner of affirmation entailed in Foucault's late invocation of rights, but is this affirmation a simple embrace of the ideology of liberalism—with its operative assumptions about subjectivity and sovereignty—that Foucault had been at such pains to contest for so long? Or is it something else?

The short answer is that Foucault's politics of rights is indeed something else, and the shorthand phrase I adopt in this book to describe what he is attempting to do in his late work on rights is to generate a critical counter-conduct of rights. My use of the word "critical" signals at least two different aspects of this reading. First, and in a more general (and less technical) sense of the word, I am marking a certain distance on Foucault's part from an orthodox liberal politics of rights (with its valorization and protection of the individual subject, its protection or enlargement of that subject's originary freedom, its paradoxical restraint of and yet reliance upon state sovereignty, and so forth). Rather than interpreting his late work on rights as expressing a return, or a capitulation, to liberalism, I intend to read that work as indicative of a critical distance between Foucault and liberalism.[66] It will be apparent already from some of my remarks, then, that the reading to which I am most opposed is that of Foucault as a belated convert to a liberal philosophy of the subject and of sovereignty. In my reading, Foucault remains faithful in his rights politics to his earlier theoretical critiques of the subject and of sovereignty. But in remaining a critic of these philosophical presuppositions of liberal political theory, he nevertheless draws tactically upon the resources, practices, and institutions of liberalism. He expresses his political interventions via the liberal idiom of rights, but perverts and "performative[ly] undermin[es]" them in the process.[67] Here we must observe that Foucault's critique of liberalism is neither a simple opposition to nor a rejection of liberalism, but rather a contrary inhabiting of it, a destabilizing "counterinvestment" which works within and against it.[68] This leads me to the more specific, and revealing, sense of critique used in this book.

Second, in engaging with rights "critically" Foucault aligns himself with a more particular, personal understanding of critique—which also implicates "counter-conduct," the term I have used to characterize Foucault's rights politics. In the next chapter I shall examine in greater depth the variety of ways of approaching Foucault's understanding and deployment of "critique." For now I want to introduce just one of these, and it relates to the question of resistance to forms of government. In the late essay "The Subject and Power," Foucault proposes an understanding of power relations in terms of the related ideas of "conduct" and "government." He argues there that to conduct means to lead others but also reminds us that the term refers to a way of acting and behaving. For him, the exercise of power represents an attempt to modify conduct, to affect behavior and actions. Such an exercise is best conceived not as a "confrontation between two adversaries or their mutual engagement," but rather as a calculated "'conduct of conducts' and a management of possibilities . . . a question of 'government.'"[69] Power is here understood as a mode of governing the conduct of others (and of oneself). In a broad sense this "definition" comprises the disciplinary relation whereby individuals are objectified together with those relations to self whereby the individual is enjoined to work upon himself in the exercise of his "autonomy."[70] This project of governing conduct is not, as he goes on to say, reducible to "political structures or to the management of states," but rather encompasses a much more diffuse domain of possible actions whereby "the conduct of individuals or groups might be directed—the government of children, of souls, of communities, of families, of the sick."[71]

But just as he had previously insisted upon the necessary entailments of power and resistance,[72] so too within the historical forms of the government of conduct there emerge for him various forms of "counter-conduct" that are deployed "as a way of suspecting them, of challenging them, of limiting them, of finding their right measure, of transforming them, of seeking to escape these arts of governing or, in any case, to displace them, as an essential reluctance."[73] And it is to this internal contestation and limitation of government that Foucault comes eventually to give the name "critique," or the critical attitude. "I would thus propose this general characterization," he says in "What

Is Critique?," a lecture delivered around the same time, "as a rather preliminary definition of critique: the art of not being governed so much."[74] Thus to be critical, in this second, more specific sense, is to pose questions of the government of conduct ("of [its] principles, . . . objectives . . . [and] methods")[75] using the available political resources and repertoire furnished by government itself, a kind of refractory turning of government against itself from within the discursive and political field of possibilities opened up by government. The critic is necessarily situated within the field of government and tries to destabilize existing governmental arrangements from this immanent vantage point, thereby freeing them up to the possibility of their being otherwise. As we shall see in the next chapter, this critical countermobilization of existing concepts rests upon some theoretical premises (articulated in Foucault's famous methods of archaeology and genealogy) concerning the historicity and promising contingency of knowledges, institutions, and social practices.

In what follows I shall be reading Foucault's deployment of rights precisely as a form of critical counter-conduct. While Foucault says that we must not "demand of politics that it restore the 'rights' of the individual"[76] (where such a demand synechdochically reduces all politics to rights), nevertheless rights do present themselves as one of a range of contingent political tools available for counter-investment and appropriation, for "strategic reversibility"[77] on behalf of different political interests and as a part of diverse political struggles. This is the general characterization of Foucault's approach to rights that this book will present. In the chapters that follow I offer a layered and detailed account of different aspects of this politics of rights—the sorts of subjects it presupposes and configures; the relations of power it reveals, contests, and transmits; the tactical and strategic uses for which it can (and cannot) profitably be deployed. Foucault's critical politics of rights is by no means a straightforward endorsement of the power and value of rights (and definitely not as a normative defense of the individual), but rather a much more selective, strategic, instrumental, shifting, and often quite ambivalent engagement with them. My account is organized around three different but related dimensions of Foucault's understanding and deployment of rights: the contingent ground of rights; the ambivalent nature of rights as simultaneously liberatory and subjectifying; and finally, the tactical and strategic possibilities of rights as political instruments. At the same time, as I have already noted, I want to think critically about just what such a politics of rights comprises and what it helps to foreclose. As we shall see in the coming pages, Foucault does some of this critical thinking for us, too.

My interpretation is one that insists upon a continuity between the critical philosophical concerns of Foucault's early and midcareer work—on the archaeology and genealogy of regimes of truth and relations of power—and those of the late work on rights.[78] But how, and how successfully, does he maintain his critical genealogical perspective in the late encounter with rights? How does his articulation of rights respond to the critiques he had made in the previous years? How and to what extent can rights, being embedded within relations of power, offer a truly critical purchase that breaks with the logic of the power relations within which they are situated? What limits are encountered when one attempts tactically to redeploy a politically hegemonic discourse such as rights? These are all crucial (even critical) questions engendered by Foucault's politics of rights, and my answers to them will be given in the coming pages.

On Reading Foucault

Before proceeding to outline my argument, I want briefly to make a few methodological remarks, in order, first, to explain how I approach the task of reading Foucault, and second, to provide a caveat as to what *not* to expect from this book. To start with, the argument about Foucault's politics of rights presented here makes no pretensions to the status of a unified and systematic "theory" of rights (one which, for example, might claim to explain whence rights derive their normative authority, what they are in their essence, how they are to be applied in all circumstances, how different rights might be related to or balanced against each other, and so forth). This would be an odd thing to expect of a book about a thinker who on repeated occasions abjured the role of "theoretician" and characterized his work in supposedly opposed terms (as "neither a theory nor a methodology,"[79] or, for example, as an "analytics" of power as opposed to a "theory"[80]). Of course, much turns on what one understands in this connection by "theory." I do take Foucault to be making theoretical observations about rights in his work, and inescapably so, but for me this does not make his position untenable or incoherent. Rather, I interpret his resistance to theory not to theory *tout court*, but rather, and more narrowly, to the brand of theorization to which he refers in his "'Society Must Be Defended'" lectures. There Foucault takes aim at "totalitarian theories, or at least—what I mean is—all-encompassing and global theories."[81] Here he has psychoanalysis and a scientistic Marxism primarily in mind as theories that in their putative universalism are necessarily reductive and exclusionary in operation and effect. Foucault does reflect theoretically on rights (on their contingency, on their imbrications with power relations, on their subjectifying and regulatory dimensions), but such a theory does not—and the point is, it need not, in order to merit the label—amount to a structured, systematic account of the nature of rights.[82]

Second, what is presented here is not a coherent template for political action. Again, Foucault does not purport—either via his engagement with rights or more broadly in his reflections on power—to arrive at a "politics" in the perhaps more commonly accepted sense of a coherent ideological position or set of values that might dictate the assumption of certain concrete positions or the desirability of a particular future state of affairs. In the famous answer to a question posed to him in the interview titled "Polemics, Politics, and Problematizations" concerning his political affiliations ("Where *do* you stand?" asks his interviewer), he asserts: "I think I have in fact been situated in most of the squares on the political checkerboard, one after the other and sometimes simultaneously: as anarchist, leftist, ostentatious or disguised Marxist, nihilist, explicit or secret anti-Marxist, technocrat in the service of Gaullism, new liberal, and so on."[83] He continues in the same interview to characterize his own politics in terms precisely of a problematization of politics itself, of posing genealogical questions to politics. Properly speaking, if there is a politics in Foucault, it is methodologically prior to the establishment of any given political position—in the form of an archaeological or genealogical inquiry that asks after the founding circumscriptions of "the political" and what it excludes, represses, and disavows (but also, of course, what it enables in terms of the objects it articulates and the subjects it generates).[84] For Wendy Brown, "this is the space—harbouring no particular political aims but replete with challenging exposures and destabilizations—of genealogical politics."[85] Foucault's genealogical politics, when it comes to rights, does not dictate the assumption of a given policy or advocacy position. As a theoretical matter, Foucault views rights as contingent historical artifacts that are (more or less, depending on the strategic and institutional balance of forces) available for political contest and deployment. When it comes to his own deployment or advocacy of given rights in particular situations, we shall see that he views the attainment and enforcement of these rights not as normative ends in themselves, but rather as part of an ongoing and often diffuse struggle conducted on a number of different fronts. It is not possible, I believe, to characterize the various "aims" of Foucault's rights struggles (the recognition of different affective relations, the establishment of rights for prisoners or "the governed," and so forth) as belonging to a unitary normative political goal or vision of the world. Consistent with his own philosophical refusal to legislate moral or political ends, there is neither any overarching principle that can predict how rights will be used nor anything that can safeguard them from what we might judge normatively unappealing or "illegitimate" uses. Just as Foucault tends to bracket questions of legitimacy, so too am I, in trying to make sense of his late body of work on rights and in calling the interpretation I have arrived at a "Foucauldian politics of rights," focused much more on how rights are constructed and deployed and on the political effects they produce than on what they are engaged for or on why they are so engaged. On these former levels, I shall argue, it is possible to detect commonalities among Foucault's different rights claims, and moreover, these commonalities are themselves reflective of his long-standing yet evolving positions on discourse, power, and the subject.

Finally, the interpretive approach I shall take to this late body of work on rights—a collection of philosophical works that engage with rights as a subject of analysis, but also more directly political texts such as activist statements, interviews, and journalism—is twofold. First, I endeavor to interpret this latter body of directly political texts in the light of (or in a way that is consonant with) Foucault's more elaborated theoretical positions. In the face of the oft-remarked discontinuities between the two bodies of work it is tempting, as many have done,[86] to sever them.[87] I feel that this is an unsatisfactory way to proceed. For a start, it appears to be based upon what is not only a somewhat ungenerous interpretive premise (namely, assuming Foucault to have deliberately cultivated inconsistency between the different orders of his own discourse), but also an arguably incorrect one, in that Foucault, it turns out, paid scrupulous attention to the continuity of his work on multiple occasions.[88] To separate the two types of work thus elides the theoretical import of the more directly political texts. Second, and this flows from the comment just made, I shall try not only to address the theoretical significance of the political texts, but also to foreground the political importance of the philosophical texts. Put another way, without collapsing the distinctions between the two types of text or failing to attend to their different exigencies or material requirements,[89] I hope to complicate the very distinction between theory and practice in Foucault's work. For me, the political texts are not the direct practical application of a pre-announced theory; rather, they are themselves theoretical contributions, disclosing theoretical insights about rights even in the instant of their claiming or mobilizing them. Similarly, his theoretical remarks about rights made in the course of the philosophical texts are themselves speech acts that are intended to have "political" performative effects and force. Thinking and doing rights are here necessarily intertwined in the scene of Foucault's various *énoncés*.

The Chapters

In Chapter 1 I aim to achieve three goals. In the first part of the chapter, I propose a theoretical framework for thinking about the meaning and the function of critique in Foucault's work. Here I shall suggest that the Foucauldian style of critique is best understood primarily as a labor of destabilization. Critique as destabilization functions to expose the contingency of social and political arrangements and thus, potentially, to open them to alternative possibilities. Importantly, then, this style of critique is not simply a negative rejection of the present, but represents instead a profoundly affirmative and enabling enterprise, one that allows us to begin to think the present—and the past and future—differently. This understanding of critique provides a way of grasping Foucault's politics of rights as a tactical re-using of rights for new and different purposes. In the second part of the chapter, I expand upon some of the material introduced in the foregoing pages concerning Foucault's theoretical challenge to the two underlying presuppositions of liberal rights theory: subjectivity and sovereignty. Simply put, it is important to grasp what Foucault's critique of these fundamental elements of liberal rights theory consists of in order to understand how he does, or does not, move away from these positions. The treatment of these two interrelated topics is largely expository in nature and intended as background material to the arguments I make in subsequent chapters. I conclude the chapter by introducing in more detail Foucault's specific concept of "counter-conduct," which serves as a kind of conceptual or theoretical lens through which to interpret his politics of rights in the following chapters.

My account of Foucault's politics of rights in the remainder of the book is developed through a series of readings of particular rights, or of political claims or issues to which rights present a response, in order to elucidate a different dimension of his rights politics. Chapter 2 focuses on the issue of Foucault's advocacy of human rights in a number of different contexts. This serves to introduce the first dimension of Foucault's rights politics, namely, their being contingent and ungrounded. Here I make the argument that the rights for which he contends are contingent and ungrounded in the sense that they consciously disavow the conventional normative grounds of rights—whether that be envisioned as reason, will, intention, or even (in the case of human rights) bare humanity itself. Foucault, as I have already indicated, consistently refuses the notion of any "anthropological constant"[90] that might serve as an enduring or essential ground for rights claims. However, rather than seeing this refusal as an insuperable problem for his deployment of rights in the late work (as have many normative theorists of rights and those critical of Foucault on this score), I argue that Foucault's advocacy of the contingent, artifactual, and revisable grounds of rights claims actually constitutes a particular and conscious ethico-political choice on his part, and more to the point, one that opens up future political possibilities in and through rights rather than destabilizing or circumscribing them. (Here I read Foucault's work alongside that of Judith Butler on rearticulating the human of human rights and Jacques Rancière on the politics of rights claiming.)[91]

In Chapter 3, in order to illustrate the second dimension of Foucault's politics of rights, namely, their ambivalent quality, I present a reading of rights of or to "difference" or "identity" within political communities, with a particular focus on gay and lesbian rights activism. Here I develop the argument that Foucault theorizes rights as ambivalent (and that he attempts to navigate this ambivalence in his political practices of rights claiming). What I mean by the idea that Foucault perceives rights as ambivalent is that they have a dual function. On the one hand, they can enlarge, expand, or protect the sphere of action of subjects (as well as bring new worlds and communities into being). On the other, and simultaneously with the above function, they can constitute those very subjects and communities in particular ways and hence work to reinscribe them within existing forms of power, recuperating and domesticating the political challenges they might pose. A particular focus of this chapter will be Foucault's engagement with issues of identity formation through rights and with what I call the "regulatory dimension of rights regimes." (Here I read Foucault alongside some of the early work of political theorist Wendy Brown and subsequent debates in the political theory literature around rights claiming as a performative political practice.)[92] One of the questions raised here concerns the way in which political actors tactically negotiate this ambivalent space of rights. This thematization of tactics then leads into the discussion in the next chapter.

Chapter 4 is organized around a discussion of different political contexts— joined by the question of life and death under conditions of biopolitical rule.

In the first, concerned with the debate around the "right to die," Foucault has recourse to rights in order to achieve particular political aims. In the second, which deals with the debate around France's abolition of the death penalty, Foucault noticeably refuses to engage "rights talk." I use these related political contexts in order to think through the third and final dimension of my account, namely, that Foucault's rights claims are intended to constitute tactical deployments and interventions. However, in so characterizing them I want to reflect not only upon their tactical qualities but also on their broader strategic aspirations and effects. By "tactical," I refer to the ways in which Foucault deploys rights not as a means to satisfy political demands within the extant parameters of a liberal system (of law and state), but rather as an instrument to achieve other political aims. By "strategic," I mean to capture the extent to which these tactical deployments can be articulated in order to support wider political goals (of contestation or rupture of given power relations or forms of subjectivity). Here the theoretical foils to my particular reading of Foucault are provided by Marxist engagements with the question of political strategy, as well as more recent attempts in critical legal theory to develop a legal strategy of "rupture" (especially as found in the work of the legal theorist Émilios Christodoulidis).[93]

Finally, the Conclusion brings my account of Foucault's rights politics to an end by, as it were, shifting into a different, more openly historicizing, diagnostic, and reflective register. Here, assisted by the recent historiographies of human rights that I discussed at the beginning of this Introduction, I try to situate Foucault's turn to rights in the late 1970s and early 1980s in a political and historical context. I want to bring the book to an end not simply by restating my interpretation of Foucault but by beginning to pose some questions about the emergence, and contemporary afterlife and influence, of Foucault's critical counter-conduct of rights down to the present day. Ultimately, these are questions which point beyond the limits of the present study and toward future research.

This book thus starts with Foucault but ends by gesturing beyond him. In the following chapters I propose a particular reading of Foucault, and yet the wider political stakes of that reading present themselves all too clearly. Are Foucault's late works to be read as consonant with the liberal humanism of much contemporary rights talk or as a criticism of it? And what might such a critique amount to? Does it betoken the political or theoretical failure of the genealogical project in the face of the hegemony of rights, or a subtle continuation of that project through different means and media? Is Foucault to be assimilated into a general trend in revisionist, anti-revolutionary 1970s French intellectual circles which sees former foes now reconciled to the *droits de l'homme,* or indeed human rights? Here we might recall the *nouveaux philosophes* as testament to and symptom of this "antitotalitarian moment" in French thought.[94] Or might something more than a simple return to liberalism be made of Foucault's engagements with rights? What, ultimately, is to be made of those (re)turns to rights (of which Foucault's is but one) that seek not to glorify or naturalize them, but rather to occupy them, to appropriate and resignify them? It is to these questions and to that indicative "something more" that I want now to turn. The first step is to revisit in detail Foucault's twin critiques of subjectivity and of sovereignty. These are the necessary background to an understanding of his later political deployment of rights and are the subject matter of Chapter 1.

CHAPTER 1

CRITICAL COUNTER-CONDUCTS

I can't help but dream about a kind of criticism that would try not to
judge, but to bring an oeuvre, a book, a sentence, an idea to life;
it would light fires, watch the grass grow, listen to the wind, and catch
the sea-foam in the breeze and scatter it.

Michel Foucault

From Critique to Acceptance?

There is a common and, at first glance, perfectly plausible explanation for the
puzzle of Foucault's late engagement with rights discourse. It proceeds by setting Foucault's engagements with rights within a major shift in the late work
(his "ethical turn" or "return to the subject"). This frequently invoked shift,
from the so-called power to the "ethical" phase of his writing, is one in which
Foucault supposedly retreats from critiquing to eventually accepting the normative importance of the subject.[1] Such readings are plainly revisionist in intent—after all, what could possibly be more critical a subject to the Foucauldian
legacy than the very critique of the subject, one of the leitmotifs of Foucault's
project as it unfolded throughout the 1970s?[2] "At the time of Foucault's death
in 1984," writes Richard Wolin with evident satisfaction, "prominent observers
noted the irony that the ex-structuralist and 'death of man' prophet had played
a pivotal role in the French acceptance of political liberalism."[3] Having on this
view rashly consigned the subject to its grave as early as the mid-1960s in a fit of
(post)structuralist pique, Foucault is embarrassingly forced to exhume it only a
decade later for compelling moral and political reasons—a seemingly remarkable "capitulation in the face of the moral superiority of humanism."[4] For many,
this supposed shift—from critique to acceptance of the subject—provides a
convenient and almost self-evident lens through which to view the thinker's late
engagements with rights.[5] Of course, so goes the argument, if the later Foucault
comes finally to formulate what the intellectual historian Eric Paras has hailed

as a "prediscursive subject" unmarked by power and knowledge,[6] then it follows that his contemporaneous resorts to rights discourse come to be understood in an orthodox liberal individualist fashion—namely, as juridical protections for certain pre-political qualities of the subject (its inalienable dignity, originary liberty, and so forth). For me, once such an interpretive schema is adopted in order to read Foucault's deployments of rights, then this interesting, disparate, ambivalent, and challenging late political body of work is unhelpfully reduced to a unitary and extended paean to liberalism—which is precisely what Wolin intends by such a reading when he approvingly (yet provocatively) refers to Foucault, in another piece, as a "neohumanist."[7]

But something more—at once more politically challenging and more faithful to the critical and transformative intent of Foucault's thought—can yet be made of this late work.[8] In what follows I construct an alternative conceptual lens through which to view the late work on rights. I proceed in three steps. First, I articulate a general understanding of what critique means and how it functions in Foucault's work. As intimated earlier, the understanding I propose here is intended to foreground the *affirmative* dimensions of Foucault's critical approach—to him, critique is a form of disassembly that productively opens the contingent present to an undetermined future. Then, moving from a general and principled statement about the intent of Foucault's critical method to some particular instantiations of it, I revisit in greater detail material outlined in the Introduction—that is, Foucault's related critiques of subjectivity and of sovereignty. In this section I shall necessarily traverse some fairly well-trodden Foucauldian territory, both historical and conceptual (disciplinary power and biopolitics) and methodological (archaeology and genealogy) in nature. Finally, I shall offer a more detailed discussion of Foucault's mature conception of power as the affecting of "conduct" and the crucial notion of "counter-conduct" that such a conception brings with it. My overall aim in this chapter is hence to present an understanding of critique in Foucault's work and then to relate this understanding to his more specific concept of "counter-conduct." I hope to show how the resistant and affirmative potential embodied in this concept, a concept that looks to make sense of his late politics of rights, itself rests upon the theoretical premises of Foucault's own understanding of (archaeological and genealogical) critique.

Both this chapter and Chapter 2 together constitute an attack upon the idea that Foucault, when it comes to the subject, moves from a posture of critique to one of acceptance—an idea central to the misreading of Foucault as a belated convert to a liberal political philosophy of rights. But if Foucault, as I maintain, consistently adopts a critical stance well into his later work, then it is necessary to start by examining in some detail precisely what is meant here by critique. If, as I contend, a certain (mis)understanding of critique contours the reception of Foucault in the liberal misreadings to which I have just referred, then I am obliged to articulate a proper understanding of just what it is that Foucault intends, and more to the point, does *not* intend, by critique. It is to this task that I now turn.

What Is Foucauldian Critique?

What precisely does Foucault mean by "critique"? My premise is that one way of understanding the contention that Foucault moves toward an unlikely rapprochement with liberalism in the late work is to approach his alleged "turn" through the prism of critique itself. By commencing in this way—that is, by distinguishing the specifically Foucauldian idiom of critique from other critical traditions, with their attendant understandings of the role of the critic and of the social function of critique itself—we shall begin to see a little more clearly just what the intent, the uses, and (perhaps even) the limitations of Foucault's particular critical project might be. It will show that any claim that he reverts approvingly to liberal individualism in the late work is untenable.

No doubt an entire book could be written on Foucault's various critical practices and his serial formulations of what it means to be engaged in critique. Thankfully, Foucault himself rescues me from such a task: in the late essay "What Is Enlightenment?"[9] he provides a synoptic (and cumulative) account of his different methodological approaches. I shall accordingly take this text, an "apologia" in the "classical sense,"[10] as a distillation of Foucault's critical methods and of what he believes the work of the critic to be. As is common with Foucault, he proceeds in this essay to construct his own position by reference to the position of another thinker.[11] As is somewhat less common, the thinker on this occasion is Immanuel Kant—and quite remarkably, Foucault begins by implicitly aligning his own critical enterprise with the Kantian philosophical tradition.[12] What exactly does Foucault mean by this? He opens with a brief reading of Kant's famous 1784 essay, *Was ist Aufklärung?* (What is enlightenment?), in which Kant—in answer to the *Berlinische Monatschrift*'s question—proposed that enlightenment represents the release of man from his self-incurred tutelage and his accession to a state of intellectual maturity, in

which, now daring to know, he uses his own powers of reason and no longer acquiesces unthinkingly to the dogmas of religion, tradition, or authority.[13]
Foucault links this definition of enlightenment as the mature, autonomous use
of reason to Kant's three philosophical *Critiques* (in particular the first, *The
Critique of Pure Reason*). For him, the former necessitates the latter in that the
vertiginous moment at which man's reason is finally to be deployed upon its
own account, as it were, requires the critical policing of this selfsame reason,
lest humanity's newly acquired faculty go awry: "Its role is that of defining the
conditions under which the use of reason is legitimate in order to determine
what can be known [*connaître*], what must be done, and what may be hoped.
. . . The critique [Kant's *Critique*] is, in a sense, the handbook of reason."[14]

For Foucault, the importance of Kant's text resides in the fact that it poses a
particular question—that of the philosopher's relationship to the present—and
that in so doing it inaugurates a particular style of modern philosophy whose
questions we (Foucault included) are still asking today. Foucault observes:

> It is the reflection on 'today' as difference in history and as motive for a particu-
> lar task that the novelty of this text appears to me to lie. And, by looking at it in
> this way, it seems to me that we may recognize a point of departure: the outline
> of what one might call the attitude of modernity.[15]

According to Foucault, the modern attitude that Kant's philosophical essay en-
capsulates is a "mode of relating to contemporary reality."[16] In his own essay,
Foucault argues that the "thread which may connect us to the Enlightenment
is not faithfulness to doctrinal elements but, rather, the permanent reactiva-
tion of an attitude—that is, of a philosophical ethos that could be described as
a permanent critique of our historical era."[17] By so doing, Foucault provocatively situates his own critical historical analyses—his archaeologies, genealogies, and problematizations—within a Kantian orbit: he is a Kantian in spirit, if
not exactly in the arid "doctrinal" letter, in that he seeks to reactivate modern
philosophy's problematic of interrogating the historical present. He character-
izes his own attempt to take up these questions—an attempt that he variously
figures within the text as an ethos, a task, a philosophical life, a historical ontology, and finally, as critique itself—in both negative and positive terms. Let me
reverse the order of the text's presentation and begin by addressing the positive
dimension of Foucault's critical project.

In describing his own project affirmatively, then, Foucault again employs
terms drawn from Kant, but now he gives them a different meaning. He de-

scribes the philosophical ethos of modernity as a "limit-attitude" and proposes critique as a means to analyze, reflect upon, and breach those limits. Whereas for Kant critique consisted in an attempt to "know[. . .] [*savoir*] what limits knowledge [*connaissance*] must renounce exceeding," for Foucault the point of contemporary critique is not to establish transcendental limits to knowledge but rather to historicize and dissolve them. He thus asks:

> In what is given to us as universal, necessary, obligatory, what place is occu-
> pied by whatever is singular, contingent, and the product of arbitrary con-
> straints? The point, in brief, is to transform the critique conducted in the form
> of necessary limitation into a practical critique that takes the form of a possible
> crossing-over [*franchissement*].[18]

For Foucault critique thus dispenses with the (Kantian) search "for formal structures with universal value." In its place he proposes "a historical investigation into the events that have led us to constitute ourselves and to recognize ourselves as subjects of what we are doing, thinking, saying."[19] Such a form of critique, he stresses, is "at once archaeological and genealogical."[20] It is "archaeological—and not transcendental—in the sense that it . . . treat[s] the instances of discourse that articulate what we think, say, and do as so many historical events," and it is "genealogical in the sense that it will not deduce from the form of what we are what it is impossible for us to do and to know; but it will separate out, from the contingency that has made us what we are, the possibility of no longer being, doing or thinking what we are, do, or think."[21]

For Foucault, then, critique consists in the work of historicizing and rendering contingent the discourses and modes of being that have come to define our present (and our relations to our present). The purpose of such a critique is not simply to explain the various historical processes that have led to the current conjuncture of why we are, behave, or think in a particular way, but rather, and more pertinently, to defamiliarize and destabilize that conjuncture, to explain how it was produced and, by doing so, open it to the possibility of its being otherwise. As he puts it toward the end of the essay, joining these two moments of analysis and disassembly, "The critique of what we are is at one and the same time the historical analysis of the limits imposed upon us and an experiment with the possibility of going beyond them [*de leur franchissement possible*]."[22]

Foucault's "negative" presentation of critique in "What Is Enlightenment?" is no less revealing. Here he is concerned to clear a space for a type of critique that neither judges (after Kant, perhaps)[23] nor negates (with Hegel or Marx), but rather, as we have just seen, simply excavates and renders unstable.[24] He expresses his objection to the constraints of these dominant ways of thinking critique in terms of an act of Manichaean "blackmail": the critic must necessarily be either in favor of or against the object of critical analysis. Worried that such a requirement reduces the possible modalities and valences of critique to a static forensic binary,[25] he insists that to situate oneself within the historical inheritance of an event such as the Enlightenment, while simultaneously critiquing it,

> does not mean that one has to be "for" or "against" the Enlightenment. It even means precisely that one must refuse everything that might present itself in the form of a simplistic and authoritarian alternative: you either accept the Enlightenment and remain within the tradition of its rationalism . . . , or else you criticize the Enlightenment and then try to escape from its principles of rationality.[26]

According to this view the critic is not removed from the contingency of the present into some pure vantage point, passing judgment aperspectivally or transcendentally, but rather is located immanently within the social field and so is necessarily invested and implicated in the object under critique. One way in which Foucault expresses this unavoidably situated dimension of critique is to draw elsewhere in his work upon a distinction between "general" and "specific" intellectuals and the different kinds of knowledge claims that each type of intellectual professes. In the interview "Truth and Power," for example, Foucault contrasts the classical Enlightenment figure of the intellectual as "master of truth and justice" and as "spokesman of the universal" (here he has a historical figure such as Voltaire in mind, while Sartre is doubtless his contemporary target) with an intellectual conceived as working "not in the modality of the 'universal,' the 'exemplary,' the 'just-and-true-for-all,' but within specific sectors, at the precise points where [her] own conditions of life or work situate [her]."[27]

In sum, we can see that Foucault's critique, as a socially situated practice, entails a historical exposure of the contingency of our present and of how it was composed. At the same time, and by virtue of this, it also exposes the possibility of thinking, acting, and doing that present otherwise. Clearly such a critical challenge to existent arrangements does not rest upon a "positive" (substantial and substantializing) normative vision of what the world ought to be. For Foucault, such possible visions have the perverse effect of constraining political practice in the present, and so he insists that if critique is to have any relationship to a future, then it must instead "be a means for a future or a truth that it will not know nor happen to be."[28] The premise upon which his critical practice rests is indeed an affirmation (of the possibility of things being otherwise than they are), but this is self-avowedly a "nonpositive affirmation."[29] "Critique doesn't have to be the premise of a deduction which concludes: this then is what needs to be done," he insists elsewhere. Rather, "it should be an instrument for those who fight, those who resist and refuse what is. Its use should be in processes of conflict and confrontation, essays in refusal."[30] The most important point to appreciate here, no doubt, is that such a refusal has a generative and affirmative quality in that the moment of (archaeological and genealogical) destabilization prizes present social arrangements and practices open to a horizon of alternative possible futures.

In the passage quoted above from "What Is Enlightenment?," Foucault links his two most famous methodological approaches—archaeology, very much indebted to French philosophers and historians of science,[31] and genealogy, largely a derivation from Nietzsche—in a unitary critical endeavor. Foucault uses these methodologies to critique the two integral and co-implicated elements of liberal rights discourse outlined in the Introduction: a foundationalist account of subjectivity and a juridical theory of sovereignty. Without adherence to these traditional premises, many of his readers insist that Foucault is normatively hamstrung and unable to generate a meaningful, let alone useful, account or practice of rights. One thing to be borne in mind, however, is that Foucault's critical stance commits him to neither advocacy nor rejection of either of these elements of rights discourse. Rather, the point of the critique is directed toward freeing them up for different uses, at exposing their contingent foundations and entailments, and hence at rendering them vulnerable to contestation, reform, or radical overcoming.

Foucault's Critiques of Subjectivity and of Sovereignty

Most studies of Foucault are organized into what has become a standard tripartite division of his oeuvre: an archaeological phase, a genealogical phase, and an ethical phase. The first of these phases covers work largely undertaken in the 1960s (see, for example, *The Birth of the Clinic*, *The Order of Things*, and *The Archaeology of Knowledge*); the second deals with work of the early to mid-1970s (*Discipline and Punish* and volume 1 of the *History of Sexuality*); and the last with work of the late 1970s until the early 1980s (volumes 2 and 3 of the *History of Sexuality*). In each of these phases, according to the now common reading,

Foucault develops a particular analytic method and applies it to a particular set of questions, before moving on in the next phase to develop a different method that is in its turn applied to a different set of questions, and so forth. Thus, simplifying matters somewhat, in the first phase the chosen method is archaeology and the question addressed is the constitution of knowledge in discourses within a given historical period. In the middle phase genealogy takes over as the preferred method of studying relations of power in modern society, while in the final phase of his work Foucault returns to classical antiquity in order to produce a history of ethical problematizations, that is, a study of the ways in which different aspects of subjective behavior are reflected upon as problems by a self-reflective, ethical subject (or a study of what Foucault calls "technologies of the self").[32] In order to examine in more depth the ways in which Foucault mobilizes different methodological approaches to enable him to critique liberal conceptions of subjectivity and of sovereignty, some preliminary discussion will be necessary to contextualize and make sense of his changes of approach over the course of his career. Let us begin with the question of the subject as it emerges in Foucault's archaeological work on discourse in the 1960s.

The Order of Things is the book that established Foucault's intellectual reputation in France in 1966 and is still perhaps the best-known example of his archaeological method (the subtitle reads: *An Archaeology of the Human Sciences*). What is the relationship between the archaeological method and the critique of the subject posed by this text (and in other examples of Foucauldian archaeology)? In the foreword to the English edition of the book, after having asserted that scientific discourse presents such a complex reality that it demands to be studied at many different levels and according to many different methods, Foucault qualifies this methodological pluralism when it comes to the topic of the subject itself. "If there is one approach that I do reject," he writes, tellingly, "it is that . . . which gives absolute priority to the observing subject, which attributes a constituent role to an act, which places its own point of view at the origin of all historicity—which, in short, leads to a transcendental consciousness." By contrast, Foucault insists that the "the historical analysis of scientific discourse should, in the last resort, be subject, not to a theory of the knowing subject, but rather to a theory of discursive practice."[33]

A theory of discursive practice (that is, as he comes to formulate it, archaeology) seeks to displace the epistemic privilege of the knowing and seeing subject in favor of a domain that he labels "discourse." For him, discourses are formalized and institutionally produced bodies of knowledge.[34] He is not interested in studying "everyday" or informal speech, but rather in examining what we might call, simply, scientific or social scientific bodies of knowledge.[35] In *The Birth of the Clinic*, for example, he analyses the discourse of medical perception in modernity, while, famously, in *The Order of Things* he examines, among other examples, the discourses of general grammar, natural history, and the analysis of wealth in the Classical Age.[36] Crucially, discourses in Foucault's understanding do not transparently represent a pre-existing reality, but rather order the perception of that reality in historically contingent and particular ways. In his well-known description, discourses are not simply "groups of signs (signifying elements referring to contents or representations)," but rather, crucially, "practices that systematically form the objects of which they speak."[37] What he means by this claim is that discourses are governed by particular institutional practices of constraint and (often implicit) rules concerning the production of valid knowledge within the discourse about given objects, as well as rules for the qualification of subjects to speak about those objects. For Foucault, it is because of these rules and practices that certain objects appear in a certain light and are circulated in a certain way.[38]

"Archaeology" is the name that Foucault gives to the excavation of this constitutive dimension of discourse and the unearthing of the rules by which discourse silently establishes "the limits of enunciability" (what can be said by whom, and of what, and when it will qualify as proper knowledge).[39] It is a consciously ironic term for the theoretical work that he intends this method to perform because the intent of Foucauldian archaeology is by no means to seek the *archē*, the origin, of knowledge itself. Rather, the archaeologist refuses transcendental explanations of the constitution and limits of human knowledge and seeks instead a thoroughly historical accounting of the ways in which certain objects are rendered thinkable (and others unthinkable) and certain speaking positions opened up (while others are foreclosed) at a given moment in time. Archaeology, Foucault remarks in the interview titled "Politics and the Study of Discourse," is "the description of an *archive*." However, as with his playful reference to "archaeology" itself, Foucault does not intend the ordinary, textual-institutional meaning of the word "archive." "By this word," he explains, "I do not mean the mass of texts gathered together at a given period, those from some past epoch that have survived erasure." Rather, for him the archive signifies something more constitutive, namely, "the set of rules which at a given period and for a given society define" what can be said and thought about given objects; how these sayings and thoughts are circulated (or restricted);

who has access to them and on what terms—indeed, even who is permitted to make them in the first place.[40]

Foucault's archaeology of discursive knowledge is designed, as he puts it in the interview just quoted, "to challenge the idea of a sovereign subject."[41] For him it is discourse and discursive relations that dictate the emergence of objects of study—and not the constituent acts of a perceiving subject. Discursive relations—and not subjective properties of insight or originality, for example— are what permit us "to speak of this or that object, in order to deal with them, name them, analyse them, classify them, explain them, etc."[42] We cannot simply "speak of anything at any time," he says in *The Archaeology of Knowledge*; "it is not easy to say something new; it is not enough for us to open our eyes, to pay attention, or to be aware, for new objects suddenly to light up and emerge out of the ground."[43] "Discourse is not," therefore, "the majestically unfolding manifestation of a thinking, knowing, speaking subject, but, on the contrary, a totality, in which the dispersion of the subject and his discontinuity with himself may be determined."[44]

If Foucault's archaeology emphasizes the dispersion of the "thinking, knowing, speaking subject," then the next, genealogical phase of his work addresses this fractured and finite subject from a different angle, as it were. Here the subject receives a different critical treatment, emerging not simply as a creature historically endowed with a certain way of thinking about, knowing, and seeing the world, but as the sedimented result of a range of political techniques applied to the body (themselves informed, traversed, and invested by various knowledges)—not, that is, simply an artifact of discursive relations, but a product, famously, of power relations. No matter how one understands the shift in Foucault's work in the early 1970s, there clearly is a significant change of emphasis around the beginning of the decade, which, as we have seen, is commonly understood as a shift from an archaeology of knowledge to a genealogy of power relations.[45] "Orders of Discourse," his inaugural professorial lecture at the Collège de France in 1970, is usually taken to mark the shift in his thinking. Having previously emphasized the ways in which knowledge is formed in various discursive settings, from this point onward Foucault becomes increasingly interested not so much in what we might call the "internal" dynamics of discourse, but rather in the question of how discourse is articulated with and upon the extra-discursive: the political dimension of knowledge production, dissemination, and instrumentalization. As he puts it late in the 1970 lecture, implicitly distancing himself from his earlier attempts to study discourse throughout the 1960s as a quasi-autonomous phenomenon, he now accords the "material, technical and instrumental investment in knowledge" a more central explanatory role in his work.[46] Consequently, the ways in which knowledge of the human subject comes to be joined with various techniques for the objectification and disposition of the subject—or in Foucault's emblematic hyphenated formulation, the nexus of "power-knowledge"[47]—now become a central preoccupation in the next phase of his work.

The analysis of "power," his central concern from the early to mid-1970s, is probably the feature of his work for which Foucault is best known—at least in the humanities and social sciences. Indeed, if there is a term most readily associated with him, it would have to be "power" or "power relations." Marcelo Hoffman quips that "the name 'Foucault' and the word 'power' appear to have become so densely intertwined that it is difficult to even imagine a sustained discussion of one without reference, at least, to the other."[48] Numerous studies have been devoted to the philosophical reconceptualization or retheorization of power that he developed during this period[49]—in spite of his own insistence, both at the time and subsequently, that he was not interested in power per se and, at any rate, definitely not as something that would give rise to a conceptual or theoretical analysis. For example, in the space of a short passage in the interview "Critical Theory/Intellectual History," Foucault stresses three times that "in studying these power relations, [he] in no way construct[s] a theory of Power," that he is "far from being a theoretician of power," and that, finally, he is "not developing a theory of power."[50] Moreover, in the late, methodologically reflective 1982 essay "The Subject and Power," he goes so far as to deny that the thematic of power was central to his work during the previous twenty years: "I would like to say, first of all, what has been the goal of my work during the last twenty years. It has not been to analyze the phenomena of power, nor to elaborate the foundations of such an analysis."[51] What accounts for the importance of "power" in this middle period, then, is neither the fact that he addresses power as an autonomous domain of intellectual analysis, nor that he presents a new and improved theory of power superior to previous accounts, but that he refuses to do either of these things. In light of his clearly articulated problems with a certain type of abstract, idealist, and "totalitarian" theory (as noted in the Introduction),[52] to read Foucault's 1970s work as an attempt to lay the groundwork for a metaphysics or an ontology of power is misguided.[53] We should rather see him as committed to reframing the analysis of power by looking at it in a new and different way—that is, as he puts it, *penser autrement* about the question of power,[54] to try to think power differently by displacing the frames by and through which it is customarily thought.

In my view, then, the methodological reframing of the question of power is a defining feature of Foucault's work in the 1970s, which permits him to bring into analytic focus several new dimensions of the phenomenon. He insists on approaching the question of power not via the traditional ontological route of asking "What is it?" (as if the entity named "power" were possessed of a pre-existing and inherent nature that was knowable), but rather, and famously, by asking the "flat and empirical little question" of "how it functions":

> To put it bluntly, I would say that to begin the analysis with a "how" is to introduce the suspicion that power as such does not exist. It is, in any case, to ask oneself what contents one has in mind when using this grand, all-embracing, and reifying term; it is to suspect that an extremely complex configuration of realities is allowed to escape while one endlessly marks time before the double question: what is power, and where does power come from? The flat and empirical little question, "What happens?" is not designed to introduce by stealth a metaphysics or an ontology of power but, rather, to undertake a critical investigation of the thematics of power.[55]

By insisting on "studying the 'how of power,' or . . . trying to understand its mechanisms,"[56] Foucault is evading some of the blind spots and conceptual entailments of many traditional, philosophical approaches to the question of power.[57] Here the domain of analysis that preoccupies him is the level of embodied and material social practices. He is interested in the various mechanisms, tactics, techniques, and political technologies (each of which implies and necessitates certain forms of knowledge) for instantiating, maintaining, and reproducing power relations between subjects. While for Foucault the ontology of power allows, as he says above, "a complex reality to escape" (to paraphrase him), a properly situated program of "power analytics"[58] permits the would-be student of power to capture something of that reality and so perceive how subjects are led to govern themselves and each other through diverse and often unacknowledged material practices—practices that are often irreducible to those institutional and juridical practices of law, rights, and the state.

Foucault's work in the 1970s famously presents a series of critical histories, or genealogies, of these practices. While a project of power analytics examines the ways in which practices of power function (by analyzing the "how of power"), the work of genealogy seeks to historicize these practices and to explain how they came to be. For the genealogist, however, their historical coming-to-be is a function neither of logical historical necessity nor of teleology, but rather of accident, discontinuity, and unpredictable political struggle. But just as Foucault's choice of "archaeology" for the title of his analysis of the unacknowledged discursive structures and limits of knowledge is deliberately ironic, so too is his choice of "genealogy"—a borrowing from Nietzsche. While the Foucauldian archaeologist refuses the search for a transcendental *archē* of knowledge, similarly the Foucauldian genealogist abjures the traditional genealogist's quest for an origin that (it is hoped) will validate present practices in a remote and glorious past.[59] Foucault takes over this critical intent from Nietzsche.[60] Genealogy, Foucault writes, "rejects the metahistorical deployment of ideal significations and indefinite teleologies."[61] According to this view, the meaning and value of contemporary practices and institutions cannot be secured in a distant origin and transmitted seamlessly to the present age. If genealogy "opposes itself to the search for 'origins,'"[62] it is because such an endeavor represents the flawed "attempt to capture the exact essence of things, their purest possibilities, and their carefully protected identities, because this search assumes the existence of immobile forms that precede the external world of accident and succession."[63] The misguided search for such an origin reveals instead a more profound secret about the world of things: "not a timeless and essential secret, but the secret that they have no essence or that their essence was fabricated in a piecemeal fashion from alien forms."[64] Genealogy describes a tumultuous history of "invasions, struggles, plundering, disguises, ploys,"[65] in which values, institutions, practices, and identities are constantly remade and recontested over time. A historiographical task of this sort does not aim at the "erecting of foundations: on the contrary, it disturbs what was previously considered immobile; it fragments what was thought unified; it shows the heterogeneity of what was imagined consistent with itself."[66] And this dispersion, predictably, extends to the subject itself. Genealogy, as we have seen, "differs from traditional history in its being without constants"[67]—especially of the anthropological kind. "Nothing in man—not even his body—is sufficiently stable to serve as the basis of self-recognition or for understanding other men," Foucault argues.[68] "We believe that feelings are immutable, but every sentiment, particularly the noblest and most disinterested, has a history."[69] The body itself, if indeed it can be spoken of as any kind of unity, is not a biological reality outside of history but is rather "molded by a great many distinct regimes; it is broken down by the rhythms of work, rest and holidays; it is poisoned by food or values, through eating habits or moral laws."[70]

The genealogist's methodological suspicion thereby "introduces discontinuity into our very being—as it divides our emotions, dramatizes our instincts, multiplies our body and sets it against itself . . . depriv[ing] the self of the reassuring stability of life and nature."[71] According to this rigorous and vertiginous historicization, then, history is not a temporal continuity, but rather a series of ruptures and events (the product of arbitrary and "haphazard conflicts");[72] practices, institutions, and identities have no stable essence extended over time, but rather are constantly made and remade (by "substitutions, displacements, disguised conquests, and systematic reversals");[73] and as a result of this, the subject's unity is ultimately "dissolved."[74] What emerges from the genealogical accounts of Nietzsche and Foucault is a heteronymous subject historically forged, imposed upon, made, and constantly redirected—a subjected subject. If in his *On the Genealogy of Morality* Nietzsche broaches a particular narrative about how the human subject came to be a promising animal,[75] then in his best-known genealogies of the mid-1970s Foucault proposes a neo-Nietzschean narrative about how the modern subject was fabricated as docile and self-responsible in and by a set of particular political technologies. It is to these celebrated writings that I want briefly now to turn, linking Foucault's approaches of "power analytics" (the methodological focus upon the operative workings of practices of power) and genealogy (the historicization of those practices). My intention is not to provide an exhaustive account of this body of work but rather to elucidate, in line with my theme, how Foucault's reframing of the question of power articulates a critique of subjectivity and sovereignty.

In books such as *Discipline and Punish* and the first volume of the *History of Sexuality*, as well as in the more recently published Collège de France lectures, Foucault develops a distinctive account of the growth and operation of power in modernity. Recalling that his analytic focus is not on the normative legitimacy of power, but rather on how power operates (and relatedly, on how we conceptualize and problematize its operation), his analyses revolve around the general claim that power undergoes a "very profound transformation" in modernity.[76] In this well-known if somewhat reductive historical narrative, Foucault describes an epochal transition from a pre-modernity defined by sovereignty and its law to a modernity in which sovereignty has been transcended or transformed into something more generative and finely regulatory of (individual and collective) life. Whereas classical and negative sovereignty operated according to a principle of "deduction" (negation, limit, seizure, blockage), in modernity "'deduction' has tended to be no longer the major form of power but merely one element among others, working to incite, reinforce, control, monitor, optimize, and organize the forces under it: a power bent on generating forces, making them grow, and ordering them, rather than one dedicated to impeding them, making them submit, or destroying them."[77]

Foucault's basic argument, then, is that in modernity the political technology of sovereignty comes to be supplanted by (or better, supplemented with) a series of other technologies.[78] The first of these, the first modification that modernity introduces into the classical field of sovereignty, as it were, is the disciplinary. This is Foucault's famous thesis about the disciplinary character of modern power. Against the discontinuous, "ostentatious" logic of sovereignty,[79] Foucault details (in *Discipline and Punish* and elsewhere) the "humble modalities" and "minor procedures" of an anti-spectacular form of power.[80] Such a form of power is embedded in the quotidian spatio-temporal routine of institutions. Moreover, it does not address itself coercively to a juridical subject, but rather seizes upon and constitutes material bodies in order to form them, control them, and maximize their capacities. As he puts it, power under disciplinary conditions "is no longer exercised through ritual, but through permanent mechanisms of surveillance and control."[81] Those mechanisms—instantiated in institutions as diverse as prisons, factory workshops, schools, barracks, hospitals, and monasteries—are deployed in order to inculcate certain patterns of behavior and self-understanding in the individual subjects who live or work there. The inculcation of the relevant behavioral norm is achieved through a series of disciplinary interventions that Foucault documents in great detail in *Discipline and Punish*—the minutely regulated disposition of individual bodies in time and space; the hierarchical ranking of individuals; the iterative training of bodily aptitudes (*dressage*); the intense surveillance, examination, and recording of individual capacities. In short, in Foucault's account, the subject of discipline is produced through the iterative application of the norm.

That Foucault conceives of discipline precisely as a normalizing power indexes the two related theoretical challenges to subjectivity and sovereignty that I have been discussing in this chapter and in the Introduction. On the question of the production of subjectivity, Foucault famously writes that "the individual is . . . a reality fabricated by this specific technology of power that I have called 'discipline.'" Disciplinary normalization, in his view, does not function on a negative level by way of exclusion, repression, censorship, and so forth, but rather on a productive level: "It produces reality; it produces domains of objects and rituals of truth. The individual and the knowledge that may be gained of him belong to this production."[82] Elsewhere in *Discipline and Punish*, recalling his genealogical premise that the subject has no essence and that it cannot, *pace* liberal accounts, be normatively opposed to a power that stands above and apart from it, Foucault writes that "it is not that the beautiful totality of the individual is amputated, repressed, altered by our social order, it is rather that the individual is carefully fabricated within it, according to a whole technique of forces and bodies."[83] As regards the problematic of sovereignty, the disciplines operate according to a form and a logic irreducible to law and sovereignty. Not only does the disciplinary distribution around a norm mark a break with the binary juridical logic of the law,[84] but these very disciplinary practices and procedures operate in the shadows and the interstices of law and formal state apparatuses. Discipline, Foucault insists more than once, is a kind of "infra-law"[85] and exists on the "underside of the law."[86] In sum, the invention of disciplinary power at the turn of the modern period marks a profound mutation in the operation of power. No longer is the abstract juridical subject the exclusive point of application of power. Rather, and more profoundly, *homo juridicus* now becomes disciplinarily doubled.[87] The material, embodied disciplinary subject, that contingent complex of "forces and bodies," becomes the focus of an elaborate technical investment and control by an ensemble of techniques and knowledges that is subjacent to the formal juridical armature of law.

But the invention of discipline is not the only modulation that the old, juridical model of sovereignty undergoes in modernity. Accordingly, Foucault describes a second shift in the organization of modern power. This new apparatus operates on a different scale, according to a different temporality, and is oriented toward a different political object—this time not the embodied individual whose aptitudes are to be disciplined and normalized, but the population, or the species, the vagaries of whose life are to be regulated. Foucault gives to this second apparatus the name "biopolitics."[88] With the advent of biopolitics the life of the population itself becomes directly political in so far as it emerges as a modifiable object of political attention and control. As with the technology of discipline, to which it is functionally related but from which it differs in several key respects, biopolitics is an ensemble of knowledge and power. One of the key ways in which the population is made known is through the emerging science of state: statistics.[89] More precisely, and recalling my earlier discussion of the constitutive status of discursive knowledge, the "population" is itself epistemically fabricated as an object of knowledge within the discourse of statistics. It is clearly not a matter of claiming that human collectivities are legislated into existence by the knowledge claims of statistics (a species of radical discursive idealism), but rather of making the more nuanced claim that the discourse of statistics develops the conceptual category of the "population" in order to understand such collectivities and their internal and environmental interactions (and, moreover, claiming that from this contingent and particular understanding there emerges a range of available political interventions). While juridical sovereignty knows only an abstract subject, and disciplinary power via the human sciences knows an embodied individual with certain proclivities and aptitudes, biopolitics is enabled, in part through the discursive agency of statistics, to know a living population with a specific density and "life" of its own that is possessed of observable and modifiable regularities irreducible to the lives of each of its constituent individuals.

If the population is thus made known through the discourse of statistics, then it is governed by means of a range of regulatory interventions and mechanisms that no longer take the subject or the individual-to-be-corrected as their point of application but rather address the population, or pertinent sections of it. The purpose of such regulatory interventions is neither to forbid nor to circumscribe allowable behaviors (per law), nor to mold the behavior of errant individuals, but to "establish an equilibrium, maintain an average, establish a sort of homeostasis, and compensate for variations within this general population and its aleatory field." It hence addresses itself neither to abstract juridical subjects nor to material disciplinary subjects but rather to the milieu within which the population lives. By making regulatory adjustments to this milieu the "mortality rate [can be] modified or lowered; life expectancy [can] be increased; the birth rate [can be] stimulated," and so forth.[90] The regulatory interventions and mechanisms of biopolitics such as natalist, public health, or sanitation policies thus operate on a wider scale and function according to a very different temporality. While discipline is applied from minute to minute, the collective phenomena of biopolitics ("propagation, births and mortality, the level of health, life expectancy and longevity, with all the conditions that can cause these to vary")[91] are "serial phenomena . . . aleatory events that occur within a population that exists over a period of time."[92] Foucault, it should be stressed, did not envision the wholesale replacement of juridical sovereignty with mechanisms of discipline and biopolitics in modernity, but rather an apparatus that comprises the different dimensions of sovereign, disciplinary, and biopolitical rule.[93] Nevertheless, it is clear that the account he gives of the invention of this "great bipolar technology,"[94] which disciplines the life of the individual even as it regularizes the life of populations, presents certain critical challenges to received accounts of the subject and of sovereignty—challenges that seek to displace and reframe the operative concepts of subjectivity and sovereignty rather than to vitiate them. We are now in a position to conclude this section by recounting the different elements of these critiques and relating them to an understanding of rights.

To do this it might be helpful to join these two critiques of Foucault's by saying that what he is most concerned to distance himself from in the middle phase of his work is a conception of power that he labels "juridico-discursive." It is this theory of power that he has in mind when, as noted in the Introduction, he calls for the King's head to be cut off.[95] In the first volume of the *History of Sexuality*, Foucault takes issue with what he calls "the repressive hypothesis,"[96] according to which, he alleges, sexuality exists prior to the advent of social customs, laws, and practices and is consequently, according to their form and intensity, either more or less repressed by them. By contrast, it is his belief that those very customs, laws, and practices themselves directly produce, incite, and contour sexuality. In other words, sexuality is not a pre-existing "thing in itself," but rather a highly contingent artifact and product of discourse and power, something that only has meaning within and not outside of or before these culturally variable normative frameworks. Foucault argues that the "repressive hypothesis" still mistakenly continues to structure and animate contemporary thinking about power. According to such a view, power operates by stating a rule: "Power acts by laying down the rule. . . . It speaks, and that is the rule."[97] Yet thinking power in this way tends to elide its constitutive dimension, resulting in an impoverished understanding of the way power operates in modern societies. According to such a conception the exercise of power is simply the repression of pre-existent objects:

> It is a power that only has the force of the negative on its side, a power to say no; in no condition to produce, capable only of posting limits, it is basically anti-energy. . . . It is a power *whose model is essentially juridical, centred on nothing more than the statement of the law* and the operation of taboos.[98]

In addition, thinking power in this way prompts us to ask (what are for Foucault rather circular) questions about the legitimacy of power. If power is not in some ways formative of the object on which it is being brought to bear, then that object can provide a ready-made normative standard by which to assess the limits and application of power. In the social contract tradition, for example, the life and welfare of the subjects, or the respect of their inalienable rights, is seen to furnish a measure by which to assess the limits of sovereign power. The exercise of power by the sovereign is legitimate to the extent that it respects such limits. Hence Foucault will argue that "the essential role of the theory of right has been to establish the legitimacy of power," since it not only "masks" the violence of sovereignty and "dissolves" the "element of domination" proper to it, but does so by making the question of power revolve around "the legitimate rights of the sovereign on the one hand, and the legal obligation to obey on the other."[99]

For Foucault, this orthodox theoretical conception of power renders legitimate and simultaneously re-performs the operation of sovereignty, and does so at the cost of hiding the productive dimension of power. As he says, power is therefore rendered "tolerable only on condition that it mask a substantial part of itself."[100] In contrast to this theoretical edifice of sovereignty and its legitimate limits, Foucault's genealogies of discipline and biopolitics illuminate the ways in which power is not simply repressive of a pre-given object of control, but is in crucial respects formative of that object. For him, power is "*already productive* power, forming the very object that will be suitable for control and then, in an act that effectively disavows that production, claiming to discover that [object] outside of power."[101] And that object, famously, includes the subject— which for Foucault is precisely never "outside of power," but rather is generated within and by it. His work in this period accordingly details the emergence of a range of political technologies in modernity that are productive and regulative of subjectivity and cannot simply be assimilated into existing juridical models of law, state, and right. These new modalities of power do not operate in a repressive, "top down" fashion,[102] bringing a pre-given sovereign law to bear upon a juridical subject, but function in a much more diffuse, lateral way, insinuating themselves into the bodies, gestures, and self-conceptions of the very subjects they form and govern. This body of work consequently represents a theoretical critique of essentialist and foundationalist conceptions of the subject at the same time as it proposes a challenge to juridical theories of power.

What, then, are we to conclude from this survey of the different strands of Foucault's work up until the late 1970s? I have been arguing that it is a body of work that constitutes a rich and suggestive critique of the subject and of sovereignty: two central elements of a liberal individualist theory of rights. But what manner of critique is this? What exactly are we left with after Foucault's critique if we want to think through and deploy rights? Do these critiques, as some critics maintain, mean that Foucault is himself not entitled to engage with or deploy rights? Or do they simply help us to problematize and displace certain concepts in rights discourse and in the process open them up to new and different formulations?

In what follows I want to suggest the second of these possibilities. Foucault's critique does not commend a global rejection of the terms or the object under critical investigation, but rather destabilizes that object and lays it open to the possibility of being otherwise. Briefly returning to his early work on discourse helps to illuminate this point. In *The Archaeology of Knowledge*, Foucault writes critically of the "anthropological constraints" of the traditional history of ideas.[103] Key among these constraints are the seductively common-sensical figures of the author, the book, and the oeuvre. However, accepting the self-evidence of such figures only obscures the more important operations of discourse. For the archaeologist, it is precisely the operation of discursive rules that represents the effective conditions of possibility of knowledge in a given time and place: "We must question those ready-made syntheses, those groupings that we normally accept before any examination, those links whose validity is recognized from the outset."[104] But to "suspend" their putative self-evidence and to submit them to an archaeological critique which asks after their discursive construction is by no means to reject them out of hand. Foucault again:

> These pre-existing forms of continuity, all these syntheses that are accepted without question, must remain in suspense. They must not be rejected definitively of course, but the tranquility with which they are accepted must be disturbed; we must show that they do not come about of themselves, but are always the result of a construction the rules of which must be known, and the justifications of which must be scrutinized.[105]

The object or objects under critique—here the founding subjectivities of the history of ideas—are not erased but displaced. Not being "definitively rejected," they remain, but in remaining they cannot help but remain differently. To put the matter in language that Foucault will not adopt explicitly until later in the decade but that underwrites the above analysis, such concepts, practices, and technologies as authority, subjectivity, and sovereignty remain available to tactical reappropriation, reinvestment, and reimagining after the moment of critique. In that it works a suspension and a reorientation of these familiar concepts, Foucault's critique is profoundly affirmative. Having thus been critically defamiliarized, the newly estranged objects of Foucault's critique are subsequently freed for different uses and meanings.

The remainder of this book sets out to describe, and to assess, the different ways in which Foucault seeks to accomplish this task with the available political technology of rights. In the concluding section of the present chapter, I want to link the general meaning of "critique" in Foucault's work and the affirmation of contingency that it embodies to a specific concept that enters his philosophical lexicon in 1978, the concept of counter-conduct. What I hope to show is that his mobilization of the ever-present, immanent, resistant capacities latent in forms of conduct (that is, precisely, the possibility of a counter-conduct) rests upon— and is a concrete instantiation of—his archaeological and genealogical com-mitments to a form of critique understood as ruptural and affirmative of plural, contingent possibilities for the future. Importantly, this is a form of critique that does not measure and thereby attempt to change existent arrangements by holding them up to universal normative standards that transcend them, but rather one that tries to isolate and mobilize the particular possibilities for change and contestation disclosed within and by those practices themselves.

What Is a Counter-Conduct?

As is often noted, Foucault's annual Collège de France lectures "Security, Ter-ritory, Population" and "The Birth of Biopolitics," delivered in 1978 and 1979, respectively, occur on the cusp of his investigations of ethics and technologies of the self, topics that will occupy him until his death in 1984.[106] This makes them particularly significant for scholars anxious to understand not only the motivations behind the transition but also the precise way in which Foucault's migration from a study of practices of objectification (discipline and biopoli-tics) to a study of practices of self-initiated subjectification (ethics) unfolds.[107] In the previous section I discussed Foucault's analytical and genealogical inves-tigations into particular political technologies characteristic of modernity: dis-cipline and biopolitics. In the years after 1979, as we shall see in Chapter 2, his attention turns away from this time period and back to classical antiquity. In so doing, Foucault addresses a new set of concerns—namely, the ways in which the subject constitutes itself as a subject of ethical action by means of the ap-plication to itself of a series of ascetic techniques. Reflecting on this conceptual transition in a 1982 seminar, he observes: "Perhaps I've insisted too much on the technology of domination and power. I am more and more interested in the interaction between oneself and others, and in the technologies of individual domination, in the mode of action that an individual exercises upon himself by means of the technologies of the self."[108] In other words, he says, he did not make a change of direction but rather of emphasis, a gentle self-correction, as a result of having "insisted too much" on the dimensions of human objectification via apparatuses of power-knowledge and not enough on the ways in which subjects turn themselves into subjects. The 1978 and 1979 lectures introduce a theme that helps us to make sense of this transition and the resulting change of emphasis, one that is familiar to students of Foucault: the problematic of governmentality.

Governmentality studies is, and has been for some time, a very productive "school" of work, largely in the social sciences.[109] It took its initial bearings from a lecture Foucault gave on 1 February 1978, the fourth in the series titled "Security, Territory, Population."[110] Like a number of other Collège de France lectures, such as the first two in the 1976 course "'Society Must Be Defended,'" this was published as a stand-alone lecture—well in advance of the entire course becoming available to a reading public.[111] In both the 1978 and 1979 lectures— they form a pair—Foucault constructs a sprawling genealogy of practices of governmentality that encompasses the beginnings of the Christian pastorate, Renaissance political theory, the modern nation-state, and finally, the contemporary refashioning of the state under conditions of neoliberal rule. The "ugly" neologism "governmentality" (Foucault's own)[112] is intended to signify the irreducible connection between practices of governing (*gouverner*) and the styles or modes of thought (*mentalité*) that underpin those practices.

It is doubtless accurate to interpret these lectures and the history of practices of governing that they contain as a response to certain of Foucault's critics who, throughout the middle of the 1970s but particularly after the publication of *Discipline and Punish*,[113] had criticized him for having illegitimately omitted the state from his analyses of modern political technologies.[114] But it is a characteristically playful and indirect Foucauldian "reply to critics," one that refuses and reframes the terms of the debate on the origins and functions of the state. Simply, the genealogy of governmentality is not the history of the state. He ends the ninth of the 1978 lectures with the announcement that "the emergence of the state as a fundamental political issue can in fact be situated within a more general history of governmentality, or, if you like, in the field of practices of power." Thus reversing the conceptual and terminological order of priority, Foucault accuses his imagined interlocutors of reifying and fetishizing the state and of "develop[ing] the ontology of this thing that would be the state." But, asks Foucault:

> What if the state were nothing more than a way of governing? What if the state were nothing more than a type of governmentality? What if all these relations of power that gradually take shape on the basis of multiple and very diverse processes which gradually coagulate and form an effect, what if these practices of government were precisely the basis on which the state was constituted?[115]

As historian Paul Veyne has noted, Foucault's historiographical wager in the 1978–79 lectures is to refuse purportedly universal, transhistorical categories such as this non-thing called "the state" and instead to insist on the centrality of practices of governing.[116] Seen in this way, "the state," Foucault says, is nothing more than "an episode in [the genealogy of] governmentality."[117] If the state *qua* explanatory universal does not exist, then what properly does exist for the genealogist, and therefore what can be the subject of an effective history, is the domain of governmental practice. For Foucault, then, governing is by no means coextensive with the state, sovereignty, or law. Just as with the "capillary" location of discipline beyond the routine theatres of state power,[118] his genealogy of governmental practice locates "governing" in a similarly dispersed range of sites: one governs the sick, one governs one's family, one governs children, one governs the soul, and one governs one's self. And "assuming that 'governing' is different from 'reigning or ruling,' and not the same as 'commanding' or 'laying down the law,' or being a sovereign, suzerain, lord, judge, general, land-owner, master, or a teacher," he writes, and "assuming therefore that governing is a specific activity, we now need to know something about the type of power the notion covers."[119] In short, for Foucault, the modality proper to governing is conducting. To govern is to conduct. Government is the conduct of one's (and others') conduct, the very "conduct of conducts":[120]

> Conduct is the activity of conducting (*conduire*), of conduction (*la conduction*) if you like, but it is equally the way in which one conducts oneself (*se conduit*), lets oneself be conducted (*se laisse conduire*), is conducted (*est conduit*), and finally, in which one behaves (*se comporter*) as an effect of a form of conduct (*une conduite*) as the action of conducting or of conduction (*conduction*).[121]

"One already sees here," Arnold I. Davidson writes of this passage, "the double dimension of conduct, namely the activity of conducting an individual, conduction as a relation between individuals, and the way in which an individual conducts 'himself' or is conducted, 'his' conduct or behavior in the narrower sense of the term."[122] It follows therefore that we can begin to see how this shift toward conceptualizing the operation of power as the government of conduct permits Foucault to open up an analysis not simply of the operation of power over others in an objectifying register, but also of the operation of power over oneself, in a (self-)subjectifying register. Conduct emerges as the conceptual pivot upon which the late work turns: from power to ethics.

It would be useful at this point to bring the contrary dimension of conduct into analytic relief, for we are concerned here not simply with forms or manners of "conduct," but rather with their "counter-strokes,"[123] with that which opposes them from within. However, it is not until 1 March 1978, in the eighth of his 1978 lectures, that Foucault explicitly introduces this resistant concept of "counter-conduct" into his critical vocabulary. The reason for this is that the particular discussion of counter-conducts begun in lecture 8 makes sense only within a wider history of a specific form of conduct that the lecture course as a whole, "Security, Territory, Population," attempts to trace—and that form is what Foucault labels "pastoral power."[124] Briefly, pastoral power is a particular technology of power that first arises in the Christian pastorate but that subsequently, according to Foucault's account, comes to be transposed, and thereby modified, into the statist doctrine of *raison d'État* in sixteenth- and seventeenth-century Europe.[125] The genealogy he develops in "Security, Territory, Population," then, is of the progressive institutional intensification and secular appropriation of an originally theological technology. If the pastorate, that elaborate "art of conducting, directing, leading, guiding, taking in hand, and manipulating men . . . collectively and individually throughout their life and at each moment of their existence,"[126] comes to be assimilated into modern and contemporary forms of governmentality (indeed to serve, as Foucault puts it, as their "background" and "prelude"),[127] then this for him evidences not so much a secular overcoming of the theological, but rather a continuing indebtedness and repetition—the history of the pastorate is a history from which Western modernity, despite its secular pretensions, has by no means managed to disentangle itself.

But how does Foucault characterize that form of power (originally) proper to the Christian pastorate? Such a pastoral form of power was, he maintains in an initial general discussion, characterized in the following way: first, it was exercised over a flock of people on the move, rather than over a static territory; second, it was a fundamentally beneficent power according to which the duty of the pastor (to the point of self-sacrifice) was the salvation of the flock; and finally, it was an individualizing power, in that the pastor was obliged to care for each and every member of the flock singly.[128] In the pastoral relation there hence operates a complex reciprocity binding the pastor and his sheep, with the pastor exercising a precise and meticulous accounting of the actions of each and all of his charges in order to assure their salvation: "The pastor must really take charge of and observe daily life in order to form a never-ending knowledge of the behaviour and conduct of the members of the flock he supervises."[129] The pastor's concern for the everyday life of his sheep must also extend to the "spiritual direction" (*direction de conscience*) of the thoughts of his flock, a procedure involving the production and extraction of "a particular truth through which one will be bound to the person who directs one's conscience."[130] Foucault illustrates a model of power, then, in which there is a complex and thoroughly affective tie between the pastor who exercises a minute and careful jurisdiction over the bodily actions and souls of his flock in order to assure their salvation, and those who, each of them in turn, must owe him "a kind of exhaustive, total, and permanent relationship of individual obedience."[131] In short, the pastorate revolves around the notions of salvation, obedience, and truth.

It is precisely over the meaning and direction of these three operative elements of the pastorate that counter-conducts internal to the pastorate itself begin to emerge. "If it is true that the pastorate is a highly specific form of power with the object of conducting men—I mean, that takes as its instrument the methods that allow one to direct them (*les conduire*), and as its target the way in which they conduct themselves, the way in which they behave—if the objective of the pastorate is men's conduct," wagers Foucault, then "I think equally specific movements of resistance and insubordination appeared in correlation with this that could be called specific revolts of conduct."[132] He discusses how, in the Middle Ages, there were "five main forms of counter-conduct, all of which tend to redistribute, reverse, nullify, and partially or totally discredit pastoral power in the systems of salvation, obedience, and truth, that is to say, in the three domains . . . which characterize . . . the objective, the domain of intervention of pastoral power."[133] These five were: asceticism, the formation of communities, mysticism, the return to scripture, and finally, eschatology. In their different ways, each of these counter-conducts seeks to utilize available elements of the pastoral modality of power in order to contest the official pastorate itself. To take just one example, the practice of asceticism has traditionally meant the renunciation of the ascetic's will and his "unquestioning obedience" to the rule of a spiritual director,[134] but this particular understanding and organization of the practice of asceticism does not exhaust the possibilities of asceticism per se. "What was at stake [in the official pastoral organization of asceticism] was limiting anything that could be boundless in asceticism, or at any rate everything incompatible with the organization of power," Foucault argues.[135] Against this restrained, hierarchical, and obedience-demanding formulation, a range of religious communities (such as the Benedictines and heterodox groups such as the Taboriates or the Waldensians) sought to reclaim the resistant potential of asceticism. Asceticism in their hands worked as a kind of radical withdrawal from the hierarchical relation between director and penitent, such that "in asceticism there is a specific excess that denies access to an external power."[136] The ascetic is constantly engaged in an unruly, unpredictable, highly personal, and corporeal struggle (with himself) which ultimately eludes the control of the spiritual director. This ascetic withdrawal proves to be such a significant component of pastoral counter-conducts that Foucault observes: "Whenever and wherever pastoral counter-conducts develop in the Middle Ages, asceticism [is] one of their points of support and instruments against the pastorate."[137] The important theoretical point to be extracted from Foucault's discussion of asceticism as a form of counter-conduct in "Security, Territory, Population" is that "asceticism is rather a sort of tactical element, an element of reversal by which certain themes of Christian theology or religious experience are utilized against these structures of power."[138] This is also the case with the other examples Foucault gives in the lecture course—each in their way represents a kind of taking up of received, orthodox practices and doctrines and a turning of them against orthodoxy.

Why does this notion of counter-conduct, buried in Foucault's historical presentation of the somewhat marginal practices of some medieval Christian circles in his 1978 Collège course, present a useful way for thinking about his late engagements with rights? Let me offer three answers to this question. The first and simplest reason is chronological: this is the conceptualization of power relations and their reversibility with which Foucault is working at the time he begins to engage with rights discourse. It is hence contemporaneous with many of the rights struggles with which he aligns himself and in which he participates. But we can be both a little more specific and more conceptual about the notion of counter-conduct than this. The second reason is that the notion of the counter-conduct represents both a continuation and a refinement of Foucault's earlier, midcareer theorizations of power and resistance. One of the key premises underlying Foucault's analysis of power relations in works such as *Discipline and Punish* and the first volume of *The History of Sexuality* was that, as he put it in the latter text, "resistance is never in a position of exteriority in relation to power." In that same well-known passage he insists on the "strictly *relational* character of power relations," such that "power" and "resistance" enter into a kind of back-and-forth engagement wherein each faces off against the other but is simultaneously "dependent" upon the other.[139] And yet on the very next page of that book Foucault also describes power and resistance as being interlocked, such that resistance is "inscribed in [power] as an irreducible opposite."[140] That these descriptions are somewhat at variance doubtless goes some way to explaining the consternation of many of Foucault's critics and commentators when it comes to explaining where resistance comes from and how it can indeed take place.[141] The later notions of conduct and counter-conduct (which I interpret as a development and refinement of the thematic of power, and not, *pace* some scholars, as a radical break)[142] arguably present a clearer approach to this question. This is because they foreground the ways in which it is the very forms of conduct that themselves disclose the possibilities for their contrary deployment or subversive appropriation (that is, it is not a question of power versus resistance, as linked or as interlocking as the case may be, but of a variable field of conduct multiply and internally divided against itself). In relation to the question of rights, specifically, this later notion of counter-conduct hence better captures the sense that rights are simultaneously forms of regulation and resistance. Finally, the third reason that the notion of counter-conduct is helpful for theorizing Foucault's late politics of rights is that it clearly expresses the sense that what is being governed or conducted is the behavior, attitudes, and range of options both of others and of the self doing the governing or conducting. Foucault develops the idea of counter-conduct at a point of transition between his midcareer work on power relations and his later work on ethics and on technologies of the self. As such, it indexes a more nuanced concern with the way in which practices of government simultaneously perform both these (objectifying and subjectifying, for want of better words) functions. We can readily perceive the relevance of such a formulation in the context of rights claims: the assertion of a right both functions to remake and contest relations with others but at the same time establishes a particular relation to, and conception of, the rights holder herself.

In order to lay the theoretical groundwork for an understanding of Foucault's politics of rights, this chapter has sought to connect a reading of critique in Foucault's work to his late concept of counter-conduct. Critique, on Foucault's account, is not (indeed, cannot be) an instance of pure negation or rejection, but is rather best understood as an affirmative exposure of human possibilities that are forgotten when contingent social and political formations come to be naturalized and rendered commonsensical. On this view critique is a form of excavation. What critique excavates is the hidden margin of freedom immanent in all contingent human arrangements, and what it thereby demonstrates is the sustaining possibility of their being otherwise than they are now—so as to show, as Foucault puts it, that people are "much freer than they feel."[143] It is on this affirmative dimension of Foucault's critical project—as represented in both archaeology and genealogy—that the possibility and viability of counter-conducts rests. That is to say, it is precisely by virtue of the fact that concepts, institutions, practices, and indeed, even identities are not susceptible of one final and determinative meaning, but rather present themselves as unstable opportunities for re-articulation, reinvestment and countermobilization, that elements of forms of government can be appropriated to radically different ends. Listing his reasons for focusing in detail on the different forms of medieval counter-conduct, in the eighth lecture of "Security, Territory, Population" Foucault argues that "these themes that have been fundamental elements in these counter-conducts are clearly not absolutely external to Christianity, but are actually border-elements . . . which have been continually re-utilized, re-implanted, and taken up again in one or another direction." This form of immanent critique of the pastorate consists, for him, in "the permanent use of tactical elements that are pertinent in the anti-pastoral struggle, insofar as they fall within, in a marginal way, the general horizon of Christianity."[144] Although he may do so, the critic of the pastorate is not obliged to source the grounds of critique external to the pastorate.[145] Rather, Foucault's point is that the meaning, function, and direction of various elements of the pastorate itself are open to productive reinterpretation and struggle from within.

It is according to this understanding of the critical, appropriatory practice of counter-conducts that I propose to read Foucault's politics of rights in the next three chapters. Such an understanding explains how Foucault moves from a position of being critical of rights to one of affirming them himself precisely by showing how critique is always already affirmation. It is not a matter of his relinquishing critique for something else, something more conciliatory, practical, or pragmatic—but rather a matter of realizing through the very movement of critique the latent political possibilities of rights. It is with this in mind that

I would propose a rather mundane answer to the rhetorical question Foucault poses toward the end of the second lecture of "'Society Must Be Defended.'" Readers will recall that this is where he asserts the possibility—without defining it—of a "new right."[146] Rather than realizing (or as his detractors contend, failing to realize) a substantive new form of right,[147] his subsequent politics of rights realizes the principle of potential newness inherent in rights discourse as a political artifact. Simply put, for the genealogist rights can be made anew and reinvented (as, of course, can other technologies) with each new exercise, with each new making. It is time now to examine the various dimensions of Foucault's reinventions of rights, starting, in the next chapter, with the question of the ungroundedness of rights.

CHAPTER 2

WHO IS THE SUBJECT OF

(FOUCAULT'S HUMAN) RIGHTS?

And what form of rights claims have the temerity to sacrifice an
absolutist or naturalized status in order to carry this possibility?

Wendy Brown

The Continuity of Foucault's Discourse

This chapter begins to develop my account of Foucault's politics of rights as a
form of critical counter-conduct, and in order to better orient the ensuing discussion, it opens with a reading of a particular type of rights claim. I propose to
start where traditional discussions of rights tend, for obvious reasons, to begin,
namely, with a consideration of the underlying grounds of rights. According to
most orthodox normative accounts, it is the grounds of rights that supposedly
guarantee their normative appeal and structural integrity. Yet, contrary to the
tenor of such accounts, what I shall suggest is that in his late work Foucault
has the anti-normative temerity to insist on making rights claims in the con-
spicuous absence of any of the traditionally accepted grounds of rights. It is
with this contingent and quite deliberate ungrounded dimension of Foucault's
rights politics that the present chapter deals. To be clear: I do not read the absence of an account of the grounds of rights as a failure of any kind. I am thus
not interested in saving Foucault from himself or in normatively reconstructing
him. Rather, I want to ask a different set of questions, which revolve around
the political possibilities enlivened by Foucault's contingent and ungrounded
rights claims. What happens to rights when Foucault deliberately speaks of
them as having no stable and delimitable ground, no subjective referent? What
might it mean for him, committed as he is to a non-anthropologically grounded
and anti-essentialist form of politics, to invoke rights in this way? What political effects does this contingent framing and mobilization of rights produce?

Moreover, what possibilities does such an approach help to open up—and what limits might it engender and encounter? (I pause here to mention that this approach is not one limited to Foucault and that other theorists conceive of rights in groundless terms, some of whom I discuss in the following pages.)[1] These are the interlinked and overlapping questions that the present chapter begins to answer, and it does so primarily through a consideration of Foucault's late and, for many, maddening invocations of human rights.

As the most commonly claimed ground of rights is the subject, or some property (for example, rationality or dignity) said to be proper to that subject, I cannot help but discuss this fundamental problematic. However, in doing so, I intend to focus not on subjectivity in general but on one particular (and highly contested) figuration of subjectivity: the late Foucauldian subject. The importance of this much-discussed interpretive question for an understanding of Foucault's politics of rights is fairly self-evident. The late work on rights is contemporaneous with the late 1970s work on forms of liberal governmentality and early 1980s work on ethics and technologies of the self, in which Foucault is alleged to have tacitly reintroduced some sort of liberal humanist subject. According to this view, the late Foucault surreptitiously ushers in a kind of core self, untrammeled, or at any rate significantly less determined, by the formative effects of power-knowledge apparatuses upon which he had insisted so forcefully in the mid-1970s. If this is the case, so goes the argument, then his late work on rights can plausibly be understood as a retreat to a politics of liberalism and a normative defense of the individual against the power of the state or of other individuals. This rather anodyne conclusion, entirely at variance with Foucault's preceding critical work, is one that I have already expressed my intention to revise. Accordingly, my aim here is to take up the question of the status and function of the subject in Foucault's late work in order to lay the basis for a very different understanding of his late political engagement with rights discourse. In my view, Foucault continues, even into the late work, to understand subjectivity as an effect of power and knowledge, with several ramifications for an understanding of his politics of rights. What some take to be a return to a fairly traditional subjective ground of rights is really, I believe, a much more contingent and ungrounded "ground" of rights. A proper appreciation of this should not only make us hesitate to assimilate Foucault's late work on rights to liberalism, but also prompt us to consider the ways in which such a conception of rights itself actually facilitates a range of different political possibilities beyond, and potentially critical and transformative of, liberalism itself.

Ironically, motivating this question of the subject in the late Foucault is a question of continuity, namely, the continuity of Foucault's own discourse. (I say "ironically" as Foucault is frequently, though not always fairly or accurately, read as a philosopher of discontinuity.) In turn, what is at stake in the present question of continuity is the political character and effect of the late work as understood in relation to what precedes it. The question of continuity thus directly raises questions regarding the political interpretation of the late work and, by implication, the political conclusion to—and legacy of—Foucault's thought as a whole. Recalling that he often invokes rhetorically the discontinuity between different regimes of knowledge and power by means of juxtaposition (think, for example, of the celebrated openings to *The Order of Things* and *Discipline and Punish*),[2] I want now to do something similar myself in order to concretize this political question of continuity and its implications for a reading of the late work. What follow are the closing remarks of two texts, separated by eighteen years and expressing what seems a radically different philosophical and political idiom. The first is relatively well known (if often misunderstood):[3]

> As the archaeology of our thought easily shows, man is an invention of recent date. And one perhaps nearing its end. If those arrangements were to disappear as they appeared, if some event of which we can at the moment do no more than sense the possibility—without knowing what its form will be or what it promises—were to cause them to crumble, as the ground of Classical thought did, at the end of the eighteenth century, then one can certainly wager that man would be erased, like a face drawn in sand at the edge of the sea.

The second is perhaps less well known:

> We must reject the division of labor so often proposed to us: individuals can get indignant and talk; governments will reflect and act. It's true that good governments appreciate the holy indignation of the governed, provided it remains lyrical. I think we need to be aware that very often it is those who govern who talk, are capable only of talking, and want only to talk. Experience shows that one can and must refuse the theoretical role of pure and simple indignation that is proposed to us. Amnesty International, Terre des Hommes, and Médecins du [M]onde are initiatives that have created this new right—that of private individuals to effectively intervene in the sphere of international policy and strategy. The will of individuals must make a place for itself in a reality that governments have attempted to reserve for themselves, that monopoly which we need to wrest from them little by little and day by day.

Both texts are written, of course, by Foucault[4]—and it is the alleged discontinuity within his own discourse now, between the Nietzschean glee of the archaeologist at man's coming erasure in the closing pages of *The Order of Things* in 1966 and the worthy collaboration with international human rights groups in 1984 marked by the text "Confronting Governments: Human Rights," that provides the spur for this chapter. What is it that separates these two texts, politically, philosophically, and strategically, in the Foucauldian oeuvre? What has happened to him in the eighteen years between *The Order of Things* and "Confronting Governments: Human Rights," in that curious movement from archaeology to Amnesty International? Can we discern in the latter text, as several critics have, the baffling figure of "Foucault the Neohumanist"?[5] Or can we not try, paraphrasing Foucault, to "resolve [this] problem of discontinuity"[6] without recourse to a founding subject? And what would that latter prospect mean for a reading of rights?

In what follows I take as my critical foil an influential contribution to the ongoing debate about the late Foucauldian subject: Eric Paras's 2006 *Foucault 2.0: Beyond Power and Knowledge*. Against Paras (and others) I insist upon the continuity of Foucault's archaeological and genealogical insights about subjectivity and their extension into the late work. That is, for me, the late Foucauldian subject continues to be an artifact of power and knowledge, not something that somehow pre-exists or transcends them. Armed with such an anti-essentialist understanding of the subject, I then propose a different reading of Foucault's own late invocations of human rights as a very decisive ethico-political intervention that neither circumscribes nor undermines rights, but rather productively exposes them to a range of different political futures. But let me start with this question of the subject.

The Critique (or Return?) of the Subject in the Late Foucault

The French intellectual historian François Dosse clearly articulates what is at stake intellectually and politically in the question of the subject. He writes in his compendious *History of Structuralism* that in the late 1970s and early 1980s Foucault's changeable thought pivoted once more (and possibly for the final, determinative time). On this occasion the conceptual pivot was nothing other than the subject itself, and his thought consequently slunk toward an endorsement of the then newly ascendant values of rights, human rights, and political liberalism. "In 1968," writes Dosse, "he had shifted from epistemes to discursive practices, but this time, current events led him to call the subject into question, a subject he had always circumscribed and considered so unimportant that he had simply eliminated it from his philosophical considerations." "Not only was the subject back," he continues dramatically, "but so was Foucault the individual, in the most profound way."[7] By linking in this way his theoretical and personal political commitments of the time, Dosse argues that Foucault's rethinking of subjectivity in the late work on classical Greece and ancient Rome is not simply some scholarly detour, but in fact a purposeful reorientation of his historical scholarship toward contemporary political events ("Foucault had always been attentive to the way theory and practice came together in response to the demands of the present," Dosse recalls).[8] Whether the rethinking of the subject opens the way to the political endorsement of rights, or whether the latter necessitates the former, the political manifestation of this theoretical re-articulation of the subject is at any rate very clear to Dosse: "In the late seventies and early eighties, Foucault embraced the cause of human rights."[9] For Dosse, then, the return of the subject vacates the genealogical critique of juridico-political form and paves the way for a thoroughgoing liberal affirmation of rights. Enter the subject and its rights, belatedly; exit critique, confusedly.

Others have accepted this narrative of a return to the subject in his late work and used it to strengthen an argument about Foucault's affirmation of a liberal politics of rights at this time. Perhaps the most developed and provocative attempt to do so in recent years has been by Eric Paras in *Foucault 2.0: Beyond Power and Knowledge*. Both his title and subtitle are immediately revealing—Paras's is a rebadged and updated Foucault, for whom the subject comes to be understood as somehow existing before and untouched by social and political customs, that is to say, in his terms, a somewhat unlikely Foucauldian subject subsisting somewhere "beyond power and knowledge." Paras announces his revisionist project as follows:

> We know a great deal about the constellation within which Foucault moved when he challenged the hegemony of "man," [but] we are comparatively ignorant of the process by which he abandoned his hard structuralist position and later embraced ideas he had labored to undermine: liberty, individualism, "human rights," and even the thinking subject. It is Foucault's migration away from the fire-eating antihumanism of 1968 and his asymptotic approach toward a style of thinking that countenanced a partially autonomous and reflexive subject that form the substance of this study.[10]

Paras's language of partial autonomy and reflexivity is somewhat misleading, for elsewhere and more consistently he insists on locating in the late Foucault a much more classically Kantian and fully autonomous figure of subjectivity. For example, he goes on to frame the above-mentioned transition in Foucault's thought as a "move away from the 'strong' anti-subjectivity position expressed in the disciplinary hypothesis . . . [toward] the study of the subject as an independent phenomenon."[11] This subject as an independent phenomenon is then described precisely as a "'prediscursive subject': that is, a subjective nucleus that precedes any practices that might be said to construct it, and indeed one that freely chooses among those practices."[12] Whether it emerges as an independent phenomenon, a prediscursive subject, a subjective nucleus, an "independent and freestanding subject,"[13] or a "primary entity in itself,"[14] the late Foucauldian subject clearly signals for Paras a decisive break with the archaeological and genealogical theses about subjectivity as a constructed and contingent social condition.

To be clear: for Paras as well as for Dosse, this volte-face on Foucault's part betokens a very different—indeed, surprising and contentious—form of politics. "Perhaps most interestingly," writes Paras at the beginning of his book, again explicitly linking the rethinking of the subject with the positive appraisal of a liberal politics of rights, "[Foucault] shocked many by advocating for human rights—an act that would have been unthinkable for the militant antihumanist of ten years earlier."[15] The shocking nature of this shift was perhaps most evident to Foucault's allies and comrades, philosophical and political, on the French poststructuralist left. Paras once more:

> On the political level, his part in the contentious debate over the significance of the *nouveaux philosophes* divided Foucault from the French left—and even from his own recent theses on the disciplinary society—and drove him towards a rights-oriented position in which the treatment of the individual was the ultimate marker of a regime's acceptability.[16]

The language in which both Paras and Dosse frame their analysis permits neither much margin for interpretive nuance nor, more importantly, the ability to capture the genealogical spirit of Foucault's critical thought. This style of thought, as we have seen, is one that attempts both to suspend express normative commitments and at the same time to resignify concepts and practices, often at variance with their common or initially intended meanings. Bald assertions that Foucault practiced a "violent rejection of the autonomous subject"[17] or else occupied an "anti-subjectivity" position in work of the 1960s,[18] for example, are overly reductive and belie the more subtle way in which he sought not to reject concepts such as these, but to lay bare their contingent production and then rework them. Paras's interpretive approach—which has Foucault moving from a position of denunciation to affirmation—unhelpfully excludes the possibility that the terms under critical suspension (subject, subjectivity, liberty, freedom, agency, autonomy, and so forth) could possibly be reinvested with different meanings. When Paras reads Foucault writing the language of rights, he assumes that he does so in a way that is consonant with and thoroughly contained by the ordering idioms of liberal political thought—and not in ways that might seek playfully to contest, mimic, subvert, or tactically outrun them, that is, to read them performatively and put them to different, contrary uses.[19] But what is it that Paras is reading? What is Foucault doing in the late work? Let me now, as briefly as possible, sketch the outlines of this body of writing, before returning to Paras and the implications of his reading for an understanding of Foucault's late political engagements with rights.

According to the standard periodization, Foucault's ethics constitutes the third and final phase of his career. In volumes 2 and 3 of the *History of Sexuality*, *The Use of Pleasure* and *The Care of the Self*, respectively,[20] and in his 1980–84 lecture courses at the Collège de France,[21] Foucault pursues a historical study of forms of ethical self-reflection and practice in antiquity. In those texts, he returns to the writings of thinkers in classical Greece and late antiquity in order to rediscover a certain concept of ethics. However, for the ancients, and for Foucault, the concept of ethics imports neither an obligation to others nor a rational obedience to a moral law, but rather a relationship to oneself (*rapport à soi*). In "On the Genealogy of Ethics: An Overview of Work in Progress," a 1983 interview given to his American collaborators and interlocutors Hubert Dreyfus and Paul Rabinow, Foucault helpfully summarizes this conception of ethics and the scope of his historical study of the ancients. In writing of the ancients, Foucault argues that we have to make an analytic distinction between the moral code, which determines which acts are forbidden and what the positive or negative value of acts are, and people's actual behavior in relation to the moral code. He further specifies:

> And there is another side to the moral prescriptions, which most of the time is not isolated as such but is, I think, very important: the kind of relationship you ought to have with yourself, *rapport à soi*, which I call ethics, and which determines how the individual is supposed to constitute himself as a moral subject of his own actions.[22]

Foucault goes on to subdivide the properly ethical domain of the relationship to oneself, the *rapport à soi*, into four separate elements.[23] The first of these is the *ethical substance*, the part of the ethical subject's behavior that is to be problema-tized and made the subject of ethical reflection and elaboration. For example, this might be one's dietary intake, physical appearance, or sexual behavior. In his study of the ethics of the ancient Greeks in *The Use of Pleasure*, for exam-ple, Foucault finds that the subject of ethical reflection is the *aphrodisia*, or the configuration of "acts linked to pleasure and desire in their unity" (not to be confused with later Christian notions of the flesh or modern understandings of sexuality). Second, there is the mode of subjection or subjectivation, the man-ner in which "people are invited or incited to recognize their moral obligations." This might be in acknowledgment of divine law, or scripture, or some secular commandment. Third, there is the element of asceticism. Foucault's usage of asceticism differs markedly from Christian meanings, with their connotations of self-renunciation and abnegation. For him, Greek asceticism is not primarily a self-renunciating or mortificatory practice but a "self-forming activity." In short, what he intends by asceticism here is not self-denial but something much closer to self-construction—it is really a mode of working upon oneself, or rather, upon the ethical substance.[24] This practice might involve a dietary regime, a program of bodily training, or a practice of writing or stylizing the self (perhaps through the use of diaries or other media). Finally, there is the telos, or goal, of this ethi-cal self-elaboration. In applying the arts of ascesis to those aspects of themselves that are in need of elaboration or improvement, do ethical subjects intend to achieve self-mastery, purity, an ideal of beauty, or some other end?

In summary, then, Foucault's reading of ancient Greek ethics locates ethics as a subset of a larger domain of morality. What is definitive about the ethi-cal domain, according to this view, is neither (*pace* Kant) the ethical subject's relationship to a universal moral code nor (*pace* Levinas) his relationship to another who is to be accorded some kind of ontological-ethical priority.[25] Nor, indeed, is it the relationship of such behavior to a juridical rule. Rather, the priority is the self's relationship to itself, as practiced through a series of ascetic technologies that aim to elaborate, improve, and re-form the self along certain lines in order to engender and maintain a certain state of being. Foucauldian ethics, as derived from the ancients, is thus better understood as an ethos, a way of being and acting. Continuous with his genealogies of the political tech-nologies of modernity carried out in the 1970s, Foucault's analytic emphasis is once again placed on the domain of practice. Ethics for him primarily represent a set of practices of self-formation and self-refinement. They are a form of what he calls "technologies of the self,"[26] ways in which the self can work upon itself as the object of a sort of *technē*[27]—conscious reflection, problematization of conduct, and calibrated attention to action.

Clearly, there is a change of idiom here on Foucault's part. We can discern a much finer-grained attention to the way in which subjects are to orient themselves in the world (as opposed to being oriented and regulated by objectivizing political technologies such as discipline or biopolitics) and to take themselves as the object of (self-)critical attention (again, as opposed to being constituted as an object of knowledge and investment for external apparatuses of power). Paras contends that the subject envisioned or implied in Foucault's late accounts of ethics in antiquity is radically different from its more epistemically and politically determined precursors of the 1970s. This Foucauldian subject, he maintains, "precedes any practices that might be said to construct it, and indeed . . . freely chooses among those practices."[28]

In Paras's account, the turning point in Foucault's conception of subjectivity first becomes apparent in his Collège de France lectures on liberal governmentality in 1979, "The Birth of Biopolitics." These lectures, whose title implies an intention to trace the genealogy of the modern political technology of biopolitics, actually provide an account of forms of liberal discourse. Foucault treats liberalism not so much as an ideology but rather as a way of governing, that is, in his terms, as a governmentality.[29] These lectures hence develop the thematic of governmentality inaugurated in the previous year's lectures, "Security, Territory, Population." In so doing Foucault extends his historical analysis into the twentieth century with a discussion of the German school of *Ordoliberalism* (or the Freiburg School, which included economic theorists such as Walter Eucken and Franz Böhm) and the Chicago neoliberals of the 1970s and 1980s (such as Gary Becker). Unlike the governmentalities of pastoral power or *raison d'État* discussed in the 1978 lectures, these latter forms of neoliberal governmentality are said to function not through meticulous and corrective disciplinary attention to the behavior of individual subjects, but through governmental interventions aimed at creating and sustaining a market environment in which enterprise will flourish and individual subjects are left to their own, supposedly rational-calculative devices: that is, precisely, a form of laissez-faire economic governmentality that itself represents a critique of the disciplinary administrative state for not governing properly or appropriately. Paras is hence right to isolate this moment (the formulation of the problematic of governmentality) as portending a shift in Foucault's work and as opening the way to the late work on ethics. He interprets it in a radical way, however, as the beginning of a wholesale reintro-duction of liberal subjectivity that continues into and underpins all of Foucault's late work on ethics and on rights. To this end he quotes a 1984 interview with Alessandro Fontana, a close collaborator of Foucault's at the time of the "Birth of Biopolitics" lectures: "We said to ourselves then: through a reflection on liberal-ism, Foucault is going to give us a book on politics. Liberalism seemed to also be a detour to rediscover the individual outside of mechanisms of power."[30]

It is notoriously difficult to impute a clear "position" to Foucault on the basis of his archaeological and genealogical analyses, which frequently involve a critique of historical texts but much less frequently involve a straightforward presentation of "his own" views. Paras is thus careful to acknowledge that Fou-cault's genealogy of forms of government and, in the later work, of forms of ethical self-training that assume or take as their point of application the indi-vidual subject, does not in itself necessarily commit Foucault himself to such an individualist ontology:

> Foucault spoke as though he might remain agnostic on the actual existence of subjects, [and] his questions . . . were addressed merely to the processes that he alternately called *subjectivation* and *assujetissement*; his concern for the process by which different forms of "subjectivity" were constituted likewise implied no belief in a "subject" per se."[31]

Rather, it is Paras's argument that this methodological way of approaching the subject—as an effect of power, the subject *of* a particular apparatus of power, rather than as a subject in its own right—does not make sense in the context of arguments that the subject works upon itself in order to transform itself ac-cording to a set of ethical-cum-aesthetic protocols. There must, for Paras and *contra* Nietzsche's famous dictum,[32] precisely be a doer behind the deed:

> Foucault's way of posing the problem . . . tacitly assumed some kind of already-present subject that could act upon itself. The alternative—the notion of a non-subject that performs techniques upon itself—is contradictory. But on the other hand, if we truly are to believe that subjects are formed—all the way down—by techniques of subjectivation, how are we to make sense of the idea of *individuals who elect to engage in such techniques*? Or worse, not to engage in them? . . . If subjectivity is the target of techniques rather than the product of techniques, then we are entitled to wonder where that subjectivity comes from in the first place. Without acknowledging it, Foucault had posited a free subject

prior to any "technical elaboration": a subject free to choose itself, to build its own *subjectival modality*.[33]

Finally, then, for Paras the structure of Foucault's account of ethical self-formation in the late work necessarily commits the philosopher to accepting a subject of autonomy and self-reflexivity, irrespective of genealogical declamations to the contrary. But Paras's twin *topoi* of depth ("all the way down") and of origin ("in the first place") are unhelpful ways of approaching the late Foucauldian problematic of the subject, and in the remainder of this section I shall propose an alternative understanding of this work.

As a first step, let us start with Foucault's own reflexive accounts of this work. These reveal that he understands the shift from an analysis of the disciplinary formation of subjectivity to one of ethical self-formation, via governmentality, as being a change of emphasis. Recall his comments in a 1982 seminar:

> Perhaps I've insisted too much on the technology of domination and power. I am more and more interested in the interaction between oneself and others, and in the technologies of individual domination, in the mode of action that an individual exercises upon himself by means of the technologies of the self.[34]

A focus on the interaction between oneself and others, and on the mode of action that one subject brings to bear on herself, clearly does not exclude an attention to the formative dimensions of disciplinary power in the above formulation. Rather, these are both aspects of the Foucauldian paradigm of power relations and subjectivity to which he has not given equal weight in previous analyses. It is a question of balance, of "too much" and "more and more," not of "either/or." Part of the problem is that Paras lays far too much emphasis on Foucault's commitment to a wholly determinative view of subjectivity in his work in the 1960s and 1970s. Accordingly, and in line with those conventional misreadings of Foucault that would have him describe a paralyzing and dystopic modernity in which subjects were the unwitting dupes of disciplinary and biopolitical logics they were doomed never to comprehend or resist,[35] the move to a view in which the subject begins to form itself can only be grasped as a salutary triumph over this depressing scenario and the belated emergence of a fully autonomous subject finally in control of itself. Putting it bluntly, such an understanding deprives both the earlier and the later works of considerable nuance. To assert, as Foucault does, that the subject of discipline is formed in and through relations of power is not to argue that subjects are wholly determined by these relations, that they are always acted upon and never acting (as is implied, for example, by Paras's imputing to Foucault a denial of the "thinking subject").[36] This was never the case. To cite just one example from *Discipline and Punish*, the supposed ur-text of this disciplinary determinism, Foucault makes it clear that the involvement of the disciplinary subject in her own subjectification is central to the operation of the Panoptic project:

> He who is subjected to a field of visibility, and who knows it, assumes responsibility for the constraints of power; he makes them play spontaneously upon himself; he inscribes in himself the power relation in which he simultaneously plays both roles; he becomes the principle of his own subjection.[37]

This, to be sure, is not "responsibility" in a classically Kantian key, but it nonetheless implies some ability on the part of the subject to integrate and bring to bear upon itself in some way the diverse demands of disciplinary power (a power dispersed across a range of institutional locales).[38] Nor are matters as voluntaristic in Foucault's ethical phase as Paras would have them, for the late Foucauldian subject is not an unmoved mover but rather constitutively attached to a range of techniques and practices that are assuredly neither of its own making nor subject to its ultimate control. Foucault again:

> I would say that if now I am interested, in fact, in the way in which the subject constitutes himself in an active fashion, by the practices of the self, these practices are nevertheless not something that the individual invents by himself. They are patterns that he finds in his culture and which are proposed, suggested and imposed on him by his culture, his society and his social group.[39]

Foucault continues into his late work to insist that the subject is not a "substance" that pre-exists the forms of subjectivity unearthed by his archaeological and genealogical analyses,[40] but one that continues to be the unsettled result of these forms. Crucially, these forms are neither motionless nor entirely predictable—they are susceptible of reflexive rearticulation and displacement. In a lecture titled "What Is Critique?: An Essay on Foucault's Virtue," Judith Butler neatly captures this dimension of the philosopher's late understanding of subjectivity when she describes the form of self-formation it variously institutes and undergoes as "both crafted and crafting," a "self-making which is never fully self-inaugurated."[41] She writes:

> We have moved quietly from the discursive notion of the subject to a more psychologically resonant notion of "self," and it may be that for Foucault the later

term carries more agency than the former. The self forms itself, but it forms itself within a set of formative practices that are characterized as modes of subjectivations. That the range of its possible forms is delimited in advance by such modes of subjectivation does not mean that the self fails to form itself, that the self is fully formed. On the contrary, it is compelled to form itself, but to form itself within forms that are already more or less in operation and underway. Or, one might say, it is compelled to form itself within practices that are more or less in place.[42]

This condition of forming oneself according to forms always already given (but not for that reason static) designates the inescapable condition of the Foucauldian subject. If this, to Paras and others,[43] spells paradox and inscrutability, then it may be because their assumptions about subjectivity still move within the sovereign logic of the juridico-discursive theory that Foucault sought to displace. As they see it, there is an inverse relationship between subjectivity and power such that more power, or more powerful power, equals less subjectivity. Yet Foucault, as we can see, consistently rejects such a view, arguing that the subject emerges in the field of power relations and is entirely immanent to and bound up with it. This does not signal the inaction or failure of the subject's agency but rather its condition of possibility. The late Foucauldian subject's capacity for action (including self-rearticulation) hence derives not from some primal pre-existent, but from the very capacity-bequeathing discourses and institutions whose norms it variously repeats, obeys, betrays, transgresses, and appropriates. The semantic ambiguity of the word "agency" itself indexes this dual and unstable condition: an agent designates not only the originator of action but also the representative of something or someone other than itself.[44] Foucault's late subject emerges, therefore, not as a stable metaphysical essence turned in upon itself, but as an always-achieved, always-unraveling effect of contradictory discourses, knowledges, and practices. And so it follows for my argument that the late affirmation of rights cannot simply be read as the assignation to the subject of its due and proper rights but must represent something else. I want in what follows to develop these reflections on Foucault's late subject and its ungroundedness and to pursue them into the political domain of rights. On whose behalf are Foucault's rights claimed, and with what rightful grounds? What does such an understanding of subjectivity mean for the project of claiming rights?

Rights as Ungrounded

According to the orthodox normative conception of them long dominant in liberal political philosophy and political theory, rights need stable and determinate grounds. Without such a grounding, which will specify to whom rights shall apply and why, the very currency of rights as a form of political discourse will become debased and open to dangerous speculation and inflation, ultimately becoming worthless.[45] According to this perspective, the special political value of rights as a particular form of juridical protection operative in liberal democratic societies is seen to be linked to the ability to circumscribe the grounds of rights, to determine who has rights, why, and under what circumstances they have them. Failure to provide such a grounding is likely to result in the dissipation of the force of rights and their transformation from the lingua franca of politics[46] into just another vernacular for the making of contested moral and political claims within and across political communities. As we have seen, not only does Foucault refuse to provide such normative reassurance but he maintains that it is precisely the absence of determinate grounds that ensures the ongoing contestability and political vitality of rights. Indeed, he argues that the political futures of rights are bound up in a very important way with their constitutive ungroundedness.

This ungrounded quality of rights, the first dimension of Foucault's rights politics, can best be understood through an analysis of, in particular, his late deployment of the discourse of *human* rights. To state the obvious, it is clear that in making such a claim about rights, and in himself making rights claims in such a way, Foucault is assuming a somewhat unorthodox position. Paul Patton, as quoted in the Introduction, makes the point succinctly:

> Foucault is well known for his reluctance to rely upon any such universalist concept of human nature or human essence. By contrast, the predominant approach to the nature of rights in contemporary moral and political philosophy supposes that these inhere in individuals by virtue of some universal "rights bearing" feature of human nature, such as sentience, rationality, interests or the capacity to form and pursue projects.[47]

If we hold him to the orthodox position, which requires one in speaking of rights to have a stable and determinate ground in order to safeguard their allocation and adjudication, then Foucault's critique of metaphysical conceptions of subjectivity—a critique that he continues (albeit in a modified form) into his late work on ethics—would seem to present him with a problem. It is a problem that arises with all of Foucault's late invocations of rights, but it emerges most obviously and in its strongest form in the context of his late affirmation of *human* rights. The problem manifests itself most vividly in the field of human rights because the maker of a human rights claim is committed, at least on the face of it, to an essentialist claim about the nature of human beings *qua* human beings. Human rights, that is, are the kind of rights, according to the tautological metaphysics one routinely encounters in the opening pages of human rights textbooks, that one has "simply because one is a human being."[48] And such a claim—human rights are the rights of humans as such—itself implies that, as Francis Fukayama puts it, one maintains "some concept of what human beings actually are like as a species."[49] And yet Foucault's persistent suspicion of anthropological constants—"all my analyses are against the idea of universal necessities in human existence"[50]—means that he is unable, indeed refuses, to provide such an account of humanity and its rights. And this is precisely why, even for those most sympathetic to his approach, thinking "of Foucault as a champion of human rights seems fraught with contradiction, if not downright perverse."[51]

And yet Foucault's late political practice of rights claiming repeatedly includes references to human rights. The immediate aftermath of his visit to Iran in 1978 furnishes the first, journalistic example of this usage of human rights discourse. He went to Iran for the first time in September 1978 as a correspondent for the Italian newspaper *Corriere della sera*, to cover the dramatic escalation of protests against Shah Pahlavi. He met with the exiled Ayatollah Khomeini in Paris a month later and returned to Iran in November to complete his journalistic commission. He filed a number of stories for the Italian newspaper while in Iran, many of them addressing (and applauding) the phenomenon of what he called the "political spirituality" that he saw as infusing the revolutionary movement against the American-backed regime of the shah and the hated SAVAK (the state security forces).[52]

But the lyrical language of revolution and political spirituality are conspicuously absent from the more chastened journalism that Foucault produces in the wake of subsequent political developments in postrevolutionary Iran. For example, in his "Open Letter to Mehdi Bazargan," published in *Le nouvel observateur* in April 1979, he addresses himself to the then Iranian prime minister. Recalling an interview that Bazargan had granted him in 1978 (when the latter was chairman of the Association for the Defense of Human Rights in Iran) at the residence of the Ayatollah Chariat Madari where "ten or twelve human rights activists had taken refuge . . . and soldiers carrying machine pistols kept watch on the entrance to the little street," he commends Bazargan's physical and political bravery.[53] But he soon criticizes Bazargan's postrevolutionary regime for its cynical failure to honor its pre-revolutionary human rights promises. "We spoke of all the regimes that oppressed people while invoking human rights," he recalls. "You expressed a hope," he continues, "that in the will, so generally affirmed by Iranians, for an Islamic government, those rights would find a real guarantee."[54] And yet for Foucault in 1979 the persecution of the regime's enemies and the conduct of political show trials are "nothing short of alarming." For him, "political trials are always touchstones" of regimes, in which "public authority shows itself without a mask, and . . . presents itself for judgment in judging its enemies."[55] And that judgment takes place beyond the borders of the sovereign nation-state. In terms that reflect the emerging consensus in the late 1970s on the moral imperative to judge regimes by recourse to the purportedly transnational and universal standards of "human rights," Foucault asks:

> I imagine you don't grant the principle of a sovereignty that would only have to answer to itself, any more than I do. . . . It is good when a person, no matter who, even someone at the other end of the world, can speak up because he or she cannot bear to see another person tortured or condemned. It does not constitute interference with a state's internal affairs. Those who protested on behalf of a single Iranian tortured in the depths of a Savak prison were interfering in the most universal affair that exists.[56]

A second example of Foucault's invocation of human rights discourse comes from his support for the Polish Solidarity movement. Once again, Foucault had himself been politically involved in Polish affairs for some time. "His experiences in Warsaw in 1958 [where he had been expelled from his post as cultural attaché because of his homosexuality]," writes biographer David Macey, "left him with an abiding affection for the country's people and dislike for its rulers."[57] Along with many French intellectuals of the time, Foucault signed numerous open letters and petitions protesting against the socialist regime in the late 1970s, but in 1982 he was part of a delegation from Médecins du Monde who, with financial support from the French government and the European Community, visited Warsaw, Cracow, and Auschwitz. They delivered food, medicine, books, and printing materials and met with government officials. In a wide-ranging interview, published in *Les nouvelles littéraires* on his return to France in October of the same year under the title "The Moral and Social Experience of the Poles Can No Longer Be Obliterated," Foucault condemns the historical partition of Europe into "two political forms that are not only incompatible but one of which is utterly intolerable":

> There are hundreds of millions of Europeans separated from us by a line that is both arbitrary in its reason for being and uncrossable in its reality: they are living in a regime of totally restricted freedoms, in a state of subright. This historical fracture of Europe is something that we must not resign ourselves to.[58]

He goes on to assert:

> If governments make human rights the structure and the very framework of their political action, that is well and good. But human rights are, above all, that which one confronts governments with. They are the limits that one places on all possible governments.[59]

The third and probably best-known example of Foucault's late invocation of human rights principles comes from his involvement in a press conference in Geneva in 1981 to mark the creation of the International Committee Against Piracy, "for which," writes another of his biographers, "he wrote and read a declaration, a sort of charter of human rights."[60] The piece was subsequently published in *Libération* in June 1984 and has been translated into English as "Confronting Governments: Human Rights," a title that echoes the above formulation of human rights ("that which one confronts governments with").[61] This short text, with which I opened this chapter, has generated considerable commentary in the legal and political theory literature.[62] Interestingly, despite its deployment of very similar tropes to that of the then-emergent human rights movement (to wit, an international citizenry with duties to bring to light the suffering of distant others, a suffering that grounds an absolute right to bear witness beyond national borders, and so forth), Foucault's declaration of rights does not so much designate itself explicitly as an instance of human rights as invoke the notion of the rights of the governed.[63] Its principal clauses read:

1. There exists an international citizenship that has its rights and its duties, and that obliges one to speak out about every abuse of power, whoever its author, whoever its victims. After all, we are all members of the community of the governed, and thereby obliged to show mutual solidarity.

2. Because they claim to be concerned with the welfare of societies, governments arrogate to themselves the right to pass off as profit or loss the human unhappiness that their decisions provoke or their negligence permits. It is a duty of this international citizenship to always bring the testimony of people's suffering to the eyes and ears of governments, sufferings for which it's untrue that they are not responsible. The suffering of men must never be a silent residue of policy. It grounds an absolute right to stand up and speak to those who hold power.

3. We must reject the division of labor so often proposed to us: individuals can get indignant and talk; governments will reflect and act. It's true that good governments appreciate the holy indignation of the governed, provided it remains lyrical. I think we need to be aware that very often it is those who govern who talk, are capable only of talking, and want only to talk. Experience shows that one can and must refuse the theatrical role of pure and simple indignation that is proposed to us. Amnesty International, Terre des Hommes, and Médecins du [M]onde are initiatives that have created this new right—that of private individuals to effectively intervene in the sphere of international policy and strategy. The will of individuals must make a place for itself in a reality of which governments have attempted to reserve a monopoly for themselves, that monopoly which we need to wrest from them little by little and day by day.[64]

What are we to make of these examples of Foucauldian human rights discourse? In form and function they appear to rehearse the orthodox moves performed by human rights: mobilizing the universal against the particular and violent sovereignty of a local regime; grounding resistance to power's transgressions on the witnessing of embodied human suffering; and posing human rights as a limit to governmental power. I want to focus on just one aspect of these articulations of human rights here: their ground, the subject they are said to presuppose. By relying on this universalist discourse does Foucault naturalize a certain figure of humanity? Or else, by citing the human of human rights, does he mobilize and contest the figure of universal humanity itself, occupying it differently and opening it to plural uses and futures? Just as with his late articulation of the subject discussed in the preceding sections of this chapter, we shall now see that the "human" of Foucault's late affirmation of human rights is an unfinished effect of power and knowledge networks—and not a stable "substance"[65] that might work to ground and circumscribe the distribution of rights.

In "Useless to Revolt?," another piece on the Iranian revolt against the shah, Foucault insists that the assertion of rights cannot be founded upon some pre-existing and enduring metaphysics of humanity, but must rest on more shifting and contested "grounds":

> All the forms of established or demanded freedom, all the rights that one as-serts, even in regard to the seemingly least important things, no doubt have a last anchor point there [namely, in the "irreducible" urge to disobey authority], one more solid and closer to experience than "natural rights."[66]

And again, in his statement at the United Nations in Geneva, cited above, he begins: "We are just private individuals here, with no other grounds for speak-ing, or for speaking together, than a certain shared difficulty in what is taking place."[67] The claimed right issues not from an entitlement (bare humanity, rea-son, membership of an existing community) that would ground and guarantee their speech, but from a particular, contingent difficulty shared in common, one that arises from their similar location with respect to existing formations of global government. It is an artifact of their own making and claiming—indeed, their speech begins in the very absence of grounds. The signatories are hence not carriers of universal humanity (not, as Foucault puts it elsewhere, "spokesm[e]n of the universal"),[68] and their right was granted them precisely by "no one."[69] As Thomas Keenan observes of Foucault's statement, "There is no original owner or possessor of rights, no self-present source here medi-ated or represented in its (temporary and ultimately accidental) absence."[70] Foucault's human rights claims would therefore seem to call into question any easy assumption about a naturalized ground of humanity. Rather, these are rights claims that openly disavow any foundational status and so are guaran-teed by nothing. The only "guarantee" such rights are granted is in their very own exercise:

> Liberty is a *practice*. . . . The liberty of men is never assured by the institutions and laws intended to guarantee them. This is why almost all of these laws and institutions are quite capable of being turned around—not because they are am-biguous, but simply because "liberty" is what must be exercised. . . . I think that it can never be inherent in the structure of things to guarantee the exercise of freedom. The guarantee of freedom is freedom.[71]

Here Foucault gestures toward a performative account of rights claiming in which there is no recourse to the foundational status of the subject and its universal attributes.[72] Instead, the social and political practice of rights claiming itself establishes and contours the ground of rights. Rights are there to be seized:

> It is not because there are laws, and not because I have rights, that I am entitled to defend myself; it is because I defend myself that my rights exist and the law respects me. It is thus first of all the dynamic of defence which is able to give law and rights the value which is indispensable for us. A right is nothing unless it comes to life in the defence which occasions its invocation.[73]

"It is this act of assuming one's rights, in the widest sense," observes Philippe Chevallier in commenting on the above passage, "which gives right its amplitude and effective universality."[74] Here the universality of rights, including obviously human rights, is an effect of, a product of, the investment made in rights by those who claim them—not a pre-existing characteristic of their being. Such a thinking of rights challenges the very *topos* of ground itself, which becomes not a pre-existing substance, but rather something wrought in and through the thoroughly political motions of rights claiming. Ground becomes an unstable and revisable aftereffect. To return briefly to the Polish example instanced above, we can see Foucault recall this exact understanding of the seizing and making of rights claims as a performative exercise at the beginning of the discussion, and he does so in a way that qualifies his later references to human rights in the interview:

> What is remarkable about this whole history of the Solidarity movement is that people have not only struggled for freedom, democracy, and the exercise of basic rights but they have done so by exercising rights, freedom, and democracy. The movement's form and its purpose coincide. Look what's happening right now: the workshops of Gdansk reply to the antistrike law by staging a strike.[75]

We can now begin to appreciate that Foucault works with a different—indeed, an inverted—sense of the ground of human rights, one more in the nature of a receding horizon than a determined basis or point of departure. Of course, it is this latter sense that conditions traditional understandings of the normativity of human rights. In a sensitive discussion of Foucault's ambivalent relationship to humanism in the field of human rights, Anthony Alessandrini starts from the traditional position when he asks "whether we need a form of humanism—in particular, a form that forces us to posit an essential conception of what 'man' is—to have human rights." Alessandrini answers this question tentatively in the negative on Foucault's behalf ("Perhaps not," he concludes provisionally).[76] But here I want to develop a stronger Foucauldian response. Not only is humanism of the sort mentioned by Alessandrini, namely, an essentialist humanism that specifies the limits of human being, not necessary for human rights—it is fatal for it. For Foucault, a humanism of this sort represents not the necessary ground upon which human rights can be built, but their terminal limit and the denial of their futurity. Such a conclusion may provoke surprise, but in truth were such a "grounding" of human rights to be accepted there would be no further normative work for human rights to do—no contestation, no disagreement, no development. If we are to speak in terms of political necessities, then, the undetermined human of Foucault's human rights is itself the necessary "ground" for any human rights that is to be even minimally receptive to diverse political futures. Such a fragile "ground," it bears emphasizing, cannot vouchsafe particular political outcomes (any more than more orthodox, foundationalist grounds can). Rather, my (and Foucault's) claim is that such an ungrounded grounding at the very least prizes human rights open to multiple possibilities of the human.

It is clear that in talking of human rights in the late work Foucault is indexing a certain humanism. But, as with the subject in the late work, this late articulation of humanism does not represent a retreat but rather a reimagining. His withering critiques of humanism in the early *History of Madness* and later in *Discipline and Punish* are directed toward the metaphysical closures of orthodox humanism and the political violence which that orthodoxy licenses. Whether in the guise of the specious "liberation" of the insane or the humanization of punishment, the humanism at issue here is one that works to determine and circumscribe the limits of human being. What so offends Foucault in such articulations of humanism, argues James Bernauer, is their "extraordinary diminishment of human being" (or, as Gilles Deleuze glosses Nietzsche, "man himself is a form of imprisonment for man").[77] In seeking to fix the essence of what it means to be human, humanism as political technology unavoidably denies the potentiality of that which it putatively seeks to reveal and protect. Bernauer writes:

> Foucault's work may properly be characterized as an anti-humanism, even if the term provides for many the "most scandalous aspect" of modern French thought. Although the anti-humanistic accents of Foucault's thought may always offend sensibilities, it is important to recognize that modern humanism represents for him an extraordinary diminishment of human being. Ethically, Foucault's writings were attempts to demystify the self-professed benevolence of a humanism which, in putting forward its programs for human progress and

institutional development, has actually created personal and social conducts of awesome destructiveness.[78]

Foucault's recalling of humanism in the late work on human rights is thus a calculated turning of humanism against itself in the name of its exclusions and remainders; in the name, precisely, of the not-yet-human and the human-to-come, of a human possibility *contra* the proprieties of orthodox humanism. But while Bernauer refers to such a move as "anti-" humanist, it is clear that Foucault does not situate his own critical discourse outside or beyond the discourse of humanism in any pure or straightforward sense.[79] Rather, his is a critical discourse immanent to its object, harboring an ambivalent, uncomfortable, and agonistic relationship to humanism proper, which simultaneously draws upon and seeks to contest its own lineage. In the conceptual categories I derived from Foucault in the previous chapter, such a critical thinking of humanism approaches it in the manner of a counter-conduct, tactically reordering and appropriating its elements. Foucault's own humanistic knowledge practices, then, "find [themselves] repeating and departing from the inheritances . . . [they] describe" in a "recoiling" motion that "does not advance or produce the ideas that characterize humanism, nor does it refute them . . . [but rather] puts them in question."[80]

And this ceaseless putting into question of the limits of the human of humanism is central to Foucault's own late invocation of human rights. Indeed, his mobilization of human rights is not only premised on such a questioning but is also itself one of the modalities of this questioning. In a late interview he explicitly relates the critique of humanism, understood as the determination of human essence and of necessitating a certain understanding of the species category of "the human," to a practice of claiming and expanding human rights:

> Through these different practices—psychological, medical, penitential, educational—a certain ideal or model of humanity was developed, and now this idea of man has become normative, self-evident, and is supposed to be universal. Humanism may not be universal but may be quite relative to a certain situation. What we call humanism has been used by Marxists, liberals, Nazis, Catholics. This does not mean that we have to get rid of what we call human rights or freedom, but that we can't say that freedom or human rights has to be limited at certain frontiers. For instance, if you asked eighty years ago if feminine virtue was part of universal humanism, everyone would have answered yes. What I am afraid of about humanism is that it presents a certain form of our ethics as a universal model for any kind of freedom. I think that there are more secrets,

more possible freedoms, and more inventions in our future than we can imagine in humanism as it is dogmatically represented on every side of the political rainbow: the Left, the Center, the Right.[81]

We are now, with Foucault, at a significant conceptual remove from the traditional conception of the grounding of human rights. Accordingly, it is the very impossibility of ultimately defining what it means to be human that, if not quite "grounding" human rights, nevertheless finally emerges as its political condition of possibility. For Foucault, conscious of the ways in which the human has from time to time been disciplinarily and discursively marked and produced, the putative attainment of some consensus or universal definition of the human would represent the stifling of the political promise of human rights. Such a prospect would represent the political "end" of human rights, a project that, as he sees it, is properly dedicated to holding open a space for the human to mean otherwise. Human rights for Foucault represent a stage on which the irreducibly political contests regarding the meaning of who or what is to count as a human being are played out. It would be inaccurate, however, to maintain that Foucault is alone among rights theorists in developing an account of the inescapably plural and ungrounded status of rights. For example, Foucault's treatment of the term "human" has something in common with philosopher Jacques Rancière's supple rendering of "man" and "citizen" in the *Declaration of the Rights of Man and Citizen*. For Rancière, these terms do not so much denote as invite:

> The Rights of Man are the rights of those who make something of that inscription, who decide not only to "use" their rights but also to build such and such a case for the verification of the power of the inscription. It is not only a matter of checking whether the reality confirms or denies the rights. The point is about what *confirmation* or *denial* means. *Man* and *citizen* do not designate collections of individuals. Man and citizen are political subjects. Political subjects are not definite collectivities. They are surplus names, names that set out a question or a dispute (*litige*) about who is included in their count. Consequently, *freedom* and *equality* are not predicates belonging to definite subjects. Political predicates are open predicates: they open up a dispute about what they exactly entail and whom they concern in which cases.[82]

The human as it is figured in human rights discourse is therefore an invitation to the ever-revisable work of definition. But that work, to return to a trope encountered in our discussion of Foucault's ethics, must be conceived not as completed *oeuvre* but as ongoing *travail*.[83] If human rights are to represent the vehicle for the recognition of new types of humanity and new modes of human relationality, then of necessity they must remain underdetermined. "The necessity of keeping our notion of the human open to a future articulation is essential to the project of international human rights discourse and politics," writes Judith Butler:

> We see this time and again when the very notion of the human is presupposed; the human is defined in advance, in terms that are distinctively western, very often American, and, therefore, partial and parochial. When we start with the human as a foundation, then the human at issue in human rights is already known, already defined.[84]

Like Foucault's, Butler's is a practice of engagement with human rights that insists that we (all) "be willing, in the name of the human, to allow the human to become something other than what it is traditionally assumed to be."[85] And human rights can, if they maintain this constitutive openness, be the stage for this constant "rearticulation":

> International human rights is always in the process of subjecting the human to redefinition and renegotiation. It mobilizes the human in the service of rights, but also rewrites the human and rearticulates the human when it comes up against the cultural limits of its working conception of the human, as it does and must.[86]

For Butler, then, the human of human rights does not pre-exist the texts of human rights but is made legible only within them by a political (re-)inscription; it is not an anteriority but an artifact, not a presupposition but a provocation. Such a human is never definitively installed in these texts but always beckons beyond itself; it is a human for the time being only, a "working conception," as Butler has it, always susceptible to what Foucault calls "the experiment with the possibility of going beyond."[87] The (provisional) claim to humanity begets, necessitates, counterclaims that seek to contest, displace, or expand the meaning of the human. As legal theorist Sundhya Pahuja explains,

> When a human right comes up against someone to whom the right does not apply because of the particular "human" inscribed within the right, that person embodies the limit of the right and presents to the universal an insistent factuality contesting the universal's claim to be such. This clash brings political contestation to the heart of every human right.[88]

The seeming universality of the human of human rights is thus a much more unpredictable and fragile "achievement" for Foucault than defenders of the metaphysical "inherency"[89] of human rights would allow. The finished human of rights does not come first in order to ground the rights that are subsequently bestowed upon it, but is a variable product of a much more complex and unpredictable political clash of forces. Hence Foucault will write, regarding the extradition of Klaus Croissant, the lawyer for the Baader-Meinhof German terrorist group, that this quasi universality of rights is an effect of a political mobilization that inhabits and expands rights and, in so doing, resignifies them, perhaps against their "original intent," opening them to all. "Liberties and their safeguards," he writes, "are not always conquered in a grand struggle, a triumphant morning. They are made often out of occasion, surprise or detour. It is then that they must be seized and made valid for all."[90]

Questioning the Questioning of the Human: Beyond Contingency and the Powers of Form

The reading I have proposed here presents the late Foucauldian subject not as preceding the work of power and knowledge, but as continuing to follow from it, as an unstable achievement and aftereffect. Here is Foucault again, talking of the late work on ethics:

> In the course of their history, men have never ceased to construct themselves, that is, to continually displace their subjectivity, to constitute themselves in an infinite, multiple series of different subjectivities that will never have an end and never bring us in the presence of something that would be "man." Men are perpetually engaged in a process that, in constituting objects, at the same time displaces man, deforms, transforms, and transfigures him as a subject.[91]

That transfiguration produces "not man as nature supposedly designed him, or as his essence ordains him to be—we need to produce something that doesn't exist yet, without being able to know what it will be."[92] And it is precisely this spirit of reproducing "man" in the absence of ultimate cognition or measure that underpins and animates Foucault's late politics of rights. Here it is the sustaining impossibility of grounding rights claims that, paradoxically, becomes their very "guarantee"—a guarantee not of closure and delimitation but of openness and futurity. (But, assuredly, not a stable guarantee of any given future.) For several reasons my discussion has focused on the status of the human in Foucault's late evocation of *human* rights, but my analysis applies to grounds other than the human—rationality, citizenship, sentience, the community of the governed, and so forth—grounds whose conceptual boundaries, like those of the human, cannot be policed with any certainty and which at any rate insist on being called into question. Here the human as ground of rights was productively turned upside down, as it were, or reframed, from foundation to question. To question the human of human rights is not, as discussed in the previous chapter, to erase or evacuate it, but precisely to expand its boundaries through the work of critique and countermobilization.

At least, that is the wager of Foucault's ungrounded rights claims. But here, in the spirit of Foucault's questioning of the human, we need to begin to question this very questioning itself—and our questioning will lead us onto different political terrain in the next chapter. It is clear that a critical interrogation of the ground of rights seeks to open them to certain future political possibilities, reinscriptions, and rearticulations. But it is equally clear that the exposure of contingency, however important and necessary, cannot be the resting point of a critical engagement with rights.[93] Whereas it is true that the contingency of the human betokens the radical openness and futural possibilities of human rights, it is equally true that not all futures and not all possibilities manage to install themselves with equal force within the juridical institutions of human rights. Hence we need to query how it is that certain figures of humanity come to be prioritized over others, and indeed how some figures are rendered utterly unintelligible (we might call this task the production of a semantic economy of the contingent within human rights). The theorist of international law Susan Marks helps us to begin posing these questions. Her recent work problematizes (or better, critically supplements) the notion of contingency that I have been discussing throughout this chapter. Taking her cue from Marx's famous dictum in *The Eighteenth Brumaire of Louis Bonaparte*, namely, that "[men] make their own history, but they do not make it just as they please in circumstances they choose for themselves; rather they make it in present circumstances, given and inherited," Marks identifies a "problematic tendency" in contemporary critical thought.[94] This tendency, she argues, is simply to forget the second half of Marx's equation—that the horizons for human history making are not boundless but very much bounded:

> To be clear at the outset, I believe it is quite right to hammer the point that history is a social product, not given but made . . . [and that being made] it can be remade differently. This . . . cardinal principle of all progressive thought is

as urgent as it is endless. . . . However, we may be undertaking this work in a way which causes us to neglect the equally important progressive point that possibilities are framed by circumstances. While current arrangements can be changed, change unfolds within a context that includes systematic constraints and pressures. . . . Things can be, and frequently are, contingent without being random, accidental or arbitrary.[95]

Marks, echoing Roberto Unger, names the tendency she describes in the above passage "false contingency." If, following Unger, himself following critical thinkers from Marx to Foucault, "false necessity" names the condition of turning the contingent into the supposedly necessary (to which everything from historical materialism to genealogy can serve as a useful critical antidote), then "false contingency" names the reverse condition: thinking that things can too easily be made anew, simply because they are not necessary or foreordained. This conception of "false contingency" presents a useful provocation to the critique of the grounds of rights that I, via Foucault, have laid out in this chapter—and it prepares the way for the analysis in the next chapter.

The boundedness of human action is not just a question of human finitude, but a directly political question concerning the present limits to rethinking social and political arrangements—limits often embedded and iteratively reproduced within those very arrangements themselves. I want to suggest here that one way in which those limits are manifested is in the legal form of rights themselves and the way in which that form conduces to certain understandings of human being, of human flourishing, of community—and not others. Let us remember that Foucault's premise is that the human instantiated within human rights discourse is only a concretization for the time being, only a reflection of extant power relations, only a very particular figure of humanity that neither serves to exhaust the meaning of humanity "itself" nor the latent possibilities within the human rights form ("there are more secrets, more possible freedoms, and more inventions in our future than we can imagine in humanism").[96] In the terms adopted above, Foucault's position responds admirably to the first injunction of progressive thought, namely, insisting that what appears to be a universal necessity is in fact spatially and temporally particular ("if you asked eighty years ago if feminine virtue was part of universal humanism, everyone would have answered yes").[97] But arguably he fails, or to be fair, he omits in those instances where he engages specifically with human rights, to acknowledge the "false contingency" dimension of the problem: namely, to come to terms with the operative and material dynamics (Marks's "systematic constraints and pressures") preventing certain figures of humanity, being, relation, and community from signifying within the texts of human rights. Put somewhat differently, might it be the case that while the "human" emerges from this account as an empty signifier whose meaning stands to be remade anew with every fresh political claim and counterclaim, [98] a "right" is itself a particular modality which works to contour and circumscribe the definitional possibilities of the human. Might there be something about the form and indeed, more broadly, about the operative dynamics of rights claiming as a political practice, that works to forestall or foreclose the futural and performative possibilities I have been describing? [99] Foucault appreciates these dangers, and he thematizes them through the lens of what I have called the ambivalence of rights. In the discussion of Foucault's engagements with rights to sexual difference and identity in the next chapter, we shall see how rights appear not simply as an empty space for the inscription of political possibility, but rather as a particular type of space which contours those possibilities in advance.

CHAPTER 3

THE AMBIVALENCE OF RIGHTS

It would doubtless be a mistake to say that all forms of recognition
are fugitive modes of regulation and signs of unfreedom. We have to
struggle for them at the level of law and politics, though we also have
to struggle against being totalized by them.

Judith Butler

The Subject(ion) of Rights Discourse?

Toward the end of the last chapter I compared Foucault's critical and anti-foundationalist approach to rights, and human rights in particular, to the work of another French philosopher on the same topic: Jacques Rancière.[1] For Foucault, I argued, the subject of human rights is necessarily an "unfinished" one. This is because any attempt to definitively "ground" human rights upon a given conception of humanity or attribute of the human rights bearer (dignity, reason, and so forth) can always be unmasked by the genealogist as a particular and unavoidably exclusionary interpretation of the human. Such a grounding instantiates and maintains the human precisely by delimiting and foreclosing other possible humans. And yet, as Foucault eloquently puts it, there are "more inventions in our future than we can imagine in [a] humanism"[2] that tries to fix limits to the human in this way. And so the spectral and unintelligible figures of the non- or the not-yet-human inevitably come to haunt and contest the integrity of the category from which they were constitutively excluded. Indeed, and this is the point for Foucault, it is precisely in their so doing that the political contest over who or what is to count as a human (in human rights discourse) is staged most clearly.[3] In the same vein, Rancière famously asks the question "Who is the subject of the Rights of Man?" and concludes that "the Rights of Man are not the rights of a single subject that would be at once the source and the bearer of [those] rights."[4] Rather, both "Man" and "Citizen" are what he calls "political names":

> Political names are litigious names, names whose extension and comprehension are uncertain and which open for that reason the space of a test or a verification. Political subjects build such cases of verification . . . [and] put to test the power of political names, their extension and comprehension.[5]

Thus do rights, for both thinkers, invite contests over their meaning and future jurisdiction. Rights are necessarily undetermined and unfinished, always remaining to be expanded, enforced, and contingently occupied by a political subject.

As others have recently written, this constitutive semantic openness of rights discourse harbors a democratic potential.[6] Rights present a constant solicitation to different groups within a polity to assert or to constitute themselves as rightful, co-equal members of that polity. According to such a view, the relevant question to ask is not "Who is the (pre-existing, hence ascertainable) subject of the Rights of Man?" but, more pointedly, "Who can emerge within rights discourse as a subject?" or else "Who can inscribe themselves as a subject within the juridical order of rights?" Here the borders of political inclusion and exclusion are understood as mobile and as susceptible of political change, and the subject position of the rights holder is figured as a kind of receding, yet beckoning, emptiness—its oft-critiqued abstraction now reframed as a source of political promise and open-ended possibility.[7] Not who is the singular subject, then, but who might (yet) be? And according to what logics might this process of inscription take place? Of course, this last way of posing the question opens up a different, perhaps more canonically or recognizably Foucauldian, line of inquiry, and one which picks up on the questions I began to pose toward the end of the previous chapter. We might well imagine Foucault in a different voice remarking to Rancière (and reminding us) that the proper question to ask is not who can establish and inscribe himself as a subject within the juridical sphere, but rather at what cost does this very inscription take place,[8] and under what contingent and variable conditions? This Foucault might well prefer to ask a different series of questions: "Who becomes subjectified by the rights of man?"; "What kind of subject is produced in the encounter with rights discourse (with its associated bureaucracies, institutions, regulatory frameworks, and so forth)?"; "How is that subject contoured and made the scene of power relations and subtle forms of regulatory control?" Moreover, if we grant that rights both work to expand or contest the limits of a polity as well as to produce a certain rightful subject, then how is it that rights come to perform both of these functions at once? How are rights simultaneously emancipatory and regulatory, democratic and constraining?

The present chapter takes up these questions once again from the perspective of Foucault's late politics of rights. While the previous chapter explained and analyzed the first dimension of Foucault's rights politics—its contingent ungroundedness—this chapter seeks to add to (and complicate) that discussion by explicating a second dimension of Foucault's project, namely, what I am calling a subtle appreciation of the ambivalence of rights as political instruments (that is, their being both emancipatory and regulatory). For Foucault, rights are unavoidably both emancipatory and regulatory, but these different functions or operations of rights are not dialectically related or successive modes of being of the rights form.[9] Rather, to cleave closely again to Foucault's own terms, which I am using as an interpretive lens in this book, Foucault deploys rights as a form of critical counter-conduct, insisting that rights cannot help but disclose immanent possibilities for critique and rupture alongside their more regulatory uses. Rights can enlarge, expand, or protect the sphere of action of subjects (as well as performatively bring new worlds and communities into being). But at the same time they can also be the conduit,[10] or the vehicle, for relations of power that constitute those very subjects and communities in particular ways and hence reinscribe them within existing forms of power, often recuperating and domesticating the political challenges they might pose. This is the ambivalent dimension of rights, and what I want to suggest in the remainder of this chapter is that this ambivalence is both something that Foucault theorizes in his philosophical work on rights and also something to which he is very much attuned in his own, political deployments of rights discourse as a form of critical counter-conduct. In those deployments he seeks not to transcend or to jettison rights in the face of this ambivalence, but rather to negotiate it and work through it.

In this chapter I want to explore these ideas more fully by presenting a reading of Foucault's various assertions of rights to sexuality—an issue with which he was much occupied in a series of articles and interviews published in the gay activist press in the late 1970s and early 1980s. This is clearly an issue of some personal and political importance to him at this time, but my example is dictated not by personal but rather by analytic reasons, for it is precisely in the context of rights claims to identity that what parades as a protective or emancipatory gesture also works to reinscribe the rights claimant in particular power relations, hence bringing into relief most starkly the ambivalence I am concerned with here.[11] Before pursuing this reading, however, I want to develop a clearer conceptual sense of what I am calling the ambivalence of rights discourse by turning both to Foucault's own work and to some contemporary scholarship in political theory and critical legal studies that is informed by his approach.

The Ambivalent Dimension of Rights Discourse

On Foucault's understanding, then, rights are simultaneously vehicles for political claiming and sites of regulatory control. The first side of this dynamic, as it were, is the more ideologically privileged one and represents what we might call, in liberal or democratic terms, the orthodox understanding of what it is rights are supposed to achieve. Rights are most commonly understood in the liberal political imaginary as an instrument to protect or defend the originary freedom of the subject, demarcating a zone of privacy (or conduct, belief, and so forth) safe from intrusion by the state, the community, or other subjects.[12] Rights also figure in more republican or democratic political imaginaries as tools to advance the interests of peoples—for recognition or equality, say, or for the assertion of particular values in the public sphere. In both these guises, rights are understood as broadly beneficial tools with which to make political claims—either to defend or to advance the interests of the subject or of communities of subjects acting in concert. And yet, as we saw in the Introduction, it is precisely these emancipatory qualities of rights discourse that Foucault stands accused of having marginalized or even dismissed outright.[13] His discussions of disciplinary power and its relationship to law and sovereignty, especially in the book *Discipline and Punish*,[14] have led many commentators to suppose that he doubts "the potential of rights as a language of political contestation or resistance."[15] Indeed, some have gone so far as to claim that he denies "any potential political value to tactics that seek to invoke rights against the incursions of disciplinary power and to advance or expand new rights,"[16] arguing that for him rights have "no emancipatory potential whatsoever, [and are consequently] . . . reducible without remainder to . . . [their sovereign] function."[17] Such interpretations are clearly very difficult to sustain in light of the many examples already instanced in this book of Foucault's practices of rights claiming in the late work. Clearly he did perceive a use for rights in a variety of political contexts, but instead of simply recounting the varied ways in which he advocated for rights on behalf of different constituencies (prisoners, asylum seekers, and so forth), I want to return to a particular example in his philosophical work from quite early in the period under discussion: an attempt to deploy rights discourse on behalf of a particular group that raises pertinent issues both of the relationship between rights and sovereignty and of that between rights and (the constitution and regulation of) identity.

In the early lectures of his 1976 course at the Collège de France, "'Society Must Be Defended,'" Foucault makes what is perhaps his best-known critique of the juridical discourse of sovereignty. I have already addressed this critique in both the Introduction and Chapter 1 and shall not rehearse those remarks here but shall simply recall that according to his analysis rights are inextricably bound up with the institution of sovereign power (that is, as Foucault puts it pithily, "right in the West is the King's right").[18] To assert a right against the sovereign or the state is to invoke a critical standard against certain transgressions of sovereign power while simultaneously legitimizing the very principle of sovereignty itself. Rights may demarcate the legitimate from the illegitimate exercises of sovereignty, but in so doing they "dissolve the element of domination in power and . . . replace [it] . . . with . . . the legitimate rights of the sovereign on the one hand, and the legal obligation to obey on the other."[19] In this way rights discourse launders the excesses of an irreducibly violent sovereignty, yet it does so precisely in the name of a legitimate sovereignty. This is doubtless a powerful critique of the way in which political attempts to harness the language and tools of rights end up reinforcing that which they seek to resist (a theme to which I shall return shortly). But nevertheless, several pages later in the same lecture course Foucault gives a historical example of an attempt to mobilize the discourse of rights against sovereignty in order to destabilize it and undo its claims to universal truth and legitimacy.

Foucault begins his lecture of 21 January 1976 by recounting the way in which his preceding analysis had tried to disable the juridical theory of sovereignty as a "method for analyzing power relations."[20] In place of this orthodox, sovereign grid of intelligibility, this lecture proposes a contrary hypothesis whose elucidation occupies the remainder of the course: "Can war really provide a valid analysis of power relations, and can it act as a matrix for techniques of domination?" he asks.[21] Foucault's manner of posing this question is genealogical. That is, he does not commence with a pure or ideal type of "war" and then seek to apply that concept to historical or empirical reality, but rather proceeds by historicizing the explanatory discourse of war itself. Hence, he asks:

> How, when, and why was it noticed or imagined that what is going on beneath and in power relations is a war? When, how, and why did someone come up with the idea that it is a sort of uninterrupted battle that shapes peace, and that the civil order—its basis, its essence, its essential mechanisms—is basically an order of battle?[22]

The initial answer that Foucault gives to these questions in "'Society Must Be Defended'" is to point to the emergence of what he calls "the first historico-political discourse on society" after "the end of the civil and religious wars of the sixteenth century" in both France and England.[23] In its French iterations this discourse was part of "the rearguard struggle waged by the . . . aristocracy against the establishment of the great absolute-administrative monarchy," whereas in England "it was one of the instruments used in bourgeois, petit bourgeois—and sometimes popular—struggles and polemics against the absolute monarchy, and it was a tool for political organization."[24] It is a discourse spoken by Boulainvilliers and Sieyès, by Coke and by Lilburne, and as a pointedly "historico-political" discourse it takes its name and identity in constitutive opposition to what Foucault calls "philosophico-juridical theory."[25] Whereas philosophers and jurists, that is, hypothesize fictional battles (namely, the Hobbesian *bellum omnium contra omnes*) in order to justify law and sovereignty, the various users of this dissident historico-political discourse instead assert not only that "law is born of real battles, victories, massacres, and conquests," but also that beneath contemporary legal orders "war continues to rage in all the mechanisms of power, even in the most regular."[26] The principle of this historico-political discourse hence inverts Clausewitz's famous dictum into the form "Politics is the continuation of war by other means."[27] Accordingly, "a battlefront runs through the whole of society, continuously and permanently, and it is this battlefront that puts us all on one side or the other. There is no such thing as a neutral subject. We are all inevitably someone's adversary."[28]

This discourse inscribes a heterodox relationship between universality, truth, force, and right(s). Whereas for Foucault the jurist and the philosopher characteristically speak in the unmodulated tones of the universal, *sub specie aeternitatis*, of what is true and just for all, the militant subject of this historico-political discourse speaks a more partial and particular (although for this reason more truthful) truth. "The subject who speaks in this discourse, who says 'I' or 'we,' cannot, and is in fact not trying to, occupy the position of the jurist or the philosopher, or in other words the position of a universal, totalizing, or neutral subject," explains Foucault.[29] Rather, the historico-political discourse "is always a perspectival discourse" and hence, "in a discourse such as this," he writes, "being on one side and not the other means that you are in a better position to speak the truth."[30] This is not simply a case of perspectivism or standpoint epistemology *avant la lettre*, however, but a distinctly polemical understanding of truth in which multiple truths do not just subsist together or compete in some sense, but are in a kind of epistemological battle for survival. "The truth is . . . a truth that can be deployed only from its combat position, from the perspective of the sought-for victory and ultimately, so to speak, of the survival of the speaking subject himself."[31]

The truth thus becomes "a weapon within the relationship of force," a part of the epistemic and political arsenal of the historically minded subject who "is speaking, telling the truth, recounting the story, rediscovering memories and trying not to forget anything" in order to contest unjust configurations of law, sovereignty, and political order in the present.[32] But crucially, this genealogical subject speaks his dissident truth in and as right. "Of course, he speaks the discourse of right, asserts a right and demands a right," observes Foucault:

> But what he is demanding and asserting is "his" rights—he says: "We have a right." These are singular rights, and they are strongly marked by a relationship of property, conquest, victory, or nature. It might be the right of his family or race, the right of superiority or seniority, the right of triumphal invasions, or the right of recent or ancient occupations. In all cases, it is a right that is both grounded in history and decentred from a juridical universality.[33]

This mobilization of rights discourse "establish[es] a right marked by dissymmetry, establish[es] a truth bound up with a relationship of force, [and constitutes] a truth-weapon and a singular right."[34] The aim of such a mobilization is to seize hold of rights discourse and, in a deliberately partial, particularized, and polemical way, to turn it against regimes of sovereignty in order to undo their claims to the universal. Several things are immediately noticeable about this brief historical example of a political appropriation of rights discourse in Foucault's oeuvre. The first is that while the discourse of sovereign right does function to legitimize the institution of sovereign power, it is also an available means to criticize that same sovereignty. Foucault is at pains to stress that the language of sovereignty and its rights is an available political language that gets taken up both by those who wish to solidify the claims of sovereign power and by those who wish to contest sovereignty and to expose its transgressions.[35] Many rights claims against sovereignty carry both these possibilities simultaneously, in a kind of circle of legitimation-denunciation, and of course this is precisely Foucault's critique of the limitations of this discursive tactic. Yet the historical example he speaks to here in "'Society Must Be Defended'" seeks to interrupt this circular logic, and it does so by refusing to contest sovereignty on the terrain of its proper and legitimate rights. This does not mean that it vacates the field of rights. Far from it—the historico-political discourse refuses sovereignty its rights, but it makes this move from the position of, and in the name of, *another* right. Sovereignty has no rights—or, it has lesser rights than those who challenge it in the name of *their* rights. Theirs is hence an attempted occupation and pluralization of the language of rights in order to displace the sovereign monopoly of right. This is a form of political counter-conduct that, like the examples of the Christian pastorate discussed toward the end of Chapter 1, moves within the extant discourse of rights, but that attempts to use elements of that discourse in a transgressive and destabilizing way against their dominant meanings. For this reason, writes Foucault, the attempt must be repressed and expelled:

> For philosophers and jurists, [the historico-political discourse] is an obviously external, foreign discourse. It is not even the discourse of their adversary, as they are not in dialogue with it. It is a discourse that is inevitably disqualified, that can and must be kept in the margins, precisely because its negation is the precondition for a true and just discourse that can at last begin to function . . . as a [unitary and pacifying] law.[36]

For Foucault, this rebellious usage of rights discourse remains in the margins, yet it still testifies to the malleability and reversibility of the discourse and its incipient potential to trouble sovereignty.

The second thing to note about this brief example is that when the speakers of the historico-political discourse utter rights claims, they do so not in order to reinsert themselves into a universal narrative, but rather to demarcate and protect a particular identity (recall, after all, that on Foucault's reading these are "singular rights . . . of . . . family or race"). There is hence neither a claim to the universal as such nor an attempt to contingently or "hegemonically" universalize a particular in the place of the universal for the time being.[37] Rather, this is an attempt to deploy rights discourse on behalf of a given social grouping and in advance of its particular interests (which is not to say that it succeeds in maintaining its own particularity).[38] As such, it cannot help both being "de-centred from juridical universality," as Foucault puts it in the passage quoted above, as well as displacing that juridical structure's claim to universality.

Finally, and relatedly, Foucault speaks of this mobilization of rights discourse in thoroughly instrumentalist terms. Rights are here figured not as something to which one would assent for their own sake, but rather as a means for something else—as a "truth-weapon" to achieve victory in a social struggle and, less militarily perhaps, as a "tool for political organization."[39] We have here a clear—but by no means straightforward or unproblematic—example in the Foucauldian corpus of the first aspect of rights. (And this example, it is worth noting, is simultaneously both a description of this historico-political discourse and, as Marcelo Hoffman has recently and convincingly argued, a kind of cipher for Foucault's own evolving militant conception of rights as a tool of struggle at this time.)[40] In this conception, rights are a tool for political subjects to protect or advance their interests, to make a claim for recognition, and to expand the range of their possible actions.

But as soon as rights are deployed as tools, instruments, and weapons in pursuit of particular political agendas (that is, when they become practiced and hence brought to life), then it becomes clear that their uses and effects in the social field cannot ultimately be predicted, circumscribed, or controlled. The figure of rights-as-tools presupposes a stable, intentional, effective subject who stands instrumentally before rights, who ontologically pre-exists them, whose knowable interests or freedom is thus protected by them, and who wields them in the service of those interests and of that freedom. And yet it is Foucault himself who teaches us that the user of a given technology (such as a right) is herself deployed—in various subtle and not-so-subtle ways—by that very technology. If "the individual is not, in other words, power's opposite number," he writes, but rather "one of power's first effects,"[41] then it is clear that the would-be rights claimant is not (and cannot ever be) in a simple position of mastery or instrumentalisation vis-à-vis rights. "Do not demand of politics that it re-store the 'rights' of the individual, as philosophy has defined them," he argues, precisely because "the individual is the product of power."[42] Rights produce subjects; they position, constrain, and conduct those who deploy them and subtly contour the subjectivity or self-understanding of the rights holder who is their supposed master. These functions pertain to what I have called above the second aspect of rights discourse—namely, its regulatory nature—and in the following comments I shall pursue this line of thought through some influential post-Foucauldian work in contemporary political theory and critical legal studies, as represented in some of the writings of the political theorist Wendy Brown and those in dialogue with her. (I say *post*-Foucauldian here in the sense of a body of work extending and supplementing Foucault's theoretical schema, creatively modifying it, and so forth, rather than definitively transcending or negating it.)[43] By thus supplementing the first, instrumental account of rights as available tools for the use of political subjects with this second account of rights as regulatory technologies that constitute and conduct those very political subjects, we arrive at what I have been calling the ambivalent dimension of rights discourse. Let me expand a little, then, via the work of Brown, upon this regulatory aspect of rights in order to complete the picture I have begun to sketch. To continue with the example drawn from "'Society Must Be Defended,'" the focus will be once again on rights to identity.

Wendy Brown's work on the limitations and regulatory entailments of rights discourse (particularly rights of or to a given identity) articulates a number of different strands of scholarship in contemporary political theory and critical legal studies. Key among these are the critique of identity politics and the critique of rights. As to the former, Brown creatively enlists the insights of Nietzsche (particularly the latter's concept of *ressentiment* in *The Genealogy of Morality*) in order to develop an analysis of the "wounded attachments" of contemporary forms of "politicized identity" (race, gender, sexuality).[44] For Brown, these groups reactively articulate their identity in relation to a historical injury whose wounds they are paradoxically invested in repeating. Moreover, such groups tend problematically to inflect their political claims in a moral (hence depoliticizing) register and to address them to the state, seeking juridical protection and redress from its laws.

Here I am less interested in pursuing her argument about the underlying wounded attachments of identity politics per se than I am in tracing what happens when the claims of politicized identity are made in and as claims of right. Whereas for Brown the figuring of politicized identity in terms of injury, suffering, and plaint runs afoul of Nietzsche, the particular framing of political claims in the juridical language of rights only serves to exacerbate these problems and, in so doing, implicates his most famous twentieth-century disciple. But before turning back again to Foucault, it is important to note that Brown situates her engagement with this latter question of rights against the work of two more recent legal thinkers. Brown singles out the critical race scholar Patricia Williams and the feminist legal theorist Catherine MacKinnon as two "progressive exponents in contemporary law and politics" of the idea that rights (despite their evident limitations) *can* be used to leverage equality and recognition claims on behalf of oppressed and marginalized groups.[45] For Williams, writing out of the particular US history of oppression of African-American men and women, rights serve a crucial symbolic and political function. In spite of the inherent individualism well excavated by left critiques and the inability of the civil rights movement to effect any meaningful socioeconomic redistribution and improvement in the position of many African-Americans, rights are nevertheless something to be fought for on a symbolic level. The denial of rights to blacks was so constitutive of their exclusion from the political realm that to forsake them would be to lose a "symbol . . . deeply enmeshed in the psyche of the oppressed," a symbol functioning as a "marker of our citizenship, our relation to others."[46] If rights suffer from a debilitating individualism, then the answer for Williams is not to abjure them entirely but to remetaphorize them, to pluralize them, to let them loose, to "unlock them from reification by giving them to slaves," to "give them to trees" and to "cows," to "history" and to "rivers and rocks" and "all of society's objects and untouchables."[47] For MacKinnon, whose primary intellectual and political context is the radical feminist movement in late-1980s America, rights represent an opportunity (in Brown's reading of her) to "install an *analysis* of women's sexual subordination *in* the law,"[48] to collapse (as the title of one of MacKinnon's books has it) the distance between (gendered) life and discourses of (formal) law.[49] Despite her own penetrating analysis of the ways in which the rule of law and its formal (negative) rights guarantees serve both to naturalize and re-entrench patriarchal power, MacKinnon nevertheless perceives an "opportunity" and a "crack in the wall" whereby gendered substance can be brought to juridical form and the reality of women's lives introduced into law via rights to equality.[50]

Both these progressive thinkers commence with a critical appreciation of the limitations of rights discourse for the political struggles of African-Americans or of women, respectively, only to then insist that, despite these limitations, rights still retain either a symbolic or a strategic value, or that they can nevertheless shelter (or be made to shelter) a range of different modalities of being (slaves, trees, cows, rivers, rocks—indeed, even women and African-Americans).[51] Crucially, both thinkers envision either a feminist or an African-American subject prior to the law who seeks expression within that law (hoping thereby to broaden or transform it), but decline, in their more sanguine moments, to consider the ways in which those subjectivities are produced by legal regimes such as rights.

Brown ultimately adduces both a Marxist ("rights must not be confused with equality nor legal recognition with emancipation")[52] and a Foucauldian riposte to what she perceives as Williams's and MacKinnon's problematic rapprochement with rights. The Foucauldian response starts with the concern that a certain normative ideal of identity is inscribed within law and then becomes the occasion for a disciplinary interpellation and thence regulation of the rights claimant. Brown writes:

> In short, as a regulatory fiction of a particular identity is deployed to displace the hegemonic fiction of universal personhood, we see the discourse of rights converge insidiously with the discourse of disciplinarity to produce a spectacularly potent mode of juridical-disciplinary interpellation.[53]

When and how does inscribing one's identity in rights come to function in a disciplinary register? Writing elsewhere and specifically in the context of women's rights, Brown states:

> The problem surfaces in the question of when and whether rights for women are formulated in such a way as to enable the escape of the subordinated from the site of that violation, and when and whether they build a fence around us at that site, regulating rather than challenging the conditions within. . . . *The more highly specified rights are as rights for women, the more likely they are to build that fence insofar as they are more likely to encode a definition of women premised upon our subordination in the transhistorical discourse of liberal jurisprudence.*[54]

The urge to juridify identity in rights discourse and, moreover, to specify the contours of that identity with some precision means that rights discourse becomes not the neutral mechanism for achieving liberation for oppressed social groups, but rather the occasion for constituting those groups and subjecting them to modes of surveillance and control. "Rights," that is, "produce the subject they pretend only to presuppose."[55] Would-be rights claimants are called upon to internalize and perform a particular identitarian script in the pursuit of their rights. This conundrum, writes Brown, "is the problem that Foucault painted most masterfully in his formulation of the powers of identity and of rights based on identity. To have a right *as* [for example] a woman is not to be free of being designated and subordinated by gender."[56] Indeed, it is arguably to deepen and extend it. The argument travels beyond the contemporary disciplinary production of gender, obviously, even as the workings of other vectors of power are not reducible to the model of gender subjectification. In the context of a discussion of what he calls a "reluctant critique of legal identity politics," for example, the critical legal scholar Richard T. Ford (writing in a volume of essays co-edited by Brown) draws attention to a similar phenomenon in the context of race-based rights claims. He remarks upon the way in which assertions of racial or cultural difference often enable very particular, often reactionary and exclusive cultural norms of what it means to be a member of that group. He counsels:

> The point here is that the discourse of racial difference can take on a life quite independent of the good intentions of those advancing cultural identity rights. The nature of rights discourse is that anyone can assert a right and have it tested in court. But the ill effects of the codification of bad definitions of group culture and identity will not be limited to the litigant asserting the right: they will instead be deployed to regulate all members of the group.[57]

One need not necessarily subscribe to the voluntaristic and normative language of good and bad intentions, good and bad definitions of culture, and so forth in order to agree with Ford's underlying contention that the invocation of rights discourse can redound upon the would-be claimant (and claimants to come) in ways that profoundly challenge the directionality of the liberal rights narrative of a subject standing before the law. Here, to the contrary, it is the law that configures that subject. Ford critiques the case of *Regents of University of California v Bakke*, the United States Supreme Court decision concerning affirmative action programs for university admission, which in part determined that "*only* by highlighting their own distinctiveness could minority students justify their presence in the universities that admitted them [by linking admission to normative standards of 'cultural diversity' within institutions]."[58] He writes: "By altering the character of the institutional treatment of race, it also altered the incentives surrounding racial identity and *thereby altered performance of racial identity*, at least among those directly affected by the institutions."[59] For Ford, then, rights regimes can specify and hence juridically entrench a very particular racial script that would-be claimants must adhere to and iteratively (re)produce, to the detriment of themselves and others (or at any rate, to the exclusion of other possible ways of performing that identity). However, those disciplinarily controlled "others" are not found simply within the putatively included group but outside of it as well, as the contemporary example of struggles to legislate in favor of gay marriage aptly demonstrates. As those critical of the movement maintain, the petition to include same-sex relationships within the state-sanctioned, juridical definition of marriage itself serves to bolster state power over intimate relationships and the regulation of sexuality as well as entrenching a distinction between legitimate and illegitimate queer unions.[60] "As long as people marry," writes Michael Warner in *The Trouble with Normal*, "the state will continue to regulate the sexual lives of those who do not [and legally cannot] marry."[61] In so doing, marriage, in Samuel A. Chambers's terms, "becomes much more than simply a right; it becomes a disciplinary institution."[62]

Importantly, as the last example given indicates, the disciplinary work of rights discourse is not performed solely by inscribing a given formulation of identity within the legal text, as if the legal word had some kind of interpellationary power of its own motion, but rather by the ongoing work of a whole range of actors (friends, family, activists, social workers, bureaucrats, lawyers, judges) within and without the strictly "legal" process of rights claiming.[63] As Foucault makes clear, "when I say right, I am not thinking just of the law, but of all the apparatuses, institutions, and rules that apply it."[64] On this score, Brown writes that

> the emancipatory function of rights cannot be adjudicated in abstraction from the bureaucratic juridical apparatus through which they are negotiated. Who, today, defends their rights without an army of lawyers and reams of complex legal documents? In this regard, rights, rather than being the "popular and available" currency depicted by Patricia Williams, may subject us to intense forms of bureaucratic domination and regulatory power even at the moment that we assert them in our own defense.[65]

Juridical rights and their various disciplinary modes of social-institutional realization thus particularize, producing narratives of identity formation that are unavoidably exclusionary and regulatory.[66] In doing this, they do not simply represent a pre-given or already-established identity, but rather—through the various legal and political mechanisms of representation, lobbying, enactment, and enforcement—go to constitute that very identity in the guise of its recognition.[67] This is Foucault's insight about the disciplinary, identity-producing function of rights:

> I have been trying . . . to show not only that right is an instrument of . . . domination . . . but also how, to what extent, and in what form right (and when I say right I am not thinking just of the law, but of all the apparatuses, institutions,

and rules that apply it) serves as a vehicle for and implements relations that are relations of domination ... [, namely,] the multiple subjugations that take place and function within the social body.[68]

Bringing to bear the Foucauldian insights of Brown (and others) on the image of rights as an available political tool, we hence arrive at a more layered and complex understanding of rights as ambivalent disciplinary artifacts. If they are sometimes effective in redirecting and remaking power relations, they nevertheless do so by fabricating and then regulating the very subjects who claim to rely upon them. Does this ambivalence lead Foucault to dismiss or reject rights? On the contrary, Foucault's critical counter-conduct of rights operates according to his own oft-cited principle on the reversibility and normative neutrality of power relations: "My point is not that everything is bad, but that everything is dangerous," he pronounces in an interview with Hubert Dreyfus and Paul Rabinow in 1983. The danger of rights and the possibility of their entrenching power relations and resubjugating the political subjects who seek to claim them leads Foucault to what he calls in the same interview a "hyper- and pessimistic activism," always alive to these dangers yet seeking all the same to tarry with the drawbacks and ambivalences of a critical counter-conduct of rights.[69] It is to an example of that activism that we now turn.

The Ambivalence of Rights:
From Gay Rights to the Rights of the Friend

In the early 1980s Foucault made a series of suggestive political proposals for rights struggles and linked these directly to a set of interventions into debates within the gay and lesbian communities over sexual identity, politics, and rights. These proposals and interventions were primarily, although not exclusively, made in the course of interviews in both North American (*The Advocate, Christopher Street*) and French (*Gai pied*) gay and lesbian activist periodicals. From the mid-1970s onward Foucault began to spend increasing amounts of his time in America. On the West Coast he worked at UC Berkeley, initially at the invitation of the French Department's Leo Bersani in 1975, and then from late 1979 (when he delivered the Tanner Lectures on Human Values at Stanford University) in collaboration with the philosopher Hubert Dreyfus and the anthropologist Paul Rabinow, who were to produce out of their joint discussions what is to this day still a very important text on his work.[70] On the East Coast Foucault lectured in New York. (One of his biographers, David Macey, remarks that Foucault and Derrida established between them a kind of de facto "geographical division of labour" for the diffusion of "French theory" into American academia: "Deconstructionism colonized Yale and the Ivy League universities, whereas Foucault found his audience, in which professional philosophers were usually underrepresented, in New York and on the West Coast.")[71] The attractions of America were, as many have observed, alternately cerebral and sensual. "He found intellectual life freer and more open there than in France," and, Macey observes drily, "California offered ample opportunity for the further exploration of the use of pleasures."[72] Yet it would be just as wrong to read the Frenchman's interventions into North American intellectual and political debates around gay liberation as reflecting the naive outsider's ready escape from Old World prurience into the countercultural San Franciscan pleasures of sex and drugs as it has been for others to stigmatize his much-publicized embrace of these pleasures as some form of homosexual "death wish."[73] Rather, Foucault's contributions to these political debates constitute a deeper theoretical problematization of freedom, rights, and liberation that both thematizes and navigates the ambivalence of rights as political tools laid out in the previous section.

He starts with the basic proposition that affirming the right of sexual choice (as a juridical question) is indeed important. The following excerpt is taken from an exchange in an interview published in *The Advocate*, a Los Angeles magazine, in 1984 but conducted in Toronto in June of 1982 and titled "Sex, Power, and the Politics of Identity":

> Q: Practically speaking, one of the effects of trying to uncover that secret [of a truth to one's sexual identity] has meant that the gay movement has remained at the level of demanding civil or human rights around sexuality. That is, sexual liberation has remained at the level of demanding sexual tolerance.
>
> A: Yes, but this aspect must be supported. It is important, first, to have the possibility—and the right—to choose your own sexuality. Human rights regarding sexuality are important and are still not respected in many places. We shouldn't consider that such problems are solved now.[74]

In an interview with James O'Higgins titled "Sexual Choice, Sexual Act," published in the American literary journal *Salmagundi* in 1982, Foucault similarly observes:

> I don't think we should have as our objective some sort of absolute freedom or total liberty of sexual action. However, where freedom of sexual choice is

concerned, one has to be absolutely intransigent. This includes the liberty of expression of that choice. By this I mean the liberty to manifest that choice or not to manifest it. Now, there has been considerable progress in this area on the level of legislation, certainly progress in the direction of tolerance, but there is still a lot of work to be done.[75]

There is no question, then, that Foucault believes that struggles over rights should form part of the political arsenal of gay and lesbian movements. In the language of the previous section of this chapter, rights function to defend and protect a particular way of life, and they do so by legally entrenching the "right to choose [one's] sexuality" and by allowing "the liberty to manifest that choice or not to manifest it." With their rhetorical invocation of choice, liberty, progress, and tolerance, these are strikingly liberal-sounding formulations. And yet for all his clear support for a rights-based political approach to the question of sexuality, he is equally clear that rights are both politically insufficient and themselves problematic in terms of their disciplinary and identity-producing (and -constraining) effects. In an interview titled "The Social Triumph of the Sexual Will," which was published in the flagship New York gay magazine *Christopher Street* in 1982 (yet given in October the preceding year), Foucault asserts:

> I think we should consider the battle for gay rights as an episode that cannot be the final stage. For two reasons: first because a right, in its real effects, is much more linked to attitudes and patterns of behavior than to legal formulations. There can be discrimination against homosexuals even if such discriminations are prohibited by law. . . . [And second,] it's not only a matter of integrating this strange little practice of making love with someone of the same sex into pre-existing cultures; it's a matter of constructing [*créer*] cultural forms.[76]

The first, legally postrealist insight is by now, I believe, relatively uncontentious (indeed, almost axiomatic in critical legal thinking): rights depend to a significant extent upon societal patterns of behavior and normative acceptance for their actual observance and enforcement (and not simply upon their purely legal status). But Foucault's second point is more critical. For all their utility as juridical guarantees of a particular way of life, rights actually function to produce, delimit, and circumscribe that very way of life. In the same interview, Foucault goes on to assert: "That in the name of respect of individual rights someone is allowed to do as he wants, great! But if what we want to do is to create a new way of life [*mode de vie*], then the question of individual rights is not pertinent."[77] However, far from merely being beside the point, rights are themselves directly implicated in the disciplinary process of inscribing homosexual identity. In the *Advocate* interview, Foucault is asked: "Identities help in exploring such practices and defending the right to engage in them. But are they also limiting in regards to the possibilities of individuals?" He agrees:

> If identity becomes the problem of sexual existence, and if people think they have to "uncover" their "own identity," and that their own identity has to become the law, the principle, the code of their existence . . . then, I think, they will turn back to a kind of ethics very close to the old heterosexual virility. . . . Yes, it [politicized identity] has been very useful, but it limits us.[78]

In these passages Foucault repeatedly points to the limitations of a purely juridical strategy of identity-based rights protection as compared to the more fecund and creative possibilities disclosed by the search for a gay way of life, or culture. "Not only do we have to defend ourselves, not only affirm ourselves [variously the work of rights], as an identity but as a creative force," he counsels.[79] Instead of pursuing the search for a true gay identity and attempting to protect it via rights, the political task, Foucault proposes, is to become gay. Again in the *Advocate* interview:

> Q: That's basically what you're getting at when you suggest that we should
>   try to become gay—not just to reassert ourselves as gay.
> A: Yes, that's it. We don't have to discover that we are homosexuals.
> Q: Or what the meaning of this is?
> A: Exactly. Rather, we have to create a gay life. To *become.*
> Q: And this is something without limits?
> A: Yes, sure . . .[80]

This becoming gay refuses the self-identity of the subject, insisting that "the relationships we have to have with ourselves are not ones of identity, rather, they must be relationships of differentiation, of creation, of innovation."[81] "Therefore," Foucault concludes, "we have to work at becoming homosexuals and not be obstinate about recognizing that we are."[82]

But if this aesthetic-political becoming gay is, as Foucault suggests in the above interview, "without limits," it is equally not without the domain of rights.[83] For if rights are the occasion and the vehicle of a disciplinary inscription of homosexual identity, they also emerge, ambivalently, as the scene of that inscription's potential loosening, overcoming, or displacement. While observing the problems endemic to rights, Foucault nevertheless tellingly makes a claim for what he calls "relational rights" in the 1982 *Christopher Street* interview. "Rather than arguing that rights are fundamental and natural to the individual," he suggests there, "we should try to imagine and create a new relational right that permits all possible types of relations to exist and not be prevented, blocked, or annulled by impoverished relational institutions."[84] Foucault's claim for a relational right, unlike the feminist discourse that mobilizes the same term,[85] does not rest upon an ontological claim about the fundamental connectedness and relationality of the subject. Rather, it is an attempt to use rights discourse in order to reconfigure the institutional and social possibilities for the recognition of different (possibly as-yet-uncontemplated) types of relationship. Foucault explains: "The relational right is the right to gain recognition in an institutional sense for the relations of one individual to another individual, which is not necessarily connected to the emergence of a group."[86] (He gives, as an example of a relational right, a right to adult adoption: "Or—why not?—of one adult by another. Why shouldn't I adopt a friend who's ten years younger than I am?")[87] His usage of rights discourse here is intended not simply to include gay and lesbian unions or parenting within existing institutional structures (for he argues that "the progress made is slight" if one adopts that approach), but rather to conduct a wider "fight against the impoverishment of the relational fabric," using rights to sexuality as a starting point.[88] In the *Christopher Street* interview, he says:

> We have to reverse things a bit. Rather than saying what we said at one time, "Let's try to re-introduce homosexuality into the general norm of social relations," let's say the reverse—"No! Let's escape as much as possible from the type of relations that society proposes for us and try to create in the empty space where we are new relational possibilities." By proposing a new relational *right*, we will see that nonhomosexual people can enrich their lives by changing their own schema of relations.[89]

On the one hand, rights discourse entrenches, stabilizes, and regulates identity; on the other, it discloses possibilities, as the contemporary political theorist Karen Zivi writes, for "transformation or resignification rather than either repudiation or reification."[90] The aim of the new form of relational right toward which Foucault is gesturing here is clearly not to stabilize the notion of already-existing forms of homosexual relations (although of course it always unavoidably runs this risk, and hence needs self-critically to guard against it). Rather, it is a conscious attempt to use the existing language of rights discourse in order to pluralize and "stray afield from" identity and the selfsame,[91] to carve out a space for possible relations between individuals that elude the disciplinary and nor-malizing effects of identitarian categories (of "gay man," "straight man," and so forth). These possible relations enabled through the discourse and practice of relational rights hence are not and cannot be the preserve of a determinate iden-tity called "gay" or "homosexual." Foucault evidently has something queerer in mind, and he names it "friendship." The thematic of friendship emerges as an explicit philosophical concern in the late work—it is discussed in the context of his genealogy of the ancient care of the self in the 1982 Collège course "The Hermeneutics of the Subject." There Foucault traces the different articulations of friendship in a range of classical philosophical schools such as the Epicureans and the Stoics.[92] The historical analysis of friendship in classical antiquity is also connected, for Foucault, with his important discussion of the ancient concept and practice of *parrhesia*, which, introduced in the 1982 lectures, comes to oc-cupy a central role in the lectures of the following two years. As hesitant as Fou-cault is to appropriate an anachronistic "solution" to the disciplinary problems of modernity from the milieu of the care of the self in antiquity,[93] it is equally clear that friendship has some significant contemporary political work to do for him, and we can see this in some of the late interviews and interventions I have been discussing. In Steven Garlick's words, Foucault's concept of friendship in these interviews is proffered as a "challenge to the modern gender regime and its underlying discourse of heterosexuality," that is, as a "site of gender trouble."[94] Broadly, friendship in this body of work signifies the potentiality of affective re-lations beyond (and disruptive of) the heteronormative binary with its "sadistic social hierarchies of identitarian difference."[95] In the *Gai pied* interview from 1981, "Friendship as a Way of Life," Foucault critiques the notion of homosexual-ity itself as defined by (same-)sexual desire and "getting each other off" as being too easily domesticated by regulatory heterosexual gender norms:

> There you have a kind of neat image of homosexuality without any possibility
> of generating unease, and for two reasons: it responds to a reassuring canon of
> beauty, and it cancels everything that can be troubling in affection, tenderness,
> friendship, fidelity, camaraderie, and companionship, things that our rather
> sanitized society can't allow a place for without fearing the formation of new
> alliances and the tying together of unforeseen lines of force.[96]

If, for Foucault, "the development toward which the problem of homosexual-ity tends is the one of friendship,"[97] this friendship is not one of reconciliation but rather one of agonism and rupture.[98] Friendship in his hands exposes and remakes interpersonal and wider social relationships, and it is the figure of the homosexual who inaugurates (but does not finish) this process. "Homosexuality is a historic occasion to reopen affective and relational virtualities, not so much through the intrinsic qualities of the homosexual but because the 'slant-wise' position of the latter, as it were, the diagonal lines he can lay out in the social fabric allow these virtualities to come to light."[99] Homosexuality "thus invites the creation of new forms of relationship,"[100] but it is overcome by those new forms of relationship that put its founding concepts in question.

Let us recap. An assertion of a right to sexuality, Foucault is arguing, is a crucial political move. It is incredibly important, he insists in the interviews given to the *Advocate* and *Salmagundi*, to protect a liberty of sexual choice. And yet, of course, this juridical protection also functions as a disciplinary tool that inevitably circumscribes and polices what it means to occupy the position of the desiring subject exercising that sexual choice. Rights ambivalently protect and entrench identity. But this ambivalence is not equivalent to a closed logic and a paradox that leads nowhere politically. Rather, rights are to be seized and used as counter-conducts, and Foucault himself demonstrates that they still have some creative political work to do. In and through his understanding of relational rights he tries to show how rights claims can also be the medium for contesting the limits of those identities by allowing new affective relations to form and be respected. He gives the name friendship to these affective possibilities, but the possibilities of the rights of friendship are, of course, themselves neither an institutional nor a political "answer" in any enduring sense (although they do disclose what is for Foucault an enduring ethos and practice of friendship). "We can never be sure," he responds to a question about whether new resistant sexual practices can be co-opted. "In fact, we can always be sure *it will happen*, and that everything that has been created or acquired, any ground that has been gained will, at a certain moment be used in such a way. That's the way we live, that's the way we struggle, that's the way of human history."[101] Even the rights of friendship inevitably "produce [their] countereffects."[102]

Rights and Freedom?

Finally, then, what relationship between rights and freedom arises from Foucault's critical counter-conduct of rights? In answer to a question posed in the *Advocate* interview about the political utility of identity claims, Foucault responds: "Yes, it has been very useful, but it limits us, and I think we have—and can have—a right to be free."[103] Is this the classical liberal freedom of a subject that Foucault recalls here? The originary right of a subject protected by law? It would, of course, be possible to read this brief phrase, "a right to be free," in just such an orthodox, liberal individualist way. But such a reading would be inconsistent with Foucault's understanding both of subject formation and of rights, an understanding we have traced over the preceding chapters. Instead, we can discern in this quotation that a certain understanding of rights is posed against, or is maintained in some tension with, the utility of identitarian claims ("Yes, it has been very useful, but . . . we . . . can have—a right to be free"). According to *this* reading, rights represent something other, an excess, as set against a closed logic of identity. They are both something we have and yet also something we can have: something in the present and something irreducibly futural at the same time. They can never be quite determined, and their possibilities can never be entirely extinguished. Rights are the carriers of freedom, then—not so much in the sense of a right to be free, where freedom signifies an ontologically given or an institutionally guaranteed state of affairs, but rather in the sense of a right and its exercise both relying upon and practicing freedom. But what exactly might Foucault understand by "freedom" here?

As we know, Foucault consistently refuses to endorse a juridical formulation of subjective freedom, of a freedom of the subject protected by his proper and selfsame rights. As he puts it in his lecture course for 1979, "The Birth of Biopolitics," "Freedom is not a given . . . it is not a ready-made region which has to be respected"[104] via a system of rights—indeed, on his view such a system cannot ever assure freedom.[105] Freedom is not a property of the individual subject,[106] and consequently there are for him "no [subjective] spaces of primal liberty between the meshes of [power's] network."[107] And yet in his late work on ethics and on the care of the self (and in later work where he reflects upon his conception of power as relational) he comes increasingly to talk of freedom. As I argued in Chapter 2, it would be a mistake to read such work as a belated rapprochement with a liberal ontology of the subject. Freedom here does not attach itself by right to a subject, but rather comes to designate the condition of possibility for power and, latterly, ethical relations. "Freedom is the ontological condition of ethics," he writes in "The Ethics of the Concern for Self as a Practice of Freedom."[108] And in "The Subject and Power" he asserts: "Freedom may well appear as the condition for the exercise of power (at the same time its precondition, since freedom must exist for power to be exerted, and also its permanent support, since without the possibility of recalcitrance power would be equivalent to a physical determination)."[109] If Foucauldian freedom in these later renditions does not denote an ineluctable property of human nature, then, as Johanna Oksala explains, we can instead understand it as marking "the ontological contingency of the present," conceived as "the moment of the unexpected as opposed to the normalized, the unforeseen as opposed to the determined."[110] Freedom as a precondition of, or as the condition of possibility for, power is nothing other than the constitutive instability and possibility of the reversibility of power itself, of power's always potentially being otherwise, of its never being ultimately determined. Here freedom is neither counterposed to power (as in the standard liberal formulations I have been critiquing) nor is it reducible to an "internal modality of power relations"[111] (as in the understanding of freedom as itself a vehicle of governmentality).[112] Rather, as Foucault stresses in both the formulations extracted above, freedom is the necessary precondition of power. Where there is power, for Foucault, there must also always—and precisely to the extent that there is power (and not an immoveable state of utter domination)[113]—be freedom: freedom, that is, grasped as the possibility of movement, contestation, and resistance.[114] Freedom here is the beginning and end of power, its enabling condition and limit—its inescapable contingency.

How can we (re)connect this late Foucauldian evocation of freedom to the relationship between the subject and her rights? Initially, it would seem that such a relation is circular, for the very subject of rights is always already an effect of those rights. "What happens," asks Wendy Brown perceptively, "when we understand individual rights as a form of protection against certain social powers of which the ostensibly protected individual is also an effect?"[115] From the perspective of a liberal understanding of the subject—as pre-political and before the law—this question surely poses an insoluble conundrum. However, to return to the understanding of Foucauldian subject formation articulated in the previous chapter, we can recall that that subject is neither formed once and for all nor in a single and coherent discursive/disciplinary location. Rather, that subject emerges from time to time as the unfinished and performative result of a range of different interacting and potentially conflicting processes of subjectification. It is a subject, in Judith Butler's resonant reflections on subjectivity in the late Foucault, that is simultaneously "crafted and crafting."[116] And as such, its tenuous agency is momentarily achieved both in the spatial clash of those different disciplinary logics as well as in the temporal dimension of their iteration and unfolding. It is "there" and "then" that the possibility for new formations of the subject emerge. Freedom in the Foucauldian lexicon names this very possibility, and rights—as a mechanism of power—both rely upon that freedom (as internal margin, as contingency) in order to take place and also potentially help to bring it about (as the carrier of new ways of being and relating). However, as the ambivalence of the critical counter-conduct of rights makes clear, this freedom is never a telos, never a settled state of affairs. It can never be definitively guaranteed and must constantly be practiced. It demands an ongoing and self-reflective critique in order to be actualized. Rights are a political mechanism that both produce and threaten the space of freedom. They both entrench but also, and simultaneously, help to free and to loosen power relations. As such, Foucault's conception of the relationship between freedom and rights decisively moves beyond liberal figurations. Against a liberal understanding that might see freedom as the subject's essence and destiny, and formal systems of rights as the proper institutional representation and manifestation of that freedom, Foucault sides with Nietzsche. "Liberal institutions immediately cease to be liberal," opines the latter in *Twilight of the Idols*, "as soon as they are attained: subsequently there is nothing more thoroughly harmful to freedom than liberal institutions."[117] And as Foucault remarks, "it can never be inherent in the structure of things to guarantee the exercise of freedom. The guarantee of freedom is freedom"[118]—which is to say, of course, that freedom cannot be ultimately guaranteed at all. Rather, it is only through the constant work of critique, self-interrogation, and political struggle that power relations are unpicked, made, and remade and freedom's possibilities fleetingly practiced. Otherwise, power relations set and ossify, hardening into relations of domination in which there is no possibility for reversal or contestation.[119] Such a mobile and iterative understanding of freedom refuses, as per liberal or utopian understandings, to reify the concept or to mark it as foundational or as a finished state of affairs. Freedom is a ceaseless work without any guarantee. And in its being an ongoing work, neither can it be the set preserve of any given institution or practice. Rights are but one available political means to contest those power relations and to perform that always-imperiled work of freedom. While, as Foucault shows, they do reveal their contingency and availability for political resignification, they will not for this reason alone always and necessarily present the best possible means for the contestation of power relations. Judith Butler writes of her own approach to the occupation and subversion of dominant political terms in the following way:

> Here it should become clear that I am not, in this instance [she is writing about the right to gay marriage], arguing for a view of political performativity which

holds that it is necessary to occupy the dominant norm in order to produce an internal subversion of its terms. Sometimes it is important to refuse its terms, to let the term wither, to starve it of its strength. And there is, I believe, a performativity proper to refusal which, in this instance, insists upon the reiteration of sexuality beyond the dominant terms.[120]

But when will rights, with their ambivalent logics and particular histories, present a useful means for political struggle—and when will they be best left to wither, best refused in favor of other means? These questions speak to the themes of tactical and strategical deployments of rights, which are the subject of the next chapter.

CHAPTER 4

RIGHTS BETWEEN TACTICS AND STRATEGY

All my books . . . are little toolboxes, if you will. If people are willing to
open them and make use of such and such a sentence or idea, of one
analysis or another, as they would a screwdriver or a monkeywrench,
in order to shortcircuit or disqualify systems of power, including even
possibly the ones my books come out of, well, all the better.

Michel Foucault

On (Not) Playing the Game: From Tactics to Strategy?

In one of the last interviews before his death, given in May 1984 and titled "Polemics, Politics, and Problematizations," Foucault is asked by his interviewer
(and sometime collaborator) Paul Rabinow why it is that he does not "engage
in polemics."[1] In responding to the question (and in agreeing with its premise) Foucault proposes a distinction between the respectful partner in dialogue,
who seeks the truth, and the polemicist, who manifestly does not. The distinction rests upon the metaphor of the game and, importantly, on the function of
rights in administering the game. Genuine partners in dialogue, those committed to the "search for the truth and the relation to the other," agree to take
part in "a game that is at once pleasant and difficult—in which each of the two
partners takes pains only to use the rights given him by the other and by the
accepted form of the dialogue."[2] According to such a form, the questioner "is
merely exercising the right that has been given to him: to remain unconvinced,
to perceive a contradiction, to require more information, to emphasize different
postulates, to point out faulty reasoning, and so on," while the one who answers
likewise "exercises a right that does not go beyond the discussion itself; by the
logic of his own discourse, he is tied to what he has said earlier, and by the acceptance of dialogue he is tied to the questioning of the other."[3] Thus do the
participants agree to abide by certain rules that seek both to guarantee the tenor
of the discussion itself and, in a sense, its outcome (that is, the truth, or at any
rate a more truthful discourse). Importantly, Foucault conceives of the rules of

this game of truth in the form of rights tenable by each of the participants and exercisable against the other. We have here a neat metaphor of the way in which, for example, free speech rights or rights to freedom of political expression are said to function internally to a liberal democratic polity—simultaneously guaranteeing the rights and, in turn, setting forth the responsibilities of the speaking subject and in so doing securing and legitimizing the free play of political discussion and debate (within a "marketplace of ideas," and such).[4]

Against this rights-based and dialogical model of the game Foucault counterposes the figure of the polemicist, who sets himself against the game, as it were, and thereby refuses its rights. "The polemicist . . . proceeds encased in privileges that he possesses in advance and will never agree to question."[5] There is no vulnerability to the polemicist, no openness to the other and to the risk of putting his own position into question; no frankness, *parrhesia*, risk taking, or conversion is possible for the polemicist. Hence "for him . . . the game consists not of recognizing this person as a subject having the right to speak but of abolishing him, as interlocutor, from any possible dialogue; . . . not to come as close as possible to a difficult truth but to bring about the triumph of the just cause he has been manifestly upholding from the beginning."[6] We need not accept Foucault's characterization of the polemicist[7] in order to find the distinction that he proposes in this brief interview a suggestive starting point for thinking about his own rights praxis at this time. I say that it is a "suggestive" starting point, yet it is ultimately an insufficient one for what it leaves out of account. Foucault draws a rather schematic picture. On the one hand is the dialogical use of rights that is consonant with, remains within the limits of, and is indeed functional to the reproduction of the game; on the other hand is the polemical refusal of the game and its rights. This distinction surely does capture some normative and critical orientations toward rights, yet just as surely such a stark opposition prompts us to think beyond the two alternatives and toward other critical possibilities.[8] Is there not some other way of playing the game that consists neither of acquiescence and reproduction nor of utter refusal, that is neither wholly dialogical nor utterly polemical—some way of using rights to play a different game, perhaps?

In this chapter I want to suggest, in line with the idea of a critical counterconduct of rights, that there is such a possibility and that this possibility better captures Foucault's own political use of rights in the late work. According to this possibility, one can play the game against itself, use the rules of the game in a way not envisioned by its makers, and indeed attempt to use the tools of rights in order to play a different game entirely. This third possibility between dialogue and polemics we might initially call, although in a moment we shall need to revisit and refine this terminology somewhat, a "tactical" use of rights. To use rights tactically, according to this first meaning of the phrase, is to use them instrumentally, to invoke them as a mere means to an end. Foucault repeatedly deploys this sense of "tactical" in his writings. For example, in the fourth lecture of his 1978 Collège de France course "Security, Territory, Population," he says of the status of law under governmentality that "it is not a matter of imposing a law on men, but of the disposition of things, that is to say, of employing tactics rather than laws, or, of as far as possible employing laws as tactics; arranging things so that this or that end may be achieved through a certain number of means."[9] To employ law as a tactic is to approach it not as a substantive ideal or a normative system binding on all, but rather as an assemblage of power-knowledge available for appropriation by various social actors that can be, and is, put to varying uses. An instrumental deployment of law (or any other assemblage) is a kind of insubordinate, disobedient, and potentially subversive deployment that plays the game[10] in a way that does not respect the stated purpose of the game and hence troubles and possibly undermines it.[11] Foucault echoes this idea of a tactical usage as being opposed to a proper or obedient usage elsewhere in the late lectures, in "The Hermeneutics of the Subject," when in paraphrasing a text by Seneca on rhetoric he makes a distinction between "a tactical use of rhetoric" and a "fundamental, overall, or total obedience to the rules of rhetoric."[12]

This chapter hence provides a reflection on what I call the tactical and strategic dimension of Foucault's politics of rights. My starting point is this concept (and practice) of rights being deployed in a tactical way—by which I mean, broadly, an instrumental deployment of rights that does not respect their stated role in a system but that tries to appropriate them for different, partial, and selective purposes. While I commence with this basic concept of rights as tactical instruments, I want ultimately to layer and complicate this initial understanding of the term "tactical" by bringing it back into proximity with a related concept that, while frequently confused with tactics in popular and occasionally even in academic discourse, actually takes its meaning in opposition to it: strategy. The complementary terms "tactics" and "strategy" are possibly encountered more often today in the annals of business and management consultants than they are in the writings of the theoretical left (itself revealing, of course),[13] but my first step will be to revisit the (original, canonical) meanings given to these terms in a *military* context (in the writings of Clausewitz, for example). Then we can move on to more (openly) political terrain and consider some of Foucault's writings on tactics and strategy, at the same time situating Foucault's understandings of these terms in reference to some emergent Marxist literature in the field of critical legal theory on when and how to engage in politics in a revolutionary and strategic way. My intent is neither to resuscitate the rather tired "debate" on Foucault's supposedly antagonistic relation to Marx and the Marxist tradition,[14] nor (necessarily) to see whether the two can be brought into a more productive proximity,[15] but simply to propose the more developed Marxist understanding of tactics and strategy (particularly as it relates to law and rights under capitalism) as a foil for Foucault's less elaborated but suggestive account of the same. Bringing Foucault back into dialogue with a Marxist tradition is a necessary conceptual move, but it is also a restaging of an actual dialogue. Recent Marxist and post-Marxist accounts of critical legal strategy have drawn heavily upon the influential theory of the "strategy of rupture" developed by the controversial communist and anti-colonialist lawyer Jacques Vergès—a theory articulated in his 1968 book, *De la stratégie judiciaire* and (perhaps most infamously) practiced in his career as a criminal defense lawyer during which he defended, among others, the Nazi war criminal Klaus Barbie (the infamous "Butcher of Lyon"). Foucault was himself in dialogue with Vergès in the 1980s (among other connections, writing a preface to the second edition of the latter's book) and was interested in the elaboration and application of Vergès's judicial strategies in contemporary political struggles.

Putting Foucault back in touch with this radical legal tradition helps to clarify the stakes and intentions of his own tactical and strategic interventions into rights discourse, which I shall interrogate in the following section through a reading of two different political interventions, both of them addressed to the question of life and death under biopolitical rule: his writings on suicide and the right to die, and his writings on the abolition of the death penalty in France in the early 1980s. To return to Foucault's metaphor of the game, he sought to leverage the resources of the game in order to play it differently, that is, in the sense of a tactical (read: instrumental) intervention. But in what sense might Foucault's tactical reversal or creative game playing with rights at the local level of power relations resonate with wider efforts to contest and remake overarching logics and practices of power? Is his a merely tactical reversal (in the more precise sense of the word) or a strategic intervention? And how might the two be related? These are the animating questions of this chapter, but in order to answer them I need first, via Clausewitz and his readers, to provide a more elaborated distinction between tactics and strategy.

Tactics and Strategy in Critical Legal Thinking:
From Clausewitz to Foucault via Vergès and Marx

The Prussian general and military theorist, Carl von Clausewitz, is perhaps best known today for the proposition from his work, *On War*, that war is the continuation of politics by other means—a proposition that Foucault famously inverts in the opening lecture of "'Society Must Be Defended'" to read: "Power is war, the continuation of war by other means."[16] The importance for Foucault of this reformulation of the Clausewitzian maxim is that it assists him in constructing his own, "strategic" analytic of power relations. We shall engage this Foucauldian analytic shortly, but for now we can simply recall that beyond the memorable realpolitik statement of the continuum between war and peace, Clausewitz also bequeaths to us what is surely the canonical definition of strategy itself:

> The use of the engagement to attain the object of the war. . . . It must therefore give an aim to the whole military action. The aim must be in accord with the object of the war. In other words, strategy develops the plan of the war, and to the aforesaid aim links the series of acts which are to lead to it; that is, it plans the separate campaigns and arranges the engagements to be fought in each of them.[17]

In defining the concept of strategy Clausewitz thus also defines the concept of tactics and shows both how they are related but also how they function at different levels. In military terms, then, strategy is the general, overarching plan that a commander formulates and implements in order to win the war, while tactics are the intermediate methods (such as fighting or not fighting particular battles, or conducting them in particular ways) that such a commander will employ in order to achieve that overriding goal. This basic distinction, cardinal to military engagements, has of course been carried over into the realm of politics (each of these realms being, according to Clausewitz and Foucault, reflections of the other). As the Marxist legal scholar Robert Knox argues, "many of those who used the terms 'strategy' and 'tactics' in describing politics [Lenin, Trotsky, Mao Tse-tung, Guevara] were influenced directly by . . . military theorists [such as Clausewitz]"[18] and, rather obviously from the names just recited, it has been within the radical and particularly the Marxist tradition of political theory that questions of tactics and strategy have been most fully considered. What actions will constitute a tactical political intervention and how these tactical interventions can be successfully articulated into an overall strategy are the questions this tradition asks.

From within the Marxist tradition questions of strategy have been directly indexed to systemic or structural concerns, such that a properly strategic approach is oriented toward grasping and then overcoming the structural logics of the system under critique. In formulating his understanding of the political distinction between tactics and strategy Knox, for example, draws upon the writings of the Marxist thinker best known for theorizing the political: Antonio Gramsci. Gramsci proposes a distinction between "conjunctural" and "organic" moments and the type of political criticism that each calls forth. The former are more fleeting, occasional phenomena, while the latter represent permanent elements of the political situation. "Conjunctural phenomena," writes Gramsci, "do not have any very far-reaching historical significance . . . [and consequently] give rise to a political criticism of a minor, day-to-day character," while "organic phenomena on the other hand give rise to socio-historical criticism, whose subject is wider social groupings."[19] For Knox, following Gramsci, strategy is "related to organic phenomena, that is to say those relationships which are relatively permanent [such as, for Marxists, a given society's mode of production], and serve as the basis or fundamental structure of the field in which the intervention is made," and hence "strategic questions are those that are addressed at critiquing and overturning those relationships."[20] "By contrast," he goes on to write, "tactics are concerned with conjunctural moments, that is to say those which are not structural in a direct sense . . . [and which] address those transitory conflicts and battles that occur in the political sphere . . . from an individual election, to a particular protest and so on."[21] Working within the Marxist political tradition that Knox articulates, then, allows one conceptually to separate the tactical and the strategic (in a way that permits one to say of certain interventions that they might well be pragmatic or tactical but that they are, in the temporal perspective of revolution or of structural critique, un- or even anti-strategic). It also, importantly, allows one to articulate tactics and strategy, that is, to begin to answer the question of when and in what circumstances a tactical move might also be strategic. Having sketched this Marxist conceptual distinction between the tactical and the strategic and suggested the political stakes of such a distinction, I want now to turn to Foucault's own, rather different understanding of the question of tactics and strategy. In a moment we shall bring both these perspectives to bear on the question of rights, which will return us to Jacques Vergès and his much-vaunted strategy of judicial rupture.

Foucault uses the term "strategy," in a broad sense, to describe his own analytic of power relations developed in the 1970s.[22] As I have discussed in Chapter 1, he constructs this analytic of power in response to the theoretical failings of the repressive hypothesis and the juridico-discursive model of power. For him, in contrast, power must be understood relationally and horizontally and not as emanating from a sovereign or as acting upon a pre-formed object. "Power must be understood in the first instance," writes Foucault, "as the multiplicity of force relations immanent in the sphere in which they operate . . . [and] as the process which, through ceaseless struggles and confrontations, transforms, strengthens, or reverses them."[23] In sum:

> It is a question of orienting ourselves to a conception of power which replaces the privilege of the law with the viewpoint of the objective, the privilege of prohibition with the viewpoint of tactical efficacy, the privilege of sovereignty with the analysis of a multiple and mobile field of force relations, wherein far-reaching, but never completely stable, effects of domination are produced. The strategical model, rather than the model based on law.[24]

By describing his model of power relations as "strategical," argues Amy Allen, Foucault intends to convey both that power relations "involve confrontation or struggle" and that "there is an instrumentalist logic to these confrontations or struggles, such that each party to the struggle is concerned with getting the other to do what he/she wants."[25] We might add as well that what is key to this "strategical" understanding of power is the sense of relationality and constant flux, such that the field of force relations that Foucault connotes by the word "power" is "multiple . . . mobile . . . [and] never completely stable."[26] By referring to power relations as "strategical," then, Foucault signifies that they are the momentary result of contestation and struggle and hence that, with further contestation and struggle, they can be overturned and reversed.

As Allen quickly acknowledges, this meaning of the term "strategic" is a broad one that,[27] as well as being largely synonymous with the initial meaning of "tactical" with which we started (that is, instrumental), does not really begin to engage the conceptual distinction between tactics and strategy so consequential to the military and Marxist political traditions we have just sketched. But elsewhere in Foucault's work (indeed, elsewhere in the first volume of *The History of Sexuality*) he *does* invoke, or reference, such a distinction, although in so doing he parts company with some of the ontological and political assumptions shared by writers within the Marxist tradition. For example, he specifies in the course of the interview "Power and Strategies" that there are different levels of power relations. "Dispersed, heteromorphous, localised procedures of power" are "adapted, reinforced and transformed" by what he calls "global strategies" which "adopt a more-or-less coherent and unitary strategic form."[28] He hastens to add that this wider aggregation of the local relations of power into global formations does not result in "a massive and primal condition of domination, a binary structure with 'dominators' on one side and 'dominated' on the other," but rather something much more fissiparous, fluid, and undetermined.[29] Relations of domination form at the macrolevel of strategy but are never firmly set and are always subject to reversal and overturning. While these power relations subsist at both a local and an overarching level, so too does resistance to these relations in the sense that "like power, resistance is multiple and can be integrated in global strategies."[30] Foucault hence asserts—in terms of both power and resistance—that relations formed at a local level can be and often are integrated into a more global level, to which he gives the name "strategy." In the first volume of *The History of Sexuality* he frames this relation between the local and the strategic in terms of a "rule of double conditioning," according to which

> no "local centre," no "pattern of transformation" could function if, through a series of sequences, it did not eventually enter into an over-all strategy. And inversely, no strategy could achieve comprehensive effects if it did not gain support from precise and tenuous relations serving, not as its point of application or final outcome, but as its prop and anchor point.[31]

That is, he says, "one must conceive of the double conditioning of a strategy by the specificity of possible tactics, and of tactics by the strategic envelope that makes them work."[32] So, just like the military and Marxist traditions, Foucault also sustains a distinction between the tactical and the strategic (although for him the distinction is metaphorized spatially, not temporally) and suggests that they can be and are articulated upon each other. And yet there are, of course, profound differences between Foucault and the Marxist tradition. I do not propose to rehearse these differences in their entirety here; it will suffice simply to recall a few of them which bear on the question on the use of rights in a tactical or strategic way.

The first point of difference is that for Foucault, while power relations are "intentional," they are at the same time "nonsubjective."[33] What he means by this is that while "the rationality of power is characterized by tactics that are often quite explicit at the restricted level where they are inscribed," and that often these tactics "becom[e] connected to one another ... [and] form [...] comprehensive systems [with intelligible logics, aims and objectives]," nevertheless "no one is there to have invented them" but "the great anonymous, almost unspoken strategies" themselves.[34] Such a conception of a political "strategy without strategists"[35] abjures explanatory recourse to determinate and intentional political actors or subjects (both individual or collective) just as it problematizes their political formation. "Neither the caste which governs, nor the groups which control the state apparatus, nor those who make the most important economic decisions," writes Foucault, can be said to be in control of "the entire network of power that functions in a society."[36]

Second, it is clear that in conceiving of this "entire network of power," Foucault disagrees in both an epistemological and a political sense with those Marxists who maintain that one should understand power relations to form part of a (contradictory) totality that can be grasped and overcome in toto and replaced with a new (non-alienating, emancipated) set of social relations. Rather, Foucault's conceptions of "entire networks" and "strategies" are not only desubjectified but also far less coherent and structural than orthodox Marxist versions of the same.

This, finally, leads us to the third relevant difference—namely, Foucault's critical attitude toward revolution and revolutionary tactics and strategy. Much could be written of the changing fortunes of the thematic of "revolution" (understood in its broadest senses) in Foucault's thought, and indeed how his approach to revolution and revolutions (actual, historical, and imagined) indexes shifts in his own political imaginary.[37] Here I want simply to suggest that at this point in his work he is concerned to problematize revolution (and specifically the notion of a Marxist revolution) as a means to think the political. This problematization issues in both a general critique of the notion of a revolution (the historical "experience" of which, he avers in "What Is Enlightenment?," "has led only to the return of the most dangerous traditions")[38] and a more specific critique of revolutionary tactics and strategy. As to the latter, he provides in "Power and Strategies" a critique of what he calls "the 'theory' of the weakest link," according to which a "local attack is considered to have sense and legitimacy only when directed at the element which, if broken, will allow the total breach of the chain."[39] Seeking to distance himself from "this 'Leninist' thesis,"[40] Foucault remarks that such a position essentially mortgages the tactical to a certain, for him restrictive, understanding of the strategic. According to such a view, only those tactical moves that isolate a genuine weak point will prove to have strategic merit and political purchase, considered in the light of an a priori and overarching theoretical conception of the social totality. In fact, he insists, the goal should not be to subsume local, tactical interventions under a totalizing theory of the social whole, but rather "to analyse the specificity of mechanisms of power, to locate the connections and extensions, to build little by little a strategic knowledge (*savoir*)" from the ground up, as it were.[41]

Placing Foucault in dialogue with the Marxist tradition helps to bring his project into relief. The differences are clear and important. And yet to suggest, as many have,[42] that Foucault's aversion to concepts of structure, totality, and emancipation, together with his problematization of revolution, leads him to a purely localized and tactical politics that never broaches wider interventions against more hegemonic forms of power relations would be a serious misreading. Not only does Foucault refuse to replace the strategic with the tactical (and counsel a retreat to the merely local, occasional, conjunctural, and discontinuous level in which power is inscribed), but he holds out some hope on the part of his own critical counter-conduct of rights for a more sustained, strategic opposition to wider forms of power. If the tactical, in opposition to the Leninist position he criticizes, has for Foucault a certain priority over the strategic, then this is purely temporal. Tactics seemingly come first, from the bottom up, so as to drive the articulation of strategy. In the next section I shall investigate how Foucault aims to do just this with what I have called the rights of life and death under biopolitical rule; but first I want to refocus our attention on the specific question of the politics of rights, on their tactical or strategic uses, and on the particular political possibilities that they enable or attenuate.

I have dwelt on the Marxist tradition not simply for comparative purposes but because the comparison itself reflects a contemporary theoretical dialogue (at the same time as it recalls an actual historical one) between Foucault and radical politics. We see this dialogue at play in recent work in critical legal theory that has sought to re-energize the question of strategy and, in so doing, to ask again what role law might play as part of a broader radical politics.[43] In an important article, "Strategies of Rupture," that catalyzed these concerns and was published in the journal *Law & Critique* in 2009, the legal theorist Emilios Christodoulidis formulates the question as one of how legal instruments such as rights can furnish radical possibilities under present capitalist conditions: "*What registers as resistant, neither reducible to nor cooptable by the order it seeks to resist?* And generalising it: what can break incongruently, irreducibly so, with the order of capital or, more precisely, with capitalism's economy of representation?"[44] Ultimately, Christodoulidis commends what he calls a critical strategy of rupture that uses the existing legal institutional spaces precisely so as to perform an immanent critique that breaks radically with the logic of the system.[45] Such an approach would need to contend with what Christodoulidis percipiently calls law's mechanisms of homology (concerning the expectations of what will count and what will register as legally valid knowledge) and deadlock (exclusionary forms of process, such as jurisdictional limits and rules of standing) that function to contain the possibilities of radical political change within the system.[46] Others have subsequently taken up Christoudoulidis's challenge, foregrounding the resistant potential in legal and rights-based strategies on behalf of, respectively, anti-colonialist and anti-capitalist movements in both India and Israel/Palestine and the movement against the mandatory detention of asylum seekers in Australia.[47] In taking up Christodoulidis's suggestion of prosecuting legal strategies of rupture in the present day, of course, these and other writers are drawing upon and redeploying an older archive, for Christoudoulidis takes the concept of the strategy of rupture from the notorious French criminal defense lawyer Jacques Vergès.

Broadly, Vergès's 1968 book, *De la stratégie judiciaire*, articulates a distinction between what the author calls a "strategy of connivance" and a "strategy of rupture." While the former strategy counsels an accused and her defense team to accept the law's authority and its formal rules, the latter approaches the trial politically as an opportunity to contest the law's legitimacy and its self-presentation so as to effect a rupture in the system itself.[48] Vergès postulated that the normative authority of the criminal trial was dependent upon the acquiescence of the accused; crucially, where that enabling "connivance" was withdrawn, the possibility of a confrontation with the legal order arose that allowed the lawyer to stage a political challenge to the legal system and its supposed values. Here the rules of the game, to return to the metaphor with which we started, are deployed to maximum effect in order to interrupt the game itself. "He . . . presents himself as a lawyer, he does his job as a lawyer, he uses all the resources of the law," the philosopher Jacques Derrida observed of Vergès and his strategy of rupture in a 1987 interview, "while *radically* contesting the legitimacy of this law and all of its consequences."[49] In *De la stratégie judiciaire* Vergès lists a number of historical examples of the legal strategy of rupture (Socrates, Louis XVI, and the Bulgarian communist Georgi Dimitrov, accused by the Nazis of burning down the German parliament building in 1933) yet the best-known example of Vergès's ruptural defense strategy is still the infamous one he conducted himself on behalf of Klaus Barbie ("the Butcher of Lyon") in 1987.[50] Barbie was an ex-Gestapo officer, a spectacularly unrepentant Nazi ideologue to the end, and in view of this, obviously, a singularly uncompelling accused. Charged with "crimes against humanity" for his role in carrying out the torture and murder of Jews, communists, and Resistance members in Lyon from late 1942 onward (where he was made the head of the Gestapo), Barbie's defense was not so much a defense as an offensive move against the French legal order and the colonial violence of the French state perpetrated in Algeria. "Vergès," Christodoulidis summarizes, "refused to conduct the defence in terms of the usual tactics of seeking attenuating circumstances, of stressing the only subsidiary role of the French Gestapo to the organised atrocity of the Final Solution, or of presenting the array of psychological or bureaucratic 'excuses.'"[51] Refusing these tactics, Vergès deployed other tactics—notably, and in main part, the *tu quoque*—in aid of the overall strategy of rupture, which was essentially to indict the French state with hypocrisy for purporting to charge Barbie with crimes that it routinely carried out as part of its own colonial warfare and counterinsurgency operations in Algeria. "We bow our heads also in front of the martyrdom of the children of Izieu," concluded the legal dramaturge Vergès, "because we remember the suffering of the children of Algiers."[52] By neither evading nor conniving with the charges, then, Vergès used the trial as an opportunity to conduct a radical political critique of the French state and the normative pretensions of its legal order.

It must be remembered that Vergès was a criminal defense lawyer and that the innovative strategy of rupture he developed in this particular context inevitably reflects the jurisprudential and jurisdictional limitations and opportunities of the criminal law form. Criminal law, and the "show" or political trial form in particular, discloses certain opportunities for a ruptural strategy, with its necessary invocation of morality, obligation, transgression, didacticism, and responsibility (opportunities which may or may not emerge in other legal fora). In the context of contemporary work in critical legal theory that is indebted to Vergès's strategic thinking, various scholars have posed the question of how far beyond the criminal law the latter's ideas may travel and have sought to adapt them to that end. Brenna Bhandar asks whether, for example, "there is some aspect of this strategy that could be generalized and applied to non-criminal law domains, such as the administrative, military, property, or constitutional legal orders that structure and buttress" systems of colonial and capitalist exploitation, while for his part Christodoulidis uses Vergès's reflections on the criminal trial as a means to develop a broader understanding of how to engage with the contemporary dominance of capital via a range of different legal forms (constitutional, rights-based, and so forth).[53] Can other legal forms—such as rights—sponsor a ruptural, or otherwise strategic, move?

This evolving dialogue on the legal left was one,[54] to return us to Foucault once more, that the philosopher broached back in 1981 when he was himself in dialogue with a range of activist lawyers and militants. At the time, he wrote a preface to the second edition of Vergès's *De la stratégie judiciaire* in which he commended the author for his disabused conception of the justice system as nothing other than a "battlefield" for the lawyer-as-strategist.[55] The first half of this text is a brief summary of *De la stratégie judiciaire*'s key theses and a survey of its reception in France, while its second half represents a published version of a roundtable discussion between Foucault, Vergès, the activist lawyer Christian Revon, and some others. Foucault asks two questions, both of which concern the adaptation, development, and deployment of Vergès's strategic approach. The second is most revealing:

> Your book was conceived and written in a specific historical moment and, even if its scope stretches far beyond the context of the Algerian War, nevertheless this event is still very present within the text and without doubt dictates part of your analysis. Do you not think that the practical development of a new judicial strategy calls for an analysis and critique of the global functioning of the legal system today and how do you think we might undertake this work as a group?[56]

Vergès responds that what distinguishes the strategy of rupture today is that it need not be confined in its application to "a small number of exceptional circumstances" (such as the highly mediatized political trial), but rather can be practiced in a great number of everyday legal encounters.[57] Vergès, agreeing with Foucault that this implies a rethinking of the contemporary legal order, as well as forms of political organization, concludes that this is precisely "the task that Défense [L]ibre has set itself."[58] (Défense Libre was a rather short-lived activist legal group with which Foucault was briefly involved in the early 1980s.)[59] In answer to the question raised by Vergès, Foucault sought, via a critical counter-conduct of rights, to develop a strategic response to the contemporary legal order via an engagement with two separate questions: the right to suicide and the death penalty. On their face, both represent extraordinary, or limit, cases, but Foucault's rights-based engagement with both political questions implicates questions of day-to-day life and quotidian struggles to craft an autonomous existence under disciplinary and biopolitical conditions. We have seen that Foucault was interested (in line both with his general theorization of power relations as reversible and with his genealogical understanding of critique) in instrumentally appropriating rights discourse and, in so doing, altering it. Let us look more closely at two specific examples of this rights praxis, bearing in mind the question that has oriented us so far: whether rights present an opportunity for the strategic, or merely tactical, reformulation of power relations.

The Rights of Life and Death Under Biopolitical Rule

In the space of a few pages in part 5 of the first volume of *The History of Sexuality* Foucault makes reference not only to the question of the death penalty (a somewhat sparse analysis in this context but one which he takes up again from the perspective of racism in "'Society Must Be Defended'")[60] but also to the question of suicide. It is with the latter that I want to begin my discussion here. In the era of modern biopolitics, an era in which "it is over life, throughout its unfolding, that power establishes its dominion,"[61] suicide emerges as both a curiosity of knowledge and a potential vector of resistance. Thinking doubtless of Durkheim's seminal fin de siècle treatise,[62] Foucault observes:

> It is not surprising that suicide—once a crime, since it was a way to usurp the power of death which the sovereign alone, whether the one here below or the Lord above, had the right to exercise—became, in the course of the nineteenth century, one of the first conducts to enter into the sphere of sociological analysis; it testified to the individual and private right to die, at the borders and in the interstices of power that was exercised over life. This determination to die . . . was one of the first astonishments of a society in which political power had given itself the task of administering life.[63]

Could this "individual and private right to die," exercised "at the borders and in the interstices of power that was exercised over life," represent a possible form of resistance to that power? Indeed, could such a death, as Foucault puts it in the same passage, represent "power's [very] limit"?[64] Foucault neglects to take up this question of the resistant potential of the right to die in the *History of Sexuality*, but he pursues it some years later in other writings. In a wide-ranging interview titled "The Risks of Security" that was given to Robert Bono in 1983 concerning the French social security system, Foucault ends by making a few remarks about old age and death. He is asked by his interviewer to what extent social security can "contribute to an ethic of the human person" and he responds by suggesting that it can problematize "the value of life and the way in which we face up to death."[65] This connection between the value of life and the way in which the finite subject faces up to his own mortality is both an ancient philosophical problematic and something which emerges as a distinctly political question under contemporary conditions characterized by the biopolitical management of human life, and this brings Foucault back to the question of suicide. He continues:

> The idea of bringing individuals and decision centers closer together should imply, at least as a consequence, the recognised right of each individual to kill himself when he wants to under decent conditions. . . . If I won a few billion in the lottery, I would create an institute where people who would like to die would come spend a weekend, a week, or a month in pleasure, under drugs perhaps, in order to disappear afterward, as if erased.[66]

Bono presses him: "A right to suicide?" Foucault responds: "Yes."[67] The rhetoric of the above quotation (individuals and the devolution of decision making), and indeed elsewhere throughout the interview where he invokes choice and autonomy, plainly lends itself to a liberal interpretation. According to such an interpretation, the individual rights holder exercises her right to die against the state (which holds a countervailing interest in the protection of human life) in the name of a dignified death. However, I want to suggest not only that Foucault's mobilization of the rhetoric of the right to die cannot be reduced to this liberal interpretation (indeed, it exceeds and complicates it), but also that it is an attempt to harness rights discourse in order to help construct everyday and very personal resistances to biopolitical rule. That is, in terms of the metaphor of the game introduced at the beginning of this chapter, Foucault attempts to play the game of rights but not in the (state versus individual) terms seemingly dictated by the rules of the liberal game; rather, he tries to use the game of rights to inaugurate a different game, with a different mode of relation to life. Foucault hence uses rights instrumentally (as a tactic in the broad sense), but the question remains of whether his deployment of rights is merely tactical (in the narrower sense) or strategic (in the sense of engaging and contesting wider formations of power). In order to begin answering this question, let us start by comparing Foucault's approach to the right to die to a liberal understanding of the same.

Although he does not rely on the concepts that I have been using here, such as gaming, tactics, strategy, and instrumentalization, Thomas Tierney's insightful interpretation of Foucault's approach to the right to die neatly shows how Foucault shifts the right beyond its liberal framework and deploys it for more radical uses. In the article "Suicidal Thoughts: Hobbes, Foucault and the Right to Die," Tierney argues that Foucault's assertion of the right to die problematizes the liberal dyad of state and individual. For Tierney, liberalism axiomatically weighs the harm of suicide by "balancing the right of individuals to end their lives in a manner of their own choosing, against the state's interest in preserving life."[68] Irrespective of the particular regulatory regime adopted to achieve this balance between the individual and the state, and thereby to manage the transition from life to death (via euthanasia or "physician-assisted suicide," for example), the orthodox logic of sovereign power is still reproduced in the encounter between the death-desiring individual and the biopolitical state. Whereas the standard liberal legitimation of sovereign power is to subject the sovereign exercise of power over the individual to the test of individual right, here the logic appears in inverted form wherein the individual's arrogation to himself of the right of death is submitted to the overriding (state) interest in the preservation of life. And, of course, that state interest is a quintessentially biopolitical one. As Tierney convincingly argues, it is precisely this question of biopolitics—here understood in terms of a medicalized state management of biological life—with which the liberal account fails to engage and, as a result, leaves undisturbed.

Tierney describes a contemporary "juridico-medical order of modernity" along Foucauldian biopolitical lines, one of whose

> distinctive features . . . is the tremendous extension of human life expectancy that has been accomplished largely through the development of medical knowledge and techniques. Reasonable individuals have been eager participants in this modern project of death deferral, and remain exceedingly concerned about their health and quite willing to follow the latest regimental advice disseminated by medical and fitness authorities.[69]

As rational biopolitical subjects we enlist ourselves in the medicalized project of health management and death deferral in order to prolong our lives and are, of course, biopolitically governed in the process. For Tierney, the key failing of the liberal version of the right to die is that it fails to reckon with the kinds of sub-ject, and the dispositions of this subject toward life and death, that are engen-dered by contemporary forms of biopolitical management. Nor does the liberal formulation of the right to die address itself to the kinds of medical knowledge and medical power that are routinely brought to bear on the death-deferring subjects of late modernity (rather, it ultimately appeals to and hence reinforces them). In Tierney's account, the very purpose of the liberal right to die is sim-ply to "provid[e] . . . individuals [with] enough control over their deaths so they can avoid a painful and/or degrading demise," that is to say, to enable them to die (in the titular words of the American state-based statutes on the topic) with a modicum of dignity.[70] Tierney's argument is that "by focussing on con-trolling one's death [the] liberal perspective does not foster critical reflections upon those convictions by which one lives one's life, and leaves unchallenged the role of medical authority in shaping those convictions."[71] In order to il-lustrate the liberal position and what it leaves out of account, Tierney refers to the *amicus curiae* brief written by the "Dream Team"—a collection of eminent liberal/libertarian philosophers, to wit: Ronald Dworkin, Thomas Nagel, Rob-ert Nozick, John Rawls, T. M. Scanlon, and Judith Jarvis Thomson—in support of the respondents' (ultimately unsuccessful) proposition advanced in the 1997 Supreme Court case of *Washington v Glucksberg* that the Fourteenth Amend-ment of the United States Constitution protects a liberty interest in commit-ting suicide (and hence legalizes the practice of physician-assisted suicide).[72] The details of the case are of less importance here than the kinds of argument mobilized by the philosophers, who assert in their brief to the Supreme Court the normative importance of maintaining individual control over the manner of one's own death so as to prevent the imposition of others' values and pref-erences upon one in the moment of one's greatest vulnerability (terminal ill-ness).[73] However, as Tierney points out, "in order to manage this fear of a death that is controlled and imposed by medical authority, the right to die movement ironically seeks to establish the right to medical assistance in suicide and/or euthanasia."[74] In so doing, the liberal right to die purchases a kind of individual autonomy at the cost of buttressing the biopolitical medical apparatus's claim to expertise and power (and hence to regulate and define the exercise of that very autonomy).[75] We see this most hyperbolically in the pathos-laden conclusion to the philosophers' brief itself, which inscribes what it refers to as the litigating "patient-plaintiffs" (twin subjects of medicine and law) in a milieu of desperate suffering (variously from cancer, AIDS, and emphysema) from which medicine has failed to save them and from which they now call upon law, finally, to liberate them.[76] That these subjects are figured primarily as suffering beings and in need of palliative (medico-legal) assistance, that they are precisely plaintive subjects of and to the powers of medicine and law and not disruptive political agents seeking in their own right to make something (hopeful and social) of their own deaths, is revealing of the political presuppositions and limited possibilities of the liberal right to die.[77] The liberal articulation of the right to die hence asserts an individual legal interest in controlling one's death by ceding to medical authorities the power to determine the conditions of that death. Plainly, such an approach leaves unquestioned (indeed, it reinforces) the powers of law, state, and medicine to regulate not only one's exit from life but the character and quality of that life itself.

For his part, Foucault's articulation of the right to die attempts to avoid reinforcing the powers of medicine and law as gatekeepers of individual autonomy and as generative of the very forms of biopolitical subjectivity that should remain in question. His is a creative, aesthetic, and contestatory deployment of rights that attempts to challenge the claims of medicine (backed by legal warrant and state power) and the subjectivities it fashions. He begins by refusing—in line with the standard liberal idiom of "balancing" that one routinely encounters in mainstream political and legal debates around privacy, terrorism, security, and free speech, for example[78]—to oppose the rights of the individual to the state's "unqualified interest in the preservation of human life" (the unwittingly biopolitical formulation comes from Chief Justice Rehnquist's decision in *Washington v Glucksberg*).[79] In a lecture given in 1982 at the University of Vermont, titled "The Political Technology of Individuals," Foucault explains in discussing early modern state rationality (*raison d'État*) that "right from the start, the state is both individualizing and totalitarian . . . [and hence o]pposing the individual and his interests to it is just as hazardous as opposing it with the community and its requirements."[80] If seeking to balance the rights of the individual against the interests of the biopolitical state is to commit an analytical mistake and to court political failure, then the stakes of Foucault's intervention must be found elsewhere. Tierney rightly locates them in Foucault's intent to "raise unsettling questions about the very nature of modern subjects" and thereby to effect a shift in the "nature of the subject that can assert such a right."[81] The performative effect of asserting a right to die, for Foucault, is to change ourselves in the process; once again, as with so much (if not all) of his work, the intent is to allow us to begin to alter the types of subjects we are (or have become under biopolitical rule). On this understanding of the right to die, the issue is not the correct institutional calibration of the right of the individual as against the biopolitical interest of the state, but rather the difference that claiming the right to die (and, importantly, the manner and condition of its claiming) introduces into our conceptions of who we are as living, governed beings under biopolitics. Even when framed in highly individualist terms, the political effect of rights is most commonly thought of in terms of what institutional or policy changes their exercise introduces into a polity, that is, in terms of how rights remake and contest external relations of power as opposed to what they do to the rights holder as a particular type of subject.[82] But here Foucault directs us to think of rights as an exercise in and on the self. In the previous chapter I discussed the disciplinary and subjectifying dimensions of rights, but in the present context Foucault's deployment of the right to die can be read as the attempt to use rights in order to create a space for a kind of ethical conduct, or self-transformation. What work does the right to die perform here?

If we have become such obsessive, death-deferring (and death-fearing) subjects of late modern biopolitics, each of us in thrall to the latest medical self-management directive and hyper-responsibilized for our own health as a personal project, then could it be that death, or a confrontation with or a rethinking of death, presents a limit (or stumbling block) to this form of power? And could the assertion of a right to death somehow help us to achieve this? In a brief text published in *Gai pied* in April 1979 titled "The Simplest of Pleasures," Foucault proposes: "Let's see what there is to say in favour of suicide."[83] He immediately makes it clear that he is not so much interested in questions of "legalizing it or making it 'moral,'" but rather in the more mundane, daily interactions and transactions of suicide, in the "shady affairs, humiliations, and hypocrisies . . . hastily getting boxes of pills together, finding a solid, old-fashioned razor, or licking gun store windows and entering some place pretending to be on the verge of death."[84] His proposal is that suicide should be thought of as an aesthetic and a creative act. "It's quite inconceivable," he writes, "that we not be given the chance to prepare ourselves with all the passion, intensity and detail that we wish, including the little extras that we've been dreaming about for such a long time."[85] Far from seeking, as do the self-appointed court philosophers in *Washington v Glucksberg*, to sketch the institutional parameters under which death might legitimately be managed by the state and the medical profession, Foucault suggests suicide might assume multiple, unpredictable, and Bacchanalian forms: "Suicide festivals and orgies are just two of the possible methods. There are others more intricate and learned."[86] He dreams of a heterotopic experience of suicide in which, in "places without maps or calendars," among "anonymous partners" in "the most absurd decors," one could spend "an indeterminate amount of time—seconds, weeks, months perhaps—until the moment presents itself with stunning clearness."[87] We have traveled some distance here from legal determinations of competence, of checks and balances and cooling-off periods and the solemn weighing of state interests. Foucault's is a utopian image utterly removed from palliative care and the medicalization of death—indeed, his discussion is suffused throughout with a studious sense of levity, sensuality, and what he finally calls "the shapeless shape of utterly simple pleasure."[88] But even drawing this comparison is to miss the point (although the "details" of Foucault's vision are of course themselves revealing of certain substantive disagreements with the philosophers),[89] for the intent of the exercise of claiming a right of death and in imagining death and its institutions differently is not so much to arrive at the formalization of a right of death but in the performative exercise of thought itself, in the present. He writes in "The Simplest of Pleasures" that

> we should consider ourselves lucky to have at hand (with suicide) an extremely unique experience: it's the one which above all the rest deserves the greatest attention—not that it shouldn't worry you (or comfort you)—but rather so that you can make of it a fathomless pleasure whose patient and relentless preparation will enlighten all of your life.[90]

In interpreting Foucault's invocation of suicide and of a possible future right to suicide, we need to appreciate two further and overlapping contexts to the provocation. The first context is his engagement with the Stoic (and particularly Senecan) *meletē thanatou* (a meditation on death) and what this teaches us about an approach to life. The second is that his characterization of suicide not only as a pleasurable but, more to the point, as an aesthetic and a creative act ("Make something of it, something fine," he exhorts us)[91] recalls his attempt in the late work on ancient ethics to articulate what he calls a contemporary aesthetics of existence. What each of these two contexts makes clear for us is the way in which Foucault seeks to problematize the demarcation between life and death and thereby to actualize the resistant potential of death (or a thinking of death) in and on life—that is to say, in his time, upon biopolitics. Let me briefly address them before finally characterizing Foucault's intervention into the right to die.

"The Hermeneutics of the Subject," a lecture course Foucault gave at the Collège de France in 1982, is devoted to a study of practices of "care of the self" in classical and late antiquity. He discusses a range of different philosophers and a range of different practices in the course. One of these practices is the meditation on death. "Meditating death (*meditari, meletan*), in the sense that the Greeks and Latins understand this, does not mean thinking that you are going to die," Foucault explains. Rather, more precisely,

> meditating death is placing yourself, in thought, in the situation of someone who is in the process of dying, or who is about to die, or who is living his last days. The meditation is . . . not a game the subject plays with his own thought or thoughts, but a game that thought performs on the subject himself. It is becoming, through thought, the person who is dying or whose death is imminent.[92]

The meditation on death allows "a certain form of self-awareness, or a certain form of gaze focused on oneself from this point of view of death."[93] There is in this tradition an epistemic privilege accorded not only to old age,[94] but also to the imagined moment of death itself. Death simultaneously permits the imagining subject to "take a sort of instantaneous view of the present from above" which "immobilize[s] the present in a snapshot" and hence allows the true perception of the value of the present,[95] as well as a "retrospective view over the whole of life."[96] This twin synchronic-diachronic function of the death meditation allows a crystallization and intensification of the present, but the purpose (for Foucault at any rate) of this exercise is not to provide a greater self-knowledge but actually to encourage forms of self-transformation. "The subject is shifted with regard to what he is through the effect of thought," he emphasizes.[97] The whole intent of the meditative exercise is to alter oneself, to modify one's subjectivity via the imagined encounter with death, to work out again anew what matters in the face of what will shortly no longer matter. Such an encounter necessarily represents the "actualization of death in our life"[98] and is, in the context of the lecture's genealogy of forms of self-care in antiquity, a deeply "spiritual" exercise. But in bringing death into life, potentially at every moment, these meditative practices can never be allowed to constitute a protocol on how to approach death. In the brief text on suicide from 1979 that I have been discussing, Foucault asserts that "the philosophies that promise to teach us what to think about death and how to die bore me to tears."[99] For Foucault there is no proper or authentic way of being-toward-death, of comporting oneself in the face of death. There is simply, via these meditative exercises where thought collapses the distinction between life and death, the promising opportunity to begin to rethink our lives in the face of death and to displace ourselves in the process.

Of course, rethinking our lives is the second (and wider) context into which we might place Foucault's call for a right to die. In Chapter 2 I discussed his reading of ancient Greek and early Roman sources on ethics as a form of *rapport à soi*, that is, a relation to self, a working on the self. If, as Foucault insists, "genealogy means that I begin my analysis from a question posed in the present,"[100] then we can helpfully frame this question as: How can we develop forms of subjectivity that are resistant to the normalization of life under contemporary biopolitics? Can a (re)reading of classical sources assist in the political task of pivoting away from biopolitical and ongoing disciplinary forms of capturing life? He is all too conscious of the political drawbacks of the classical approach to ethics as a care of the self ("the Greek ethics of pleasure is linked to a virile society, to dissymmetry, exclusion of the other, an obsession with penetration")[101] that make it a fairly unpalatable candidate for late twentieth-century retrieval. But of course it is not the ancients' particular answers but rather their problems and their manner of conceiving of them that interests him:

> I am not looking for an alternative; you can't find the solution of a problem in the solution of another problem raised at another moment by other people. You see, what I want to do is not the history of solutions, and that's the reason why I don't accept the word "alternative." I would like to do genealogy of problems, of *problematiques*.[102]

For Foucault, what is promising in the classical sources that he returns to—at least in the intentions of their ethics—is the fact that they did not represent attempts to discipline individuals or to normalize a population of individuals: "I don't think that we can say that this kind of ethics was an attempt to normalize the population."[103] Rather, via the notion of an aesthetics of existence, the Greeks proposed that life become the object of conscious elaboration and self-critique:

> The idea of the *bios* as a material for an aesthetic piece of art is something which fascinates me. The idea also that ethics can be a very strong structure of existence, without any relation with the juridical per se, with an authoritarian system, with a disciplinary structure. All that is very interesting.[104]

To conclude, and to bring these two related contexts to bear on Foucault's call for a right to die, we can say that his claiming of the right is a performative gesture in the sense explored by Karen Zivi in her book *Making Rights Claims: A Practice of Democratic Citizenship*. For Zivi, rights are politically important because of what happens in the very act of claiming. "It is through the making of rights claims," she argues, "that we contest and constitute the meaning of individual identity, the contours of community, and the forms that political subjectivity takes."[105] This political promise of rights cannot be reduced, or telescoped, into the moment of institutional crystallization—the legislative or judicial moment wherein rights are enacted or decided on. These moments are at any rate highly uncertain and far more contingent affairs than they are made to appear. For Foucault, the real political value of rights resides in their unpredictable afterlives—the discourses they generate and the changed attitudes they spur. Rights are not an end but rather a medium, themselves contested and contestable, for political contestation. They are a means to ventilate the political and what it might (be made to) mean. Foucault hence approaches the right to die tactically (that is, instrumentally, in the sense with which we started this chapter) and performatively. The claim to rights is not made to establish the legality of an individual taking her own life when weighed in the balance against the state's countervailing biopolitical interest or to secure the institutional conditions that would render that step as morally permissible or as risk-free as possible, but rather, and consciously, it is used as a tool to prompt us to rethink our lives and how we are led to live them under biopolitical care. The rights claim is a vehicle for a contrary imagining of death (a consciously aesthetic and creative understanding of death) which, in turn, asks us to think about the value of the life which precedes it. As Foucault suggests, it is in the contemplation of an act "whose patient and relentless preparation will enlighten all of your life"[106] that you are encouraged to think differently about that life.

Foucault uses the right to die in order to play a different game: the imaginative game of attempting to generate changes in subjectivities and attitudes toward life and death that disrupt or work against the dictates of medicalized, biopolitical self-management. Rights are hence tactically instrumentalized to this wider, more diffuse, yet at the same time highly individualized purpose. Foucault—following Vergès's suggestion that the ruptural strategy will need to be dislocated from the privileged form and juridical location of the criminal trial—seeks to incorporate the strategy of rupture into everyday experiences. Here the rights claim is obviously a tactical one, but is it also strategic? I would suggest that while Foucault's invocation of the right to die eschews the form of a direct, ruptural confrontation with the state so as to bring it into open contradiction with its own principles (*qua* immanent critique), it is nevertheless an attempt on his part to confront a wider logic of power—contemporary biopolitics—on the plane of everyday life and our day-to-day imaginings of death. In other words, rights are the tactic called in aid of the strategy of an aesthetics of existence. That this nonrevolutionary attempt of Foucault's does not obey the form of an organized collective political struggle or of immanent critique or structural analysis should not lead us to dismiss it as an isolated or nonserious attempt to contest biopolitics. If "it is true after all," as Foucault suggests, "that there is no first or final point of resistance to political power other than in the relationship one has to oneself,"[107] then this work of ethical self-creation demands to be understood precisely as a form of (social) ethics coterminous with the political work of contesting biopolitics—for which the right to die (as tactic) provides a useful and provocative starting point.

To maintain that rights are deployed as tactics implies that one does so not only consciously but selectively, and toward a particular end. It hence follows that if the tactician elects to mobilize the discourse of rights he can just as well elect not to mobilize it. And so it is with an instance of tactical refusal, wherein Foucault opts not to respond to a political question via the language of rights, that I want to conclude this chapter. My example is the question of the death penalty, and as with the example of suicide and the right to die, it implicates questions of biopolitics and of state sovereignty. Just as with his approach to the supposedly extreme case of suicide, Foucault's method regarding the death penalty is to insist on its normality and its connection to everyday forms of punishment and governing. I just proposed that political actors are equally free not to depend upon rights claims for making their interventions, but in reality, given the contemporary discursive predominance of the idiom of rights and the malleability of the discourse (such that nearly anything can in principle can be framed as a rights question), the choice not to deploy the language of rights is both a far more difficult and a far more revealing one.[108] My interest in Foucault's writings on the death penalty starts from precisely this point, then: that despite the obvious, available, and routinely invoked rights framework for contesting capital punishment, he studiously avoids problematizing the death penalty as a contravention of individual rights. I want to suggest that in so doing—that is, in retreating from the *tactical* use of rights in this case—he is ultimately being *strategic* in his assessment that the deployment of rights is not likely to advance the cause of abolition (which for him means the wider cause of prison abolition and the undoing of penal power).

A predictable yet useful starting point is provided by Foucault's graphic discussion of the death penalty in the introduction to *Discipline and Punish*, of which a hasty and overly schematic reading might suggest that for him the death penalty was an atavistic remnant of pre-modernity, a quixotic reminder of more openly violent yet historically superseded regimes of punishment. In the opening pages of the book Foucault stages an opposition between the bloodthirsty sovereignty of the *amende honorable* and the almost banal spatio-temporal discipline of the timetable.[109] Yet to suggest that discipline progressively replaces sovereign violence, rendering the death penalty a mere anomaly or anachronism, is to misread him (and to fail to appreciate that, for him, sovereignty and discipline are interrelated technologies and not exclusive stages in the teleological evolution of power).[110] Discipline and biopolitics do not historically replace sovereignty, and rather obviously, despite its biopolitical inflections, contemporary sovereignty is still exercised in multiple and violent forms—of which one example is the death penalty. As Foucault went on to observe several years later in "'Society Must Be Defended,'" under contemporary biopolitical conditions, where states are facially dedicated to the fostering and optimization of life, we witness a shift in the purpose and rationale of state killing.[111] He asks:

> If it is true that the power of sovereignty is increasingly on the retreat and that disciplinary or regulatory disciplinary power is on the advance, how will the power to kill and the function of murder operate in this technology of power, which takes life as both its object and its objective? . . . How can the power of death, the function of death, be exercised in a political system centred upon biopower?[112]

Foucault's answer is essentially that racism authorizes the biopolitical sovereign to commit murder. He defines racism not simply as a form of discrimination between different groups within a society, but rather in functional terms as "a way of introducing a break into the domain of life that is under power's control: the break between what must live and what must die."[113] Racism is a means of "fragment[ing] . . . the biological continuum addressed by biopower."[114] As a result of this internal fragmenting of life under biopolitical rule, the sovereign is empowered to kill precisely in the name of life itself:

> The fact that the other dies does not mean simply that I live in the sense that his death guarantees my safety; the death of the other, the death of the bad race,

of the inferior race (or the degenerate, or the abnormal) is something that will make life in general healthier: healthier and purer.[115]

Hence the death penalty under modern conditions of biopolitical sovereignty does not so much wither away as operate under a different sign and according to different logics: the purification of the race, the weeding out of degeneracy, and the definitive elimination of the incorrigibly dangerous. "One had the right to kill those," Foucault glosses this transition, "who represented a kind of biological danger to others."[116] The importance of this more nuanced reading is that it allows us to better explain the modern, and contemporary, continuation of the death penalty. Instead of dismissing it as an embarrassing recrudescence of violent, pre-modern sovereignty, one can begin to render the death penalty intelligible as a particular technology of state violence deployed toward the biopolitical ends of securing the safety and vitality of the population. That is, one can tie it much more closely to the operative and predominant modes of power in a modern and contemporary "normalizing society": disciplinary power and biopolitics. The critical legal theorist Adam Thurschwell adopts just this perspective when he suggests that contemporary American "abolitionists [should] turn their attention to the biopolitical disciplinary matrix that supports the death penalty today, rather than jousting with (and unintentionally reinforcing) an image of sovereignty that defines itself by its power to kill."[117]

It is precisely this close articulation of the powers of life and the power to wield death (albeit in the furtherance of a certain "life") that underpins Foucault's response to the death penalty in his own time. Indeed, by the time that the death of capital punishment had become a live political issue in French politics (it was abolished in 1981), Foucault had been critiquing the death penalty for at least a decade through the conceptual framework of penal and, more broadly, disciplinary power. His response to the guillotining of Buffet and Bontems at the beginning of this decade is exemplary (these were two prisoners caught escaping from Clairvaux Prison in 1971 who killed a nurse and a prison officer in the course of their attempt and who, after conviction and receiving the death sentence, were denied clemency by President Pompidou and put to death in June 1972). "There is something about [the guillotine]," writes Foucault in the piece "Pompidou's Two Deaths," "that is physically and politically intolerable."[118] But instead of reading capital punishment, as extreme as it doubtless is, as a necessarily exceptional and qualitatively different form of punishment from incarceration, he insists that "the guillotine is really just the visible and triumphant apex, the red and black tip, of a tall pyramid. The whole penal system is essentially pointed toward and governed by death."[119] Foucault thus tries to implicate the whole punitive apparatus of the prison in his critique of the death penalty. "A verdict of conviction does not lead, as some people think, to a sentence of prison *or* death; if it prescribes prison, this is always with a possible bonus: death."[120] In prison one is forced to live a life not worth living, subject to the reign of the penitentiary personnel, "of the arbitrary, of threats, of blackmail, of blows," which leads a young man to "beat his head against the walls or twist his shirt into a rope and try to hang himself."[121] "Prison is a death machine . . . in which [like the war machine] one learns the dreadful equivalence of life and death."[122]

Likewise, in a review of Gilles Perrault's 1978 novel about the trial and conviction of Christian Ranucci, *Le pull-over rouge*, titled "The Proper Use of Criminals," Foucault raises ideas developed at greater length elsewhere in his work about the way in which the discourse of criminal psychiatry doubles the figure of the juridically responsible individual with the knowable figure of the "dangerous individual."[123] He writes:

> A paradoxical fact: today one of the most solid roots of the death penalty is the modern, humanitarian, scientific principle that one must judge crimes not criminals. It is economically less costly, intellectually less demanding, more gratifying for the judges, more reasonable in the view of the sober-minded, and more satisfying for those keen on "understanding a man" than it is to establish the facts. And so we see a justice system that one morning, with a facile, routine, barely awake gesture, cut in two a twenty-two-year-old "criminal" whose crime had not been proven.[124]

And finally, in 1981, on the verge of the death penalty being abolished in France,[125] he returns to the theme of the humanistic, disciplinary, and penitential "roots" of the "oldest penalty in the world": "But, here and elsewhere, the way in which the death penalty is done away with is at least as important as the doing-away. The roots are deep. And many things will depend on how they are cleared out."[126] An excavation of those roots reveals that the death penalty is constitutively connected to other state institutions that wield the power of death. "The question of war, the army, compulsory military service, and so on, immediately takes shape" once one engages this perspective.[127] So too, once again, does the problem of the embeddedness of the death penalty within a wider penal apparatus now informed by the disciplinary epistemologies of *homo criminalis*. The classical criminal law's concern with the status of the act has been overtaken in modernity by the knowledge claims of criminal psychiatry and criminal anthropology:

> Penal systems . . . have claimed, since the nineteenth century, both to correct and to punish. In point of fact, these systems always assumed that there were not two kinds of crimes but two kinds of criminals: those who can be corrected by punishment, and those who could never be corrected even if they were punished indefinitely. The death penalty was the definitive punishment for the incorrigibles, and in a form so much shorter and surer than perpetual imprisonment.[128]

Several recurring and interlinked themes thus emerge from Foucault's critical interventions into the public debate on the death penalty in France. First, and as with his articulation of the right to die, he complicates the simple opposition between life and death. From this perspective the death penalty is not qualitatively different from other exercises of state power that expose subjects to death or to the risk of death. Equally, those other, supposedly more life-affirming punishments of incarceration and disciplinary correction are themselves seen to function, as he puts it above, as a "death machine." Indeed, far from a straightforward opposition between life and death, Foucault delineates a "dreadful equivalence" between the two.[129] Second, he demonstrates the death penalty's reliance upon modes of disciplinary and biopolitical knowledges that seek to apprehend the incorrigible individual. These forms of knowledge claim about the criminal individual, while often sought to be tactically appropriated by the defense, reinforce the supposedly humane, therapeutic, and scientific façade of punishment: "'Can one condemn to death a person one does not know?'"[130] Third, and flowing from the first two claims, he insists that the question of abolition should occasion a wider debate about the politics of punishment. "Accomplishing abolition is pretty good but also easy," Foucault supposedly observed to the lawyer and future justice minister Robert Badinter over dinner in November 1981; "now the essential thing to do is get rid of prisons."[131] "Do we want the debate on the death penalty to be anything other than a discussion on the best punitive techniques? Do we want it to be the occasion for and beginning of a new political reflection?"[132] Foucault wants to seize upon the anxiety produced by the death penalty and mobilize it for a wider assault upon conditions of punishment. He ends a 1977 roundtable conversation on the death penalty with the psychoanalyst Jean Laplanche and Badinter by observing: "I fear that it is dangerous to allow judges to continue to judge alone, by liberating them from their anxiety and allowing them to avoid asking themselves in the name of what they judge. . . . Let them become anxious like we become anxious. . . . The crisis of the function of justice has just been opened. Let's not close it too quickly."[133]

But, of course, besides these three positive dimensions of Foucault's critical engagements with death penalty politics there is one salient negative dimension: the absence of a recourse to rights. At first blush this is a startling omission. International human rights law, as it is institutionalized in international covenants (such as the International Covenant on Civil and Political Rights) and regional conventions (such as, in France's case, the European Convention on Human Rights), provides (and provided at the time Foucault was writing) a ready-made and quite popular normative basis for contesting the death penalty.[134] From the perspective of international human rights law the death penalty can be seen either as a contravention of the right to life or as an instance of cruel, inhuman, or degrading punishment, or both.[135] But despite a few, fleeting references not so much to the protection of these important individual rights against the state but rather to the "problem of the [state's] right to kill" itself,[136] Foucault's critique of the death penalty focuses on the way in which the practice of state killing is connected to a broader (disciplinary and biopolitical) power-knowledge apparatus of punishment at the expense of any reference to rights discourse. He never expressly discusses why he refuses to critique the death penalty through the available discourses of rights, but we do not have to search far for possible reasons, and when we do, we can see that the refusal of the tactics of rights represents a concern for strategy on his part. In short, Foucault worries that a tactical deployment of rights will lead not to the overcoming of the death penalty but either to its possible refinement or an abolition that stops short of critically engaging the penal apparatus that nourishes it. Let us begin to read this absence positively, then.

If we start our analysis of the right with its doctrinal substance or content (that is to say, with what values or objects the rights claim seeks to uphold and protect), then we can see that this is either "life" or a "dignified" or "humane" punishment by the state. There is an interesting passage in volume 1 of *The History of Sexuality, The Will to Knowledge,* that touches on the issue of a claimed "right to life." There Foucault discusses the emergent resistances to biopolitics in the nineteenth century which, "against this power that was still new . . . relied for support on the very thing it invested, that is, on life and man as a living being."[137] For these kinds of counter-conduct, "life as a political object was in a sense taken at face value and turned back against the system that was bent on controlling it." He continues:

> It was life more than the law that became the issue of political struggles, even if the latter were formulated through affirmations concerning rights. The "right" to life, to one's body, to health, to happiness, to the satisfaction of needs, and beyond all the oppressions or "alienations," the "right" to rediscover what one is and all that one can be, this "right"—which the classical juridical system was utterly incapable of comprehending—was the political response to all these new procedures of power which did not derive, either, from the traditional right of sovereignty.[138]

Foucault was hardly unaware, then, of what we might call the potential strategy of (counter-)biopolitical rights—rights of and to "life," either in the narrower civil and political framework of the classical "right to life" or in the more expansive economic, social, and cultural sense of a right to health or the material satisfaction of certain basic human needs.[139] And yet his rigorous refusal to countenance such an approach in his own work implies a wariness about so straightforwardly endorsing the politics of life as a means to counter state killing, and of thus potentially playing into the hands of biopolitics and thereby endorsing the state's claims to manage and protect life. Moreover, it suggests a strategic acknowledgment that there are potential limits to the ability of rights to leverage critical possibilities from some contexts. Those limits and those contexts are historically variable and contingent, but that Foucault hesitated to openly engage a "right to life" approach to the death penalty suggests that when it came to the death penalty, the terrain of contemporary biopolitics was not susceptible of critical rights-based subversion from within and in fact presented the significant danger of strengthening the apparatus of (capital and other) punishment. As discussed above, his reflections in "'Society Must Be Defended'" on the racial dimensions of the death penalty as a means of internally splitting the life of the population (that is, racialized killing precisely in the name of life) and on the biopolitical rationales of killing those who represent an incorrigible danger to the community clearly problematize the act of seeking to limit the death penalty through the application of a "right to life."[140] The obvious danger represented by calling on the state to better respect life is of course that it commences by acknowledging the legitimacy of the state's control of life and indeed seeks to ask the state to better live up to its biopolitical promise.

We see a similar risk presented by the other available rights claim—namely, the claim that the death penalty represents an undignified or (in the American constitutional idiom of the Eighth Amendment) a cruel and unusual punishment. Foucault's interventions into abolitionist politics were, I believe, conducted exclusively or at least predominantly in the European context,[141] but as a keen traveler to the United States from the 1970s onward and a studious observer of American culture and politics, the travails of post-*Furman* abolitionist jurisprudence in that country could barely have eluded him—indeed, they may even have informed some of his later positions. At any rate, a cursory glance at the experience of the United States from 1972 onward reveals some of the dangers of constitutional rights litigation intended to establish the claim that the death penalty represents a cruel and unusual punishment.[142] If questions of "life" and who gets to decide its value and the terms upon which it is lived are subject to endless contestation, then whether the death penalty presents an affront to evolving and variable constitutional standards of dignity and humanity offers hardly less of a dialectical opportunity for the government lawyer. Again, there could be no better chronicler of the vicissitudes and cynicism of claims of dignity and humanitarianism in punishment than Foucault, whose *Discipline and Punish* amply establishes the dangers of relying on this normative criterion for critiquing sovereign and disciplinary power. In the United States, as many have argued, the perverse result of decades of Eighth Amendment jurisprudence might actually have been, at best, to "tinker" (as Justice Blackmun famously put it in a 1994 case), or worse, to perfect "the machinery of death."[143] Particular methods of execution can always be medically improved (not eradicated); particular procedural glitches can always be juridically rectified (rendering the machine more rational); particular defendants and particular crimes can always be exempted from capital treatment (thereby confirming the heinousness of the remaining crimes)—all without disturbing the core claim of the state to put incorrigibles, convicted under a rational legal system, to death in a safe, medicalized, humane, and dignified way. That is, ultimately, if the political aim is to critique the operation of the state's power to kill but also to incarcerate and to discipline its subjects, then the rights-based invocation of life and dignity presents serious risks of recuperation, counter-investment, and stabilization by a biopolitical state that today purports to punish and indeed to kill precisely in the name of life. It is not simply that the content of the given rights—"life" and "dignified punishment"—are semantically indeterminate (although this is assuredly the case); this contingency, as Foucault insists throughout his work, can just as easily present political possibilities. It is rather that, taking the disciplinary-biopolitical penal apparatus into account, not only would a strategy that sought to use rights claims in order to contest the operation of the death penalty run the risk of perfecting the mechanism of death (by seeking to invoke some of the very biopolitical justifications the death penalty itself now relies upon), but any gains made in the field of death penalty abolition might mask, reproduce, or reinforce other disciplinary strategies (in the prison and beyond). The obvious background to this strategy on Foucault's part is his long-standing political solidarity with French prisoners and the intolerable conditions of their incarceration—a solidarity manifest both in his practical political work through the Groupe d'Information sur les Prisons and in his theoretical accounts of disciplinary power throughout the decade of the 1970s. For Foucault, one simply could not, through a rights strategy that would serve to focus and narrow the inquiry on the legitimacy of the state's right to put to death, abstract from the quotidian violence of disciplinary conditions.[144]

The Game of Rights: Everyday Strategy

For Vergès, at least as he initially formulated the problematic in *De la stratégie judiciaire*, the strategy of rupture represented an exceptional confrontation with the state and its laws conducted in order to place the system into contradiction with its own founding principles. Law was thus used in order to wage an ideological and delegitimizing battle of ideas against the state in its own fora. This direct mode of immanent critique is not Foucault's, at least not in the examples pursued here; nevertheless, I have tried to show in this chapter how Foucault—very much interested in the questions of critical legal strategy opened up by Vergès if not wedded to his answers—does try to deploy rights not just in a localized, occasional, and tactical way, but rather as connected to a broader and concerted strategic engagement with modes of power and punishment. That broader strategic engagement is always sustained with an awareness of both the limits and possibilities of rights but also of the particular terrain of state biopolitics on which those rights are sought to be deployed (and stand to be counterdeployed). In the case of suicide Foucault seeks to make use of the juridical category of the right to die but, promisingly, tries to wrest it away from a liberal formulation into a more radical questioning of forms of biopolitical subjectivity. We can connect this attempt of Foucault's to his contemporaneous interest in crafting an aesthetics of existence. In the case of his critique of the disciplinary and biopolitical roots of the death penalty, however, we see Foucault refusing to deploy rights claims where those claims potentially run the risk of re-entrenching the powers he is seeking to resist. Accordingly, Foucault frames his critiques in different terms.

We can thus perceive that the distinction between rights as tactical elements and rights as part of a broader strategic struggle is a meaningful way to analyze Foucault's rights-based political interventions in the late work (and indeed is a way in which he himself understood them). I thus want to suggest that Foucault, *pace* many easy readings of him as a proponent of sporadic and unplanned resistance, *was* a strategic political thinker and that his usage (or not) of rights bears this out in subtle and interesting ways. I now want to carry this question of strategy over into the final, concluding chapter. It is surely of the essence of strategy that it varies over time and across space—strategy by its nature is contingent, situational, and revisable (or else it is simply poor strategy). The strategist, like the genealogist, thus speaks out of and to the present. In concluding my account of Foucault's politics of rights I hence want not only to remind us of what kind of intervention it constituted in its own time, but to ask what, if any, explanatory value it retains for ours.

CONCLUSION

Westerners left the dream of revolution behind—both for themselves
and for the third world they once ruled—and adopted other tactics,
envisioning an international law of human rights as the steward of
utopian norms, and as the mechanism of their fulfilment.

Samuel Moyn

Fredric Jameson's maxim, "always historicize," appears relatively
modest next to Foucault's ambition for genealogy, which might be
summed up, historicize everything.

Wendy Brown

Today, it seems, everyone is a human rights pragmatist.

Frédéric Mégret

The History of Failed and Substitute Utopias

Historicize everything—including Foucault. "You know, I belong to a generation of people who witnessed the collapse, one after another, of most of the
utopias that had been constructed in the nineteenth and the beginning of the
twentieth century," remarked Foucault to an interviewer in 1983, before continuing and observing of his generation that they "also saw the perverse and
sometimes disastrous results that could ensue from projects that were extremely generous in their intentions."[1] We can easily capture something of this
anti-utopian resignation by juxtaposing it to the enthusiasm with which, only
five years previously, Foucault had gone in search of non-Western solutions to
the failures of Enlightenment rationalism and Marxist scientism in the crucible
of the Iranian revolution:

> We ought to have the courage to begin anew. We have to abandon every dog-
> matic principle and question one by one the validity of all the principles that
> have been the sources of oppression. From the point of view of political thought,

we are, so to speak, at point zero. We have to construct another political thought, another political imagination, and teach anew the vision of a future.[2]

This openly utopian Foucault is now an almost unrecognizable figure.[3] Whether it be the dashed hopes of 1968, the closure of the Iranian revolution's constituent "political spirituality" by the theocratic rule of the ayatollah, or the ultimately more significant ideological, geopolitical, and tragic event of the short twentieth-century's long-drawn-out failure of state socialism and revolutionary communism,[4] Foucault's generation did not have far to wander in search of utopian disenchantment by the late 1970s.

A recent and incredibly influential history of human rights has taken the vacillating fortunes of twentieth-century political utopias as its methodological starting point, and in so doing it provides an important historical reference point for the interpretation of Foucault that I have proposed in this book. In *The Last Utopia: Human Rights in History*, Samuel Moyn revisits the origin of contemporary human rights discourse.[5] His is a revisionist and genealogical account that convincingly undermines the orthodox historiography of human rights. According to the received wisdom that Moyn's book has now conclusively problematized,[6] the concept of human rights has a long and distinguished pedigree in Western thought. According to some accounts, human rights are prefigured in ancient philosophical sources;[7] according to others they are connected (more plausibly, it has to be said) to the eighteenth-century declarations of natural rights that earned the scorn of Marx, Bentham, and Burke;[8] and according to yet other versions they are an attempt to capture on a juridical and institutional level the moral response to certain horrific events of the twentieth century—World War II and the Holocaust.[9] Yet for Moyn these events are false origins. Provocatively, he suggests that human rights as we understand them today really emerge at the end of the 1970s. (Possibly succumbing to a temptation to the hyperbolic not unknown to that other genealogist, Foucault, Moyn playfully nominates a birth year, namely, 1977, being the year that commences with President Jimmy Carter's famous speech on human rights and US foreign policy and ends with the award of the Nobel Peace prize to that little-known NGO Amnesty International.)[10] Of course, much turns on how one defines human rights, and Moyn structures his account of them by recourse to what they are not. Human rights are not (as was the postrevolutionary French Declaration of the Rights of Man and Citizen) a constituent attempt to found, or more accurately, to refound, a polity. Neither are human rights political (in the sense of an attempt to articulate and produce a vision of a socially just or fair world). Rather, human rights are opposed both to the state and to politics. What they do provide is a universalist, moral, and supposedly neutral language that individuals can use in order to oppose the unjust exercise of state power in their own country but also globally, thus piercing the veil of nation-state sovereignty. A final, related rhetorical opposition is relevant here: human rights are not premised on a maximalist vision of society but rather on a minimalist vision based upon protecting the individual from harm (as distinct from connecting that individual to others or providing him with the material necessities of life). Hence, when the veil of state sovereignty is pierced by this moralizing conception of human rights, it is not to condemn the structural violence of poverty or inequality,[11] but rather to expose practices like state killing and torture. It hence aligns with a putatively minimalist program of rights protection–as–suffering prevention that enshrines a core set of traditional civil and political rights protective of the individual and her agency.[12] In Moyn's account, despite the rather obvious yet nonetheless misleading origin candidate of the Universal Declaration at midcentury, it is in fact not until the 1970s that this conception of human rights gains any political traction, and it is predominantly through the voices of Eastern European dissidents and the advocacy work of transnational NGOs like Amnesty and Helsinki Watch (now Human Rights Watch) that it does so. But if these groups, in bringing human rights to (an exponential global) prominence, are the dramatis personae of Moyn's narrative, then what is still missing from the account is what happens offstage, so to speak—indeed, what sets the historical stage itself. That missing historiographical element is signified in Moyn's title and provided by the framework of utopia: the broader political condition of possibility for the rise of human rights at this time is the failure of a certain utopia and its replacement with another.

If human rights are the last utopia, then the penultimate utopia, the utopia whose failure clears the imaginative and political way for the rise of human rights, is the leftist utopia of state socialism and revolutionary communism. Once "Westerners left the dream of revolution behind," as Moyn puts it,[13] the imaginary space vacated by the collapse of that dream was filled by the liberal conception of human rights. This conception was constructed in direct opposition to leftist visions of human emancipation and of radically de-alienated social relations in which the individual and society would be entirely remade. If these were political projects, then—so reasoned the proponents of the emergent human rights at the time—their replacement utopia was henceforth to be studiously apolitical, indeed even anti-political.[14] This would be a world in which state power over the individual would be restrained by the exercise of international laws reflecting universal moral norms. All of which is to say that human rights, on Moyn's account, is the rather pallid echo of a utopia, the kind of utopia one professes once one no longer really believes in the idea of utopia at all. The compounded contradictions of human rights at their birth (deeply political yet facially apolitical; anti-statist yet reliant on state enforcement; utopian yet not utopian; minimalist yet expansionary in application) come to fruition in later life. As a historian (of the present) Moyn is of course keenly aware of the fact that, as he puts it, "while human rights were born in antipolitics, they could not remain wholly noncommittal toward programmatic endeavours, especially as time passed,"[15] and that this tension inevitably produces a kind of identity crisis of human rights. Moyn's book ultimately recalls the putatively minimalist origins of what has subsequently become the hegemonic post–Cold War global political discourse. Importantly, his particular story about human rights is a story that could be told not solely about the rise of human rights but also about the turn to the rule of law (both domestically and in the global context of development discourse), about constitutionalism in post–Cold War or postconflict societies, about transitional justice, about rights regimes at a domestic level, and about other globalizing forms of political liberalism in the Cold War era and (subsequently) beyond it.[16]

If this vacuum of (and loss of faith in) political utopianism is the breeding ground for a resurgent global liberalism in the late 1970s and into the 1980s, then is this the proper historical frame of reference to comprehend Foucault's particular turn to rights discourse at the time? For many it is. Richard Wolin has written that "during the 1970s, Foucault developed a new understanding of politics that . . . abandoned the *gauchisme* . . . that, in the post-May era, had become the dominant political credo and turned increasingly toward a politics of human rights."[17] This Foucault, breaking not only with his previous structuralist positions (as Eric Paras has argued)[18] but also with the political positions of Marxists and the left more broadly, came to "popularize and affirm a human rights agenda"[19] and, in so doing, arrive at a "conclusion analogous to the leading representatives of the Frankfurt School: 'rule of law' or *Rechtsstaat* provides a necessary and indispensable 'magic wall' safeguarding civil society from the constant threat of authoritarian encroachments."[20] On Wolin's account, the serial exposures of communist tyranny throughout the 1970s, from Eastern Europe to the Killing Fields, provided an edifying and chastening experience that "taught the leftists—Foucault included—an important lesson: societies governed by the 'rule of law' contain internal prospects for progressive social change . . . [and] constitutional democracies remain open to the transformative potentials of 'public reason' in a way that sets them apart qualitatively from authoritarian regimes."[21] Thoroughly disciplined by the decade's experiences of tyranny and totalitarianism, then, Foucault emerges exhausted from the 1970s as a barely recognizable epigone of Rawls and Habermas. Yet if Wolin's revisionist account of the philosopher's turn to rights, written from a present in which liberalism is ideologically predominant, is reductive and dismissive of the nuances of Foucault's rights-based political interventions, it nevertheless raises two pertinent and useful questions (of accuracy and relevance). First, if Foucault is not the well-disciplined proponent of liberalism, then what is he and how can we explain his turn to rights at this time? Second, if Foucault is a liberal convert (and, more interestingly, even if he is not), then why do we continue to read him today? What are the contemporary political stakes of these foregoing interpretive questions? Surely if Foucault, in the end, gives us little more than an appreciation of public reason and the rule of law, then might we not more profitably turn to Rawls's *Political Liberalism* and Habermas's *Between Facts and Norms*? But if he gives us something more than that, then what is that something more, and how might it speak to our contemporary political concerns? To address these two related questions I shall begin with the question of how to characterize (and explain the motivations of) Foucault's interventions in the 1970s and early 1980s.

Critical Counter-Conducts in the Wake of Revolution

The interpretation of Foucault's late politics of rights that I have developed in the preceding chapters has been one framed by the notion of a critical counter-conduct of rights. By critique, as I clarified in Chapter 1, Foucault intends neither rejection nor negation of the object under critique, but rather a kind of contrary excavation and interrogation that loosens the self-evidence of that object and, in perceiving a contingency proper to it, insists upon a kind of freedom—a hidden margin of freedom and possibility. For the archaeologist and the genealogist, it follows, there is always the possibility of things—institutions, concepts, practices, identities—being otherwise. Foucault has for decades been routinely misread as a pessimistic, a nihilistic, or a self-defeating philosopher who, in the absence of a normative conception of the subject or of human freedom, cannot tell us what the good life is or how (or indeed why) to strive for it.[22] Such readings, I think, (deliberately and obtusely) miss the point, but I trust that from my discussion of his conception of critique in Chapter 1 we can appreciate what I styled his "critical affirmation": critique as the patient and relentless "yes-saying" to the possibility of current political arrangements, as well as the ways of thinking and doing that support them, being otherwise to the way they presently are. This constitutively hopeful conception of critique was then shown to underlie the notion of "counter-conducts," which he first introduces in the lecture course "Security, Territory, Population," in early 1978. This political concept of the counter-conduct starts from the conceptualization of power relations as forms of governing conduct, that is to say, forms of conducting the conduct of selves and others. Within any form of conduct, Foucault maintains, there is the immanent possibility of a counter-conduct—of something which resists, works against, subverts, or avoids the operation of the attempt to govern conduct, and that this possibility is disclosed by the workings of government itself. Where there is power, there is resistance; where there is a conduct, there is always the attendant possibility of a counter-conduct. Foucault's assumption—and this flows from the philosophical premises of his concept of critique—is that the meaning and operation of forms of governing are not set in stone but rather available for contestation, appropriation, and reversal: thus, the critical counter-conduct.

For me, this framework of the critical counter-conduct is a far more revealing (and convincing) framework with which to view Foucault's late turn to rights than one of a resigned and defeatist rapprochement with an anti-utopian liberalism of human rights and rule of law promotion. The latter simply leaves far too much unexplained about the late work. For a start, it fails to reckon with the continuities in Foucault's approach to subject formation between the mid-1970s work on power and the late-career work on ethics and technologies of the self (discussed in Chapter 2), but more important, it seeks to explain Foucault's particular and idiosyncratic engagement with rights discourse by recourse to a vague and undefined "sea change" in French—indeed Western—politics at the time, as waves of repentant and disabused leftists of all persuasions flocked toward something called liberalism. But what of Foucault's decades-long critique of liberal theories of subjectivity and the sovereign model of power? Does he really jettison these philosophical and political commitments in the space of such a short time? Or is it that the conversion-to-liberalism narrative fails to attend to the nuances of Foucault's particular engagements and is hence too quick to assimilate (and celebrate) his rights work to a liberal paradigm? The argument I have pursued here is that if we do attend a little more closely to

Foucault's rights-based political interventions in the late work, then we see not a curious and question-begging "liberal Foucault" but rather a far richer account of the ways in which Foucault, as a political actor, sought to navigate his contemporary political reality—a reality increasingly well populated with the liberal language and institutions of rights—and to use, immanently, the political tools at hand in order to make particular political problematizations, interventions, and contestations. That is to say, he proposes a critical counter-conduct of rights. And what is more, this interpretation of the late work does not constitute just a richer and more nuanced account of the period but also one that is more consonant with Foucault's long-standing (if evolving) positions on subjectivity and sovereignty. Tracking his late-career invocations of human rights, of rights to sexuality and friendship, and of the right to die, I sought to provide an account in Chapters 2, 3, and 4 of a political thinker and actor who approached rights as contingent artifacts that could be appropriated for contrary uses but that were hardly unproblematic or free of the risk of co-optation and counter-investment by power. Rights, like power, are simply "dangerous"[23]—and yet for him they still represent a potential performative political tool with which to remake relations of power and forms of subjectivity.

It is true that Foucault, on a number of occasions, problematized the value of revolution. Indeed, his late conception of political action was a specifically non-revolutionary one (although this is by no means the same thing as a purely local, marginal, and ineffective critique of power, nor does it constitute a rejection of revolution as such). But to insert Foucault—as do Wolin and others—into the Moynian narrative of a generation of 1970s leftist intellectuals desperately seeking a new outlet for idealism after the demise of the revolutionary dream, transferring their investments wholesale to the *Rechtsstaat* or to international human rights law (a narrative that nevertheless explains much), is to miss something methodologically (and maybe temperamentally) important about this late body of work. Such readings miss more than the substantive nuance and richness of his particular rights-based engagements. They miss more than the way in which he tries strategically to turn rights against state power or to deploy them for a rethinking of subjectivity. Crucially, what they miss as well (or misunderstand) is the way in which Foucault goes about his work. He does not suddenly pick up the tools of liberalism because of a Damascene, utopian faith in their possibilities.[24] Nor does he turn to rights disappointedly because revolution has failed. Neither the logic of utopia nor that of *faute de mieux* adequately captures the spirit of Foucault's approach. A certain pragmatism comes closest: the strategic pragmatism of the genealogist who seeks to use the available political resources of the time.[25] Foucault begins to engage more closely, more seriously, and more often with rights in the late 1970s and early 1980s because they become at this time (as per Moyn and others) a more "popular and available" political currency.[26] As Paul Patton has argued with respect to Foucault's conception of rights, "since genealogical critique aligns itself with 'specific transformations' underway, it inevitably relies upon particular normative choices available within the present" and thus "appeals to new rights or new forms of right will always rely upon new concepts that may be found within or derived from existing discourses of moral or political right."[27] As rights discourse becomes ubiquitous in the 1970s and into the 1980s, it should not surprise us that Foucault seeks to access the political possibilities that this emergent political repertoire discloses. This is not, I hasten to say, a kind of pragmatic accommodation to existing political reality.[28] Foucault does not simply capitulate to a certain "rights talk" because this is the predominant language of his time, but rather tries to semantically undo that rights talk and to make it mean differently. He tries to occupy rights discourse and to deploy it in a range of different directions. Foucault the genealogist seeks in present arrangements the possibilities of their overcoming, without imposing a utopian model or regulative ideal upon their becoming. "I dream," he once said, "of the intellectual destroyer of evidence and universalities, the one who, in the inertias and constraints of the present, locates and marks the weak points, the openings, the lines of power, who incessantly displaces himself, doesn't know exactly where he is heading nor what he'll think tomorrow because he is too attentive to the present."[29] That present provided a panoply of rights-based mechanisms that Foucault sought to work with and against in order to further a diverse set of political aims.

Foucault (and the Critique of Rights) Now? Back to the Future . . .

But what of *our* present? Surely there is a certain irony in continuing to read the works of a theorist today who, in his own time, studiously insisted that his writings did not generate insights about power or subjectivity that were true for all time and all places but were rather historically contingent and locally circumscribed? Addressing just this question in a paper titled "Foucault Now?," published in 2005, the philosopher Todd May humorously sets the scene:

> It has been twenty-one years since Foucault's death. Think for a moment of what this means. In 1984, there was no internet, there were no DVDs, no cell phones,

CDs were just coming into existence, TIVO was a distant dream, and we could drive around without having to deal with sport utility vehicles.[30]

It is no accident that May marks the gap between 1984 and 2005 by reference to changes in technology—and, to be more precise, largely in reference to informational and communicative technology. Many of the subsequent attempts either to update Foucault (2.0, 3.0, 4.0, ad infinitum) or to consign him to history have emphasized the rapid changes to digital technology and communicational practices consequent upon (yet also enabling of) processes of late capitalist globalization. In this regard, May references the accounts of Foucault's contemporaries, Gilles Deleuze (d. 1995) and Jean Baudrillard (d. 2007). But for him neither the "control society" nor the "hyper-reality" thesis actually serves to update Foucault. Both these putatively post-Foucauldian sociological codicils are in fact, for May, "as much pre- as post-Foucaultian."[31] They are pre-Foucauldian because they fail to heed Foucault's methodological warnings about the need to pay scrupulous genealogical attention to the present and, in so doing, to emphasize the plurality and discontinuity within that present. "Whether we are described as relays in a digital network, consumers of hyper-reality, or subjects of global capital," explains May, "we are accounted as one thing, as [a] single something that lends itself to a particular exhaustive perspective." As such, these types of generalizing accounts "have not yet reached Foucault, much less gone beyond him."[32] Foucault's contemporary use-value, then, consists not so much in *what* he said about such things as discipline and biopolitics, as if these continued unchanged into the present (although I would contend that they do continue to be relevant descriptors of our contemporary world in many important, if not unchanged, respects). Rather, Foucault is current for us in *how* he approaches his work and hence how we, in his wake, might approach ours.[33]

In writing this book I have endeavored to follow May's (and Foucault's) advice about the need to pay attention to detail and context without allowing a particular element of a situation to stand, reductively and metonymically, for the whole of that situation. I have hence tried to return to the nuance, equivocation, and ambivalence (the "corrugation," to appropriate Wendy Brown's resonant phrase)[34] of Foucault's rights-based political interventions of the late 1970s and early 1980s so as to furnish an antidote to their glib reclamation as "liberal." But there are in my opinion other dimensions of Foucault's rights politics that speak more substantively and more directly to our contemporary political situation, and here we can return again to Moyn's historical narrative about the rise and subsequent overburdening of a minimalist human rights with maximalist political agendas. While human rights came to global prominence in the 1970s on the basis of a minimalist claim simply to, in the words of one of Amnesty's advertising campaigns of the last few years, "Protect the Human," they subsequently came to serve a range of much more expansive political agendas. The story is well known; indeed, it is still being told. Human rights today are the global lingua franca of politics—ours is truly an age of human rights, if not in the sense of a universal observance of and commitment to its norms, then surely in the political and discursive sense of diverse groups articulating claims for justice or opposition to oppression in its terms. Human rights is an incredibly powerful, even hegemonic, signifier, whose authorizing force is sought by the powerful and the powerless alike.[35] So strong is the gravitational pull of human rights discourse that many critics have worried that it displaces other political languages and practices, colonizing the field of global politics.[36] And yet, while this is a concern of contemporary critics, often the same critics who make these (and other, more foundational) critiques of human rights discourse are the very same ones who ultimately recommend not the replacement of human rights with other political strategies (indeed, even other imaginaries or utopias), but rather their "transformation, re-signification, or displacement,"[37] their supplementing, modification, or redeployment.[38] A brief historical comparison might make the point more starkly. Let us suspend for a moment Moyn's (in my view, convincing) claim that contemporary human rights are qualitatively different creatures from their fin de siècle French revolutionary forebears and consult not the rights themselves but rather the critical response they engendered. Once we do so, we immediately see that the uncompromising critiques of Marx, Bentham, and Burke issued not in the attempt to refashion or internally subvert the bourgeois ideology or metaphysical nonsense of natural rights, but rather compelled their utter negation and replacement with, variously, radical human emancipation, the utilitarianism of positive legislation, or the rights of the freeborn Englishman.[39] In our own time the reigning critical orthodoxy looks very different. The international legal theorist Frédéric Mégret captures its spirit well. "Over the last few decades, coinciding with the dramatic rise of international human rights law as a force to be reckoned with," he writes, "there has emerged a significant, sustained and complex critique of the global reach of human rights." This critical discourse, he continues, "is not a project of hostility to human rights . . . but it is a project that is, at the minimum, prudent and even sceptical about some claims made relating to international human rights, even as it recognizes the particular place that human rights have come to occupy in our global legal imagination." Thus:

> Critical approaches to human rights stand in a productive dialectical tension with human rights, and their attitude can best be expressed as one of ambivalence: willing to applaud the accomplishments of human rights when those seem significant, but keen to caution against some of the limitations of the discourse—and, most importantly perhaps—dubious that the two can be disentangled.[40]

This uneasy, (self-)critical stance of complicity, entanglement, ambivalence, and pragmatism, of working within a discourse to attempt to leverage political possibilities from it, should by now feel quite familiar. If the first critiques worked on the level of negation and replacement, then this current wave of critique functions on the level of genealogical subversion and counter-conduct. It is concerned to stress the internal plurality and alternative possibilities of the discourse under critique. Foucault is paradigmatic and historically important in this regard. There is no small measure of historical irony wrapped up in this development, but it is not exactly the irony that critics charge him with. It is not that Foucault's shift from anti-humanism to humanism helps usher in a resurgent political liberalism. Things are, in my view, significantly more complicated than that. Rather, it is that Foucault, whom many continue to read as a denier of the emancipatory potential of rights, is in fact one of the first to develop a critical, subversive, appropriatory praxis of rights which, far from denying their value or utility, actually celebrates the ways in which they can be put to different, and contrary, uses. This is best understood as a critical counter-conduct of rights. Developed in the late 1970s and into the early 1980s, this approach to the politics of rights theoretically informs the work of other contemporary critical thinkers of rights whom I have discussed in this book: Judith Butler and Wendy Brown among them, but many others in a range of fields.[41] Foucault's prescient and influential approach thus commands our serious attention in the present for the diverse ways in which it continues to inform critical political engagements with rights.

But if for these reasons it commands our attention, it nevertheless cannot also demand a simplistic reproduction or application; indeed, as per May (and Foucault himself), it deserves something more. Just as the fortunes of human rights have changed, so too have the prospects of engagement with and the resignification of them. One of the salient (possibly defining) aspects of contemporary critical engagements with human rights is that they continue to articulate political projects in and through the language of human rights, albeit with an intention to subvert or resist their dominant meanings. As Foucault teaches, of course, there is no innocent and risk-free political strategy—and the same thing surely applies to a counter-conduct of rights itself. What are the risks attendant upon such a strategy? The most obvious risk is the possibility that one's efforts to subvert, appropriate, or redeploy will only result in the strengthening of the operative terms of the master discourse. Here the concern is that by continuing to make critical and emancipatory claims in the language of rights one ends up not so much displacing as reinforcing their structuring concepts. On the one hand, there could be no more familiar Foucauldian aperçu than that resistance turns out to be bound up in subtle yet determining ways with the power to which it is putatively opposed. On the other hand, of course, that risk per se never represented a sufficient reason to relinquish any given political contest for Foucault (in fact, it was merely a constitutive and inescapable feature of the strategic reversibility of power relations). "Indeed," writes Zachary Manfredi in this vein, "it could be argued that the contemporary ubiquity [and hegemonic force] of human rights language as a discursive framework for justice claims in domestic and international politics makes it a strategically essential point of engagement for left political theorizing . . . [and that by retreating from it] those on the Left appear to have conceded an extraordinarily wide array of institutions and sites of contestation to those liberal and conservative thinkers who deploy the language of rights to suit their own projects."[42] This is a compelling argument and we can see that it is one that motivates Foucault on many occasions to begin that process of contestation and reversal. But by the same token it has to be acknowledged that not all power relations are equally susceptible of strategic reversibility and recoding, not all political names as hospitable to dissonant meanings: some are significantly more supple, more protean, than others. Here the question ultimately becomes a strategic one as to when one attempts to engage and when one does not, preferring instead what Judith Butler calls the "performativity proper to refusal."[43] The ever-complex Foucault does both. We saw toward the end of the last chapter, for example, that he was unwilling to run the risk of prosecuting a rights-based opposition to the death penalty for precisely this worry about complicity and reinforcement.

Today, despite the hegemonic popularity and institutional expanse of human rights, it is very much a contested question whether human rights provide the best means with which to grapple with the world's social, economic, and political problems.[44] Can all claims be made in the language of human rights? Or are some claims less intelligible than others? What are the strategic limits of human rights? What are the limits of their contingent reappropriation? After all, to insist upon an institution's or practice's contingency is not the same thing as to always commend engagement with it. My point is neither to turn back to Foucault for an answer to this (impossible) set of questions, nor to ask "What would Foucault do *today*?" Both ways of approaching these questions do a disservice to his style of thought. Rather, the point is to acknowledge that it is always and unavoidably a question of strategy whether any given rights framework permits a margin for political contestation and critical subversion. And, if we return to the nuance of Foucault's original political engagements, we see him trying to address precisely these strategic and political concerns. It may well be that a Foucauldian strategy toward rights today actually counsels a retreat from the terrain of rights, an investment in other political struggles, and the reimagining of other possibilities and (possibly even) utopias. This is an open question. But just as Foucault did not read the Greeks for a way out, so too should we continue to read him today, and tomorrow, not for solutions but for provocations toward what he once memorably called the "permanent critique of ourselves" and of our contingent political reality.[45] This book is an invitation to do just that.

REFERENCE MATTER

NOTES

Introduction

The epigraph to the Introduction is from Michel Foucault, *Wrong-Doing, Truth Telling: The Function of Avowal in Justice*, trans. Stephen W. Sawyer (Chicago: University of Chicago Press, 2014), 265.

1. Clifford Geertz, "Stir Crazy," *New York Review of Books*, 26 January 1978, 3.

2. See Louis Henkin, *The Age of Rights* (New York: Columbia University Press, 1990); and Costas Douzinas, *The End of Human Rights: Critical Legal Thought at the Turn of the Century* (Oxford, UK: Hart, 2000), 1.

3. Quoted in Jean-Luc Nancy, *The Inoperative Community*, trans. Peter Connor et al. (Minneapolis: University of Minnesota Press, 1991), 1.

4. See the illuminating introductory chapter to *Left Legalism/Left Critique*, ed. Wendy Brown and Janet Halley (Durham, NC: Duke University Press, 2002), 1–37.

5. Costas Douzinas, "*Adikia*: On Communism and Rights," in *The Idea of Communism*, ed. Costas Douzinas and Slavoj Žižek (London: Verso, 2010), 81.

6. Claude Lefort, "Politics and Human Rights," in *The Political Forms of Modern Society: Bureaucracy, Democracy, Totalitarianism*, ed. John B. Thompson (Cambridge, MA: MIT Press, 1986); Étienne Balibar, "'Rights of Man' and 'Rights of the Citizen': The Modern Dialectic of Equality and Freedom," in *Masses, Classes, Ideas: Studies on Politics and Philosophy Before and After Marx*, trans. James Swenson (New York: Routledge, 1994); Jean-François Lyotard, "The Other's Rights," in *On Human Rights*, trans. Chris Miller and Robert Smith, ed. Stephen Shute and Susan L. Hurley (New York: Basic Books, 1993).

7. See, for example, Jacques Rancière, "Who Is the Subject of the Rights of Man?," *South Atlantic Quarterly* 103, nos. 2–3 (2004); Judith Butler, "Beside Oneself: On the Limits of Sexual Autonomy," in *Undoing Gender* (New York: Routledge, 2004); and Slavoj Žižek, "Against Human Rights," *New Left Review* 35 (July–August 2005).

8. Samuel Moyn, "Substance, Scale, and Salience: The Recent Historiography of Human Rights," *Annual Review of Law and Social Science* 8 (2012): 124.

9. Philip Alston, "Does the Past Matter? On the Origins of Human Rights," *Harvard Law Review* 126, no. 7 (2013): 2077.

10. Samuel Moyn, *The Last Utopia: Human Rights in History* (Cambridge, MA: Belknap Press of Harvard University Press, 2010). And see Micheline R. Ishay, *The History of Human Rights: From Ancient Times to the Globalization Era* (Berkeley: University of California Press, 2008); Lynn Hunt, *Inventing Human Rights: A History* (New York: Norton, 2007); and Michael Ignatieff, *Human Rights as Politics and Idolatry* (Princeton, NJ: Princeton University Press, 2001).

11. See Robert Horvath, "'The Solzhenitsyn Effect': East European Dissidents and the Demise of the Revolutionary Privilege," *Human Rights Quarterly* 29, no. 4 (2007).

12. Foucault first discusses the concept of "counter-conduct" during his 1978 Collège de France lecture course, "Security, Territory, Population," in the historical context of revolts within and against the Christian pastorate. See Michel Foucault, *Security, Territory, Population: Lectures at the Collège de France 1977–78*, trans. Graham Burchell (Basingstoke, UK: Palgrave Macmillan, 2007), 191–226. For a recent argument that the concept is central to an understanding of Foucault's shift from an analysis of power-knowledge to ethics in the late work, see Arnold I. Davidson, "In Praise of Counter-Conduct," *History of the Human Sciences* 24, no. 4 (2011). For a brief yet rich and suggestive characterization of Foucault's late work on rights as forms of counter-conduct, see Louisa Cadman, "How (Not) to Be Governed: Foucault, Critique, and the Political," *Environment and Planning D: Society and Space* 28, no. 3 (2010). See also on this score Jessica Whyte, "Confronting Governments: Human Rights?," in *New Critical Legal Thinking: Law and the Political*, ed. Matthew Stone, Illan rua Wall, and Costas Douzinas (Abingdon, UK: Routledge, 2012).

13. See Michel Foucault, *The Birth of Biopolitics: Lectures at the Collège de France 1978–79*, trans. Graham Burchell (Basingstoke, UK: Palgrave Macmillan, 2008), 20. I am especially grateful to Colin Koopman for pressing me to refine the arguments in the above paragraph.

14. Here and in what follows I adopt as a heuristic (with some qualifications that I shall explain as they arise) the fairly standard tripartite division of Foucault's work into three phases: the archaeological, the genealogical and the ethical (or, the successive engagements with discourse, power, and the ethical subject). For example, see Béatrice Han, *Foucault's Critical Project: Between the Transcendental and the Historical*, trans. Edward Pile (Stanford, CA: Stanford University Press, 2002), 1 (although see xiii for her own reservations on this score). This division is both a product of scholarly exegesis and of Foucault's own occasional (but not always consistent) retrospective (self-)fashioning. See, for example, Michel Foucault, "The Subject and Power," in *Essential Works of Foucault 1954–1984*, vol. 3, *Power*, trans. Robert Hurley et al., ed. James D. Faubion (New York: New Press, 2000), 326–27, in which distinctions are drawn between the study of sciences, the study of "dividing practices," and the study of the ways in which a "human being turns him- or herself into a subject"; and Michel Foucault, "Preface to *The His-*

tory of Sexuality, Volume Two," in *Essential Works of Foucault 1954–1984*, vol. 1, *Ethics, Subjectivity and Truth*, trans. Robert Hurley et al., ed. Paul Rabinow (Harmondsworth, UK: Allen Lane/Penguin, 1997), in which he draws a distinction between the three axes of knowledge, normativity, and relation to the self.

15. See *Discipline and Punish: The Birth of the Prison*, trans. Alan Sheridan (Harmondsworth, UK: Penguin, 1991); *The Will to Knowledge*, vol. 1 of *The History of Sexuality*, trans. Robert Hurley (Harmondsworth, UK: Penguin, 1979); *"Society Must Be Defended": Lectures at the Collège de France, 1975–76*, trans. David Macey (London: Allen Lane, 2003); *Security, Territory, Population*; and *The Birth of Biopolitics*.

16. See Foucault, *The Will to Knowledge*, 82.

17. Foucault, *Discipline and Punish*, 167, 194.

18. Foucault, *"Society Must Be Defended,"* 29–30. For a set of related reflections on methodology, see Foucault, *The Will to Knowledge*, 92–102.

19. For one example among many, see Stephen K. White's Habermasian lament that Foucault's normative failure ultimately proceeds from his inability to account for the subject: "What finally hangs on Foucault's failure to bridge the gap between the aesthetic and the juridical, while he nevertheless endorses political resistance to the normalizing processes of modern life? The most immediate implication revolves around the fact that without any way of conceptualizing juridical subjectivity, Foucault's recommendation of collective resistance has such a blind and undifferentiated character as to be almost politically irresponsible. He provides us, ultimately, with no way of distinguishing the resistance of the women's movement or the Polish Solidarity movement from, say, the Ku Klux Klan or Jim Jones's People's Temple." See "Foucault's Challenge to Critical Theory," *American Political Science Review* 80, no. 2 (1986): 430.

20. Michel Foucault, "Vérité, pouvoir et soi," in *Dits et écrits II, 1976–1988*, ed. Daniel Defert and François Ewald (Paris: Gallimard, 2001), 1598.

21. Paul Patton, "Foucault, Critique and Rights," *Critical Horizons* 6, no. 1 (2005): 269.

22. As Jack Donnelly puts it, crystallizing a widely shared—almost mantrically invoked—tautology, "human rights are the rights one has simply because one is a human being." See *Universal Human Rights in Theory and Practice*, 2nd ed. (Ithaca, NY: Cornell University Press, 2003), 1.

23. Jennifer Nedelsky, "Law, Boundaries, and the Bounded Self," *Representations* 30 (Spring 1990): 162, 167. Nedelsky's discussion focuses on property (largely but not only in the context of American constitutional discourse); but for an illuminating consideration, from an explicitly Foucauldian perspective, of the right to privacy and its operative metaphors and assumptions, see Kendall Thomas, "Beyond the Privacy Principle," *Columbia Law Review* 92, no. 6 (1992).

24. Foucault, *The Will to Knowledge*, 88–89.

25. Michel Foucault, "Truth and Power," in *Power/Knowledge: Selected Interviews and Other Writings 1972–1977*, trans. Colin Gordon et al., ed. Colin Gordon (Brighton, UK: Harvester Press, 1980), 121.

26. Ibid., 119. For a reading of Foucault which insists that he himself adhered narrowly to an undifferentiated, Austinian model of modern law, see Duncan Kennedy,

"The Stakes of Law, or Hale and Foucault!," in *Sexy Dressing Etc.* (Cambridge, MA: Harvard University Press, 1993).

27. Foucault, "Truth and Power," 121.

28. Foucault, *The Will to Knowledge*, 135.

29. Foucault, *"Society Must Be Defended,"* 26.

30. Ibid.

31. Foucault, "Truth and Power," 121.

32. Ibid., 122.

33. Foucault, *Discipline and Punish*, 222.

34. Nancy Fraser, "Foucault's Body-Language: A Post-Humanist Political Rhetoric?," *Salmagundi* 61 (Fall 1983): 56.

35. Ibid.

36. Joan M. Reynolds, "'Pragmatic Humanism' in Foucault's Later Work," *Canadian Journal of Political Science* 37, no. 4 (2004): 971.

37. As to the former claim, see, for example, Jürgen Habermas, "Some Questions Concerning the Theory of Power: Foucault Again," in *The Philosophical Discourse of Modernity: Twelve Lectures*, trans. Frederick G. Lawrence (Cambridge, UK: Polity, 1997), 282–86. As to the latter, see nn. 54–56 below and the relevant discussion in the text.

38. I have previously argued this, but now harbor some reservations about such a reading. See Ben Golder, "Foucault and the Unfinished Human of Rights," *Law, Culture and the Humanities* 6, no. 3 (2010): 362. See also the penetrating critique of Foucault's Geneva intervention (as just such a "new right") offered by Whyte in her "Confronting Governments: Human Rights?" For an interesting discussion which proceeds upon the footing that "Foucault's critique does not itself provide the basis for a new theory of right" but tries to answer Foucault's theoretical challenge by way of a rereading of the social contract tradition, see Roger Mourad, "After Foucault: A New Form of Right," *Philosophy & Social Criticism* 29, no. 4 (2003): 453.

39. Foucault, *"Society Must Be Defended,"* 39–40.

40. To clarify, I mean that Foucault subsequently makes references to rights both within the Collège lectures and in other sources, but he never explicitly returns to address the question of what might constitute a "new right" as such—and whether the various examples he adduces are candidates for such a "new right."

41. Michel Foucault, "Alternatives to the Prison: Dissemination or Decline of Social Control?," *Theory, Culture & Society* 26, no. 6 (2009): 19.

42. Quoted in Thomas Keenan, "The 'Paradox' of Knowledge and Power: Foucault on the Bias," in *Fables of Responsibility: Aberrations and Predicaments in Ethics and Politics* (Stanford, CA: Stanford University Press, 1997), 168.

43. Michel Foucault, "Letter to Certain Leaders of the Left," in *Essential Works of Foucault*, vol. 3, *Power*, 427.

44. Michel Foucault, "Open Letter to Mehdi Bazargan," in *Essential Works of Foucault*, vol. 3, *Power*, 441.

45. Michel Foucault, "The Risks of Security," in *Essential Works of Foucault*, vol. 3, *Power*, 380. See also Michel Foucault, "The Simplest of Pleasures," in *Foucault Live:*

Collected Interviews, 1961–1984, trans. Lysa Hochroth and John Johnston, ed. Sylvère Lotringer (New York: Semiotext(e), 1996).

46. Didier Eribon, *Michel Foucault*, trans. Betsy Wing (Cambridge, MA: Harvard University Press, 1991), 279.

47. Michel Foucault, "Confronting Governments: Human Rights," in *Essential Works of Foucault*, vol. 3, *Power*, 475.

48. For example, see Michel Foucault, "The Social Triumph of the Sexual Will," in *Essential Works of Foucault*, vol. 1, *Ethics*, 160, 162; Michel Foucault, "The Moral and Social Experience of the Poles Can No Longer Be Obliterated," in *Essential Works of Foucault*, vol. 3, *Power*, 465, 471, 472.

49. Keenan, "The "Paradox" of Knowledge and Power," 160–61.

50. Nancy Fraser, "Foucault on Modern Power: Empirical Insights and Normative Confusions," in *Unruly Practices: Power, Discourse, and Gender in Contemporary Social Theory* (Minneapolis: University of Minnesota Press, 1989), 31.

51. Habermas, "Some Questions Concerning the Theory of Power," 276 (emphasis in original).

52. Fraser, "Foucault on Modern Power," 20–21, 27.

53. Ibid., 29, 33. For both Fraser and Habermas, Foucault's failure to adduce proper normative grounds for his critique of modern power cannot be made good by reading him as attempting some kind of Marxian immanent critique, relying, for example, upon extant liberal norms as a presupposition of his own more radical dialectical overturning ("unmasking the humanistic self-understanding of modernity by suing for the normative content of bourgeois ideals," as Habermas neatly puts it in "Some Questions Concerning the Theory of Power," 282). Marx, writes Fraser, "is not . . . fully suspending the bourgeois norms of reciprocity and freedom. Perhaps Foucault could be read in similar fashion. Perhaps he is not fully suspending but presupposing the very liberal norms he criticizes?" ("Foucault on Modern Power," 30). However, both Habermas and Fraser ultimately rule out such a reading of Foucault. Indeed, for Habermas, while Foucault's critiques tacitly make an appeal to humanistic sentiment, the latter ultimately seeks not to resolve the pathologies of modernity but to evacuate it totally (see "Some Questions Concerning the Theory of Power," 283). This is the philosophical basis of Habermas's ill-founded and polemical charge that Foucault was a "Young Conservative." See Jürgen Habermas, "Modernity Versus Postmodernity," *New German Critique* 22 (Winter 1981): 13 (and for Fraser's significantly more nuanced response, see her "Michel Foucault: A 'Young Conservative'?," *Ethics* 96, no. 1 [1985]). I have dwelt on the Habermas (and Fraser) *contra* Foucault debate of the 1980s not because it substantively deserves a reprisal (to the contrary, as Thomas Biebricher ably shows, the "debate" proceeded on the basis of a serious misreading of Foucault by Habermas—see his "Habermas, Foucault and Nietzsche: A Double Misunderstanding," *Foucault Studies* 3 [2005]—and on a restricted range of sources). Rather, it is because the aftereffects of this debate about normativity continue to inform much of the contemporary reception of Foucault on rights.

54. Quoted in Keenan, "The 'Paradox' of Knowledge and Power," 155. For a sensitive

discussion of the relation of philosophy to politics in Foucault's later work, see David Couzens Hoy, "Foucault and Critical Theory," in *The Later Foucault*, ed. Jeremy Moss (London: SAGE, 1998), 19–22.

55. James Brusseau, *Decadence of the French Nietzsche* (Plymouth, UK: Lexington, 2005), 192. One finds a similar figuration of politico-juridical strategy in critical legal theoretical work, whereby particular (institutional and discursive) spaces invite particular approaches (which others foreclose), leading to the embrace of "multiple consciousness as judicial method." See Mari J. Matsuda, "When the First Quail Calls: Multiple Consciousness as Jurisprudential Method," *Women's Rights Law Reporter* 11, no. 1 (1989).

56. Brent Pickett, *On the Use and Abuse of Foucault for Politics* (Oxford, UK: Lexington, 2005), 97n19.

57. Thomas Biebricher, "The Practices of Theorists: Habermas and Foucault as Public Intellectuals," *Philosophy & Social Criticism* 37, no. 6 (2011): 725.

58. Kirstie McClure, "Taking Liberties in Foucault's Triangle: Sovereignty, Discipline, Governmentality, and the Subject of Rights," in *Identities, Politics, and Rights, ed.* Austin Sarat and Thomas R. Kearns (Ann Arbor: University of Michigan Press, 1995), 171.

59. Alan Hunt and Gary Wickham, *Foucault and Law: Towards a Sociology of Law as Governance* (London: Pluto, 1994), 63, 64. "It may be too harsh to say that he never returns to this topic," the authors go on to say. While admitting that Foucault does indeed "return to grapple with issues that touch on this range of issues," nevertheless they conclude that these reflections are "scattered" among (then) unpublished lectures on liberal and neoliberal government which fail to come to terms with law's role in governance (64).

60. Fraser, "Foucault's Body-Language," 65.

61. Here I am, of course, being somewhat reductive. There are several scholars whose work on Foucault and rights does not fall into the above-mentioned four interpretive categories (some of them already referenced, above). I shall deal with (and reference) their work more fully in coming chapters, often relying upon, extending, and disagreeing with their insights. Those authors who do concern themselves with the question I am addressing in this book, namely, a characterization of Foucault's approach to rights in the late work, include: Thomas Biebricher, Louisa Cadman, Philippe Chevallier, Duncan Ivison, Thomas Keenan, Paul Patton, and Jessica Whyte.

62. The classic reference point for these arguments is the work of Peter Dews. His "The Return of the Subject in Late Foucault," *Radical Philosophy* 51 (Spring 1989), is a continuation of criticisms of Foucault made in his *Logics of Disintegration: Post-Structuralist Thought and the Claims of Critical Theory* (London: Verso, 1987), esp. chaps. 5 and 6.

63. Jeffrey T. Nealon, *Foucault Beyond Foucault: Power and Its Intensifications Since 1984* (Stanford, CA: Stanford University Press, 2008), 10.

64. Timothy O'Leary, *Foucault and the Art of Ethics* (London: Continuum, 2002), 117.

65. Eric Paras, *Foucault 2.0: Beyond Power and Knowledge* (New York: Other Press, 2006), 4. See also François Dosse, *History of Structuralism*, vol. 2, *The Sign Sets, 1967–Present*, trans. Deborah Glassman (Minneapolis: University of Minnesota Press, 1997), 336. See also Alain Beaulieu, "Towards a Liberal Utopia: The Connection Between

Foucault's Reporting on the Iranian Revolution and the Ethical Turn," *Philosophy & Social Criticism* 36, no. 7 (2010). The question of narrative (and the ways in which the generic expectations of certain narratives structure the reception and interpretation of Foucault's late work) is crucial here. The religious inflections of many readings of the late work (and the religious tropes and motifs which circulate within these texts)— Foucault's Damascene moment, Foucault as recusant sinner, Foucault's deathbed conversion, Foucault's mea culpa, Foucault's putting away childish illiberal things—are rather difficult to miss (for example, see James Schmidt and Thomas E. Wartenburg, "Foucault's Enlightenment: Critique, Revolution, and the Fashioning of the Self," in *Critique and Power: Recasting the Foucault/Habermas Debate*, ed. Michael Kelly [Cambridge, MA: MIT Press, 1994], 287; and Ian Hacking, "Self Improvement," in *Foucault: A Critical Reader*, ed. David Couzens Hoy [Oxford, UK: Blackwell, 1986], 238). I am grateful to Bonnie Honig for first raising this issue with me. But alongside the religious narratives is a competing romantic narrative—in which Foucault first spurns, then flirts with, and then finally embraces, and so forth, a liberal politics (in addition to the above sources, see Michael C. Behrent, "Liberalism Without Humanism: Michel Foucault and the Free-Market Creed, 1976–1979," *Modern Intellectual History* 6, no. 3 [2009]: 541, 544, 545, 547). The point is that both of these narrations of Foucault's late work—as religious recanting and return to orthodoxy or as romantic consummation—are often underwritten by a similar teleologic in which a liberal thinking of rights emerges as the necessary but delayed conclusion to Foucault's (mature, evolved, fully worked-through) thought.

66. Cf. the recent work of Paul Patton, which effects a careful and limited rapprochement between aspects of Foucault's thought and a certain (late, more historically minded) Rawls. See Paul Patton, "Foucault and Normative Political Philosophy," in *Foucault and Philosophy*, ed. Timothy O'Leary and Christopher Falzon (Oxford, UK: Wiley-Blackwell, 2010); and Patton, "Historical Normativity and the Basis of Rights," in *Re-Reading Foucault: On Law, Power and Rights*, ed. Ben Golder (Abingdon, UK: Routledge, 2012). See also Carlos A. Ball, "Sexual Ethics and Postmodernism in Gay Rights Philosophy," *North Carolina Law Review* 80, no. 2 (2002).

67. Biebricher, "The Practices of Theorists," 725. See also Thomas Biebricher, "Foucault and the Politics of Rights," *Journal of Political Power* 5, no. 2 (2012): 310–11 (who is critical of the interpretation of Foucault's rights politics as "liberal," but is himself also critical of certain aspects and effects of Foucault's rights politics); and David F. Gruber, "Foucault's Critique of the Liberal Individual," *Journal of Philosophy* 86, no. 11 (1989) (who argues that Foucault maintains a critique of liberalism which also, it seems for him, rules out any appeal to rights). A final note on liberalism in this context. The focus of the present study is on Foucault and not on liberalism or on liberal political theory, but even so it may be objected by those better versed in the latter that I do not provide a fuller and fairer account of its more nuanced and diverse practitioners. This is true, and doubtless some of their accounts could be brought into more sympathetic alignment with Foucault in places (as, for example, does Patton, discussed in n. 66 above). Nevertheless, that is not my project here. Rather, I am trying to reconstruct a specifi-

cally Foucauldian politics of rights, and in doing so I want to suggest that it differs in important respects from the liberal conception of rights, which at its core is committed to maintaining some version of the following: that rights are an entitlement of the individual subject (she herself understood as being pre-political); that entitlement flows from certain fundamental capacities or properties of the subject; and that rights provide a mechanism to restrain (and simultaneously legitimize) the use of power against the individual subject (most classically in the sense of state coercion).

68. Foucault, *The Will to Knowledge*, 97. My reading of Foucault *contra* liberalism shares much in common with Samuel Chambers's reading of Rancière in his *The Lessons of Rancière* (New York: Oxford University Press, 2013), which, relevantly, "*seeks to disentangle democratic* [Rancièrean] *politics from liberalism* . . . [without necessarily] impugn[ing] all of liberalism" (10–11; emphasis in original).

69. Foucault, "The Subject and Power," 341.

70. Ibid., 326–27.

71. Ibid., 341.

72. For example, Foucault, *The Will to Knowledge*, 93.

73. Michel Foucault, "What Is Critique?," trans. Kevin Paul Geiman, in *What Is Enlightenment?: Eighteenth-Century Answers and Twentieth-Century Questions*, ed. James Schmidt (Berkeley: University of California Press, 1996), 384.

74. Ibid.

75. Ibid.

76. Michel Foucault, "Preface to *Anti-Oedipus*," in *Essential Works of Foucault*, Vol. 3: *Power*, 109.

77. Cited in Colin Gordon, "Governmental Rationality: An Introduction," in *The Foucault Effect: Studies in Governmentality*, ed. Graham Burchell, Colin Gordon, and Peter Miller (Chicago: University of Chicago Press, 1991), 5. And see also Foucault, *The Will to Knowledge*, 100–102.

78. See the discussion of periodization and the sources cited in n. 14 above. For a more recent and illuminating discussion of Foucault's transition from archaeology to genealogy, see chapter 1 of Colin Koopman, *Genealogy as Critique: Foucault and the Problems of Modernity* (Bloomington: Indiana University Press, 2013).

79. Foucault, "The Subject and Power," 326.

80. See Foucault, *The Will to Knowledge*, 82; but see also his comment that "I am not developing a theory of power" (Michel Foucault, "Critical Theory/Intellectual History," in *Politics, Philosophy, Culture: Interviews and Other Writings, 1977–1984*, trans. Alan Sheridan et al., ed. Lawrence D. Kritzman [London: Routledge, 1988], 39).

81. Foucault, "*Society Must Be Defended*," 6.

82. For a compelling contrary account, and one that engages the notion of "theory" on a theoretical level itself, see Peter Fitzpatrick, "Foucault's Other Law," in *Re-Reading Foucault*.

83. Michel Foucault, "Polemics, Politics and Problematizations: An Interview with Michel Foucault," in *Essential Works of Foucault*, vol. 1, *Ethics*, 113.

84. Judith Butler, "Contingent Foundations: Feminism and the Question of 'Post-

modernism,'" in *Feminists Theorize the Political*, ed. Judith Butler and Joan W. Scott (New York: Routledge, 1992), 4.

85. Wendy Brown, "Genealogical Politics," in *The Later Foucault*, 34.

86. "We suggest that there is no embarrassment in holding that some of Foucault's own political stances, such as his naïve 'abolitionist' views about criminal justice or his ill-advised enthusiasm for the regime of the mullahs in Iran, are frankly silly and barely worth debating. . . . Any serious assessment of Foucault depends not on the causes he espouses but on what those who read him can do with his enormously fertile leads and suggestions" (Hunt and Wickham, *Foucault and Law*, 36). As this quotation bears out, the temptation to treat Foucault's political interventions in this way has been felt most strongly when it comes to his engagement with the Iranian revolution and his views on criminal justice (see, for example, his views on the desexualization of rape). For a full-length critique of the former, see Janet Afary and Kevin B. Anderson, *Foucault and the Iranian Revolution: Gender and the Seductions of Islamism* (Chicago: University of Chicago Press, 2005). For a much more nuanced engagement with the latter, see Ann J. Cahill, "Foucault, Rape, and the Construction of the Feminine Body," *Hypatia* 15, no. 1 (2000).

87. Biebricher, "The Practices of Theorists," makes a strong argument—concerning both Foucault and Habermas—for integrating a reading of theoretical and political texts, but the most recent and sustained argument for reading Foucault's theorizations (of power, in particular) in relation to his militant engagements of the time is provided by Hoffman, *Foucault and Power*.

88. Foucault was, I take it—and in spite of many hyperbolic declamations to the contrary—studiously concerned with consistency and with the fashioning, and retrospective refashioning, of an intellectual oeuvre. This is no doubt itself an unfashionable observation to make of the author of "What Is an Author?" (see Michel Foucault, "What Is an Author?," trans. Joseph V. Harari, in *Modern Criticism and Theory: A Reader*, ed. David Lodge [London: Longman, 1988]), but I believe the many attempts on Foucault's part to characterize his work (as all along being about power or the subject and so forth) bear this out. See n. 14 above for some of these sources.

89. See the insightful discussion by Paul Patton of Foucault's Collège lectures as a particular form of philosophical work, the (changing) conditions under which the lectures were produced, and the ramifications that this had for Foucault's thinking on power in the mid- to late 1970s (Paul Patton, "From Resistance to Government: Foucault's Lectures 1976–1979," in *A Companion to Foucault*, ed. Christopher Falzon, Timothy O'Leary, and Jana Sawicki [Oxford, UK: Blackwell, 2013]).

90. Costas Douzinas, *Human Rights and Empire: The Political Philosophy of Cosmopolitanism* (Abingdon, UK: Routledge, 2007), 53n4.

91. See Rancière, "Who Is the Subject of the Rights of Man?"; and Butler, "Beside Oneself."

92. See, for example, Wendy Brown, *States of Injury: Power and Freedom in Late Modernity* (Princeton, NJ: Princeton University Press, 1995); Brown, "Suffering Rights as Paradoxes," *Constellations* 7, no. 2 (2000); Karen Zivi, *Making Rights Claims: A Prac-*

tice of Democratic Citizenship (New York: Oxford University Press, 2012); and Samuel Chambers, "Giving Up (on) Rights?: The Future of Rights and the Project of Radical Democracy," *American Journal of Political Science* 48, no. 2 (2004).

93. Emilios Christodoulidis, "Strategies of Rupture," *Law & Critique* 20, no. 1 (2009).

94. For an orientation to this intellectual trend and its historical context, see Michael Scott Christofferson, *French Intellectuals Against the Left: The Antitotalitarian Moment of the 1970s* (New York: Berghahn Books, 2004). For a situation of Foucault within this context, and especially in relation to the *nouveaux philosophes*, see chapter 3 of Paras, *Foucault 2.0*. I briefly return to Foucault's relationship to the *nouveaux philosophes* and his situation within this "antitotalitarian moment" in Chapter 2 (n. 16).

Chapter 1

The epigraph to this chapter is from Michel Foucault, "The Masked Philosopher," in *Politics, Philosophy, Culture: Interviews and Other Writings, 1977–1984*, trans. Alan Sheridan et al., ed. Lawrence D. Kritzman (London: Routledge, 1988), 326.

1. The periodization of his work has been a long-standing concern of Foucault scholars, as has the more specific debate over the perceived substantive and methodological differences between the thinker's late work on ethics and his earlier work on power. This latter question frequently revolves around the ontological status of the "subject" in the late, as opposed to middle, period. As discussed in the Introduction, a central reference point in that debate is Peter Dews's work in the late 1980s (see Introduction, n. 62). The most recent engagement with these issues, which explicitly takes up the question of the subject from the perspective of Foucault's Collège de France lecture courses (unavailable to Dews in published form), is provided in Paras, *Foucault 2.0*. I critically engage Paras's reading of Foucault in Chapter 2.

2. For Foucault's claim that the central objective of his work has been "to create a history of the different modes by which, in our culture, human beings are made subjects," see Foucault, "The Subject and Power," 326.

3. Richard Wolin, "From the 'Death of Man' to Human Rights: The Paradigm Change in French Intellectual Life, 1968–1986," in *The Frankfurt School Revisited, and Other Essays on Politics and Society* (New York: Routledge, 2006), 180.

4. O'Leary, *Foucault and the Art of Ethics*, 117.

5. For example, see Paras, *Foucault 2.0*, 4; and Dosse, *History of Structuralism*, 2:336.

6. Paras, *Foucault 2.0*, 14.

7. Richard Wolin, "Foucault the Neohumanist?," *Chronicle of Higher Education*, 1 September 2006, http://chronicle.com/article/Foucault-the-Neohumanist-/23118: "He [Foucault] came to realize that much of what French structuralism had during the 1960s rejected as humanist pap retained considerable ethical and political value. That re-evaluation of humanism redounds to his credit as a thinker."

8. As I hope the present chapter makes clear, I do not maintain that Foucault's work discloses a "positive" vision to transform the world. (Rather, it reveals precisely the opposite, namely, what he calls a "nonpositive" critical affirmation; see n. 29 below.) In saying this, however, I *do* maintain an interpretation of him as a thinker committed to a

restless kind of critical ethos, where critique is understood to open up spaces in which transformation can occur (but which mandates neither how such a transformation is to occur nor the principles by which it is to be guided). By suggesting that my own interpretation remains "faithful" to such an approach, I intend to signal not fidelity to a program but rather to such an understanding of critique. On the problematic of being "faithful" to Foucault, see Sergei Prozorov, *Foucault, Freedom and Sovereignty* (Aldershot, UK: Ashgate, 2007), 14–21.

9. Michel Foucault, "What Is Enlightenment?," in *Essential Works of Foucault 1954–1984*, vol. 1, *Ethics*.

10. Richard. J. Bernstein, "Foucault: Critique as a Philosophical Ethos," in *Critique and Power: Recasting the Foucault/Habermas Debate*, ed. Michael Kelly (Cambridge, MA: MIT Press, 1994), 211.

11. According to a rhetorical style arguably inherited from Nietzsche, but which at any rate is distinctly Nietzschean, Foucault frequently organizes his own presentation of a topic via the critique of a rival thinker or a given tradition's supposedly flawed conception of that same topic. Indeed, as Béatrice Han-Pile neatly puts it, Foucault was "often keener on defining his position *a contrario* than on providing a positive set of criteria" (see "The 'Death of Man': Foucault and Anti-Humanism," in *Foucault and Philosophy*, ed. Timothy O'Leary and Christopher Falzon [Oxford, UK: Wiley-Blackwell, 2010], 119). Perhaps the two best-known examples of this tendency relate to his reformulation of power *contra* the "economism" of Marx and the sovereign juridicism of Hobbes (see Foucault, *"Society Must Be Defended,"* 13, 28–29).

12. For a powerful and revealing reading of Foucault as (a historicized) Kantian, see Koopman, *Genealogy as Critique*, 109–21.

13. Immanuel Kant, "An Answer to the Question: 'What Is Enlightenment?,'" in *Political Writings*, trans. H. B. Nisbet, ed. H. S. Reiss (Cambridge: Cambridge University Press, 1970).

14. Foucault, "What Is Enlightenment?," 308.

15. Ibid., 309.

16. Ibid.

17. Ibid., 312.

18. Ibid., 315 (emphasis in original).

19. Ibid.

20. Ibid., 319.

21. Ibid., 315–16.

22. Ibid., 319.

23. I say "perhaps" advisedly, as despite the common rendering of Kantian critique as a form of judgment (for example, see n. 24 below), Judith Butler helpfully points out that "even in Kant, it is important to note that critique is not precisely a judgment, but an inquiry into the conditions of possibility that make judgment possible"; see "The Sensibility of Critique: Reply to Asad and Mahmood," in *Is Critique Secular?: Blasphemy, Injury and Free Speech*, ed. Talal Asad et al. (Berkeley, CA: Townsend Center for the Humanities, 2009), 115.

24. For helpful discussions of different genres and traditions of critique, see Costas Douzinas, "Oubliez Critique," *Law & Critique* 16, no. 1 (2005); and George Pavlich, "Experiencing Critique," in the same issue.

25. See also Foucault, "Critical Theory/Intellectual History," 27.

26. Foucault, "What Is Enlightenment?," 313.

27. Foucault, "Truth and Power," 126.

28. Foucault, "What Is Critique?," 383.

29. Michel Foucault, "A Preface to Transgression," in *Language, Counter-Memory, Practice: Selected Essays and Interviews*, trans. Donald F. Bouchard and Sherry Simon, ed. Donald F. Bouchard (Ithaca, NY: Cornell University Press, 1977), 36.

30. Michel Foucault, "Questions of Method," trans. Colin Gordon, in *The Foucault Effect*, 84.

31. Especially Gaston Bachelard (1884–1962) and Georges Canguilhem (1904–95). In this connection, see Gary Gutting, *Michel Foucault's Archaeology of Scientific Reason* (Cambridge: Cambridge University Press, 1989), 9–54.

32. Han, *Foucault's Critical Project*, 1 (although, importantly, see xiii for her own reservations on this score).

33. Michel Foucault, *The Order of Things: An Archaeology of the Human Sciences*, trans. Alan Sheridan (New York: Vintage Books, 1994), xiv.

34. See Hubert Dreyfus and Paul Rabinow, *Michel Foucault: Beyond Structuralism and Hermeneutics*, 2nd ed. (Chicago: University of Chicago Press, 1983), 48–49.

35. See Michel Foucault, "Politics and the Study of Discourse," in *The Foucault Effect*, 65; cf. Foucault, "On Power," in *Politics, Philosophy, Culture*, 106–7.

36. Foucault frequently employs the historical periodization of the Renaissance, the Classical Age, and modernity, although he is not always precise in his dating of the various periods. For example, in his *History of Madness* he is quite precise: the experience of madness in the Renaissance ends with the birth of the Classical Age, which Foucault dates from the founding of the Hôpital Général in 1657, while the modern experience of madness begins with Pinel's liberation of the mad from Bicêtre in 1794. See Michel Foucault, *History of Madness*, trans. Jonathan Murphy and Jean Khalfa (Abingdon, UK: Routledge, 2006), xxxiii. On the other hand, in *The Order of Things* he dates the commencement of the Classical Age to "roughly half-way through the seventeenth century" and the commencement of the modern era from "the beginning of the nineteenth century" (xxii).

37. Michel Foucault, *The Archaeology of Knowledge*, trans. A. M. Sheridan Smith (London: Routledge, 1972), 49.

38. See generally Michel Foucault, "Orders of Discourse," trans. Rupert Swyer, *Social Science Information* 10, no. 2 (1971).

39. Michel Foucault, "Letter to D. Defert," quoted in Paras, *Foucault 2.0*, 174n3.

40. Foucault, "Politics and the Study of Discourse," 59–60 (emphasis in original).

41. Ibid., 61.

42. Foucault, *The Archaeology of Knowledge*, 46.

43. Ibid., 44–45.

44. Ibid., 55.

45. How we interpret the shift in Foucault's method often depends on whether it is understood as the unfolding of a logic strictly endogenous to the works themselves or as a response to contemporary social and political events (such as the events of May 1968, for example). The standard textualist interpretation of the shift is provided by Dreyfus and Rabinow, who argue that Foucault's archaeological method suffers from a series of "methodological failures." In their opinion, the most important of archaeology's failures is its untenable insistence on the autonomy of discourse itself, the appreciation of which eventually leads Foucault to go in search of other methods in order to explain the institutional control and deployment of discursive knowledge (see *Beyond Structuralism*, 79–100). In contrast to these textualist approaches, Eric Paras has recently, and persuasively, argued for an interpretation of Foucault's "genealogical turn" that addresses the importance of contemporary social and political events and the way in which Foucault, in response to these currents, imports a series of Nietzschean, Deleuzian, and Marxist concepts into his own conceptual apparatus (see *Foucault 2.0*, 46–71).

46. Foucault, "Orders of Discourse," 11.

47. Foucault, *Discipline and Punish*, 27.

48. Hoffman, *Foucault and Power*, 1.

49. A recent example of an engagement with Foucault that reads him as a "conceptual" as opposed to "historical" thinker of power is Magnus Hörnqvist, *Risk, Power and the State: After Foucault* (Abingdon, UK: Routledge, 2010).

50. Foucault, "Critical Theory/Intellectual History," 38–39.

51. Foucault, "The Subject and Power," 326.

52. Foucault, "*Society Must Be Defended*," 6.

53. This has not prevented certain commentators on Foucault, such as Jürgen Habermas, from alleging that Foucault ontologizes power. See "Some Questions," 269–70.

54. See Michel Foucault, *The Use of Pleasure*, vol. 2 of *The History of Sexuality*, trans. Robert Hurley (Harmondsworth, UK: Penguin, 1992), 8–9.

55. Foucault, "The Subject and Power," 336–37.

56. Foucault, "*Society Must Be Defended*," 24.

57. For a contrary view, see Jeff Malpas, "Governing Theory: Ontology, Methodology and the Critique of Metaphysics," in *Rethinking Law, Society and Governance: Foucault's Bequest*, ed. Gary Wickham and George Pavlich (Oxford, UK: Hart Publishing, 2001), 125.

58. Foucault, *The Will to Knowledge*, 82.

59. Most famously, in the first essay of *On the Genealogy of Morality*, Nietzsche locates the origin of contemporary Judaeo-Christian moral practices of empathy and compassion in a petty and disavowed history of cruelty, festering *ressentiment*, and what he calls the "slave morality" of the weak (see Friedrich Nietzsche, *On the Genealogy of Morality*, trans. Maudemarie Clark and Alan J. Swensen [Indianapolis: Hackett, 1998]). The critical aim of Nietzsche's counter-history is precisely to arrest and disrupt the taken-for-granted-ness of the value of Judaeo-Christian morality in the present and to subject the prevailing contemporary values of his time to a counter- or transvaluation. He achieves

this rhetorically by impugning the traditional origin of Judaeo-Christian morality, suggesting it is born not in a glorious beginning but rather in a *"pudenda origo"* (Friedrich Nietzsche, *The Will to Power*, trans. Walter Kauffmann and R. J. Hollingdale [New York: Random House, 1969], § 254 [emphasis in original]). Similarly, in *Discipline and Punish*, Foucault's own book-length genealogy of the power to punish in the modern West, the counter-narrative Foucault provides (to received Whiggish accounts) of the rise of incarceration as a mode of punishment is not based on a "quantitative" increase in humanitarian sentiment ("less cruelty, less pain, more kindness, more respect, more 'humanity'" bestowed upon the prisoner), but on a fundamental change in the way in which power is organized in modernity (see *Discipline and Punish*, 16). For Foucault, "'humanity' is [merely] the respectable name given to this economy and its meticulous calculations," not the origin or engine of moral progress (ibid., 92). Of course, to avoid the imputation of a genetic fallacy to Nietzsche or Foucault, it must be noted that genealogically exposing and dispersing the origin stories of a given practice or institution does not of itself necessarily invalidate the practice or institution.

60. The relationship between Foucault and Nietzsche—and the fidelity of the former to the latter when it comes to questions such as the proper understanding of genealogy, for instance—is exegetical ground well trodden by both Foucault and Nietzsche scholars. For a critical instance, see Ken Gemes, "Post-Modernism's Use and Abuse of Nietzsche," *Philosophy and Phenomenological Research* 62, no. 2 (2001). Whether or not Foucault illegitimately interprets Nietzsche is itself part of a broader debate concerning the "reception history" of Nietzsche in the twentieth century (especially as it relates to the revisionist readings of Nietzsche pursued in the 1960s by a series of French poststructuralist philosophers such as Foucault, but importantly including Gilles Deleuze, Jacques Derrida, and Sarah Kofman). On this, see David Couzens Hoy, *Critical Resistance: From Poststructuralism to Post-Critique* (Cambridge, MA: MIT Press, 2004), 19–56. Here I pursue what I take to be a fairly uncontroversial line on Foucault's general methodological indebtedness to Nietzsche, even as it is clear that his own particular modulation of genealogy is not (how could it be?) exactly Nietzsche's in all respects. For an excellent disaggregation of the genealogies of Nietzsche ("subversive"), Foucault ("problematizing"), and Bernard Williams ("vindicatory"), see chapter 2 of Koopman, *Genealogy as Critique*. Key to Koopman's account of the force of Foucault's genealogies in the present is an insistence on his part that what Foucault teaches us is *how* (rather than simply *that*) our arrangements are contingently constructed (see 130, 144). For a recent discussion of the Maoist influences on Foucault's turn to genealogy, see Mads Peter Karlsen and Kaspar Villadsen, "Foucault, Maoism, Genealogy: The Influence of Political Militancy in Michel Foucault's Thought," *New Political Science* 37, no. 1 (2015).

61. Michel Foucault, "Nietzsche, Genealogy, History," in *Language, Counter-Memory, Practice*, 140.

62. Ibid.

63. Ibid., 142.

64. Ibid.

65. Ibid., 139.

66. Ibid., 147.

67. Ibid., 153.

68. Ibid.

69. Ibid.

70. Ibid.

71. Ibid., 154.

72. Ibid.

73. Ibid., 151.

74. Ibid., 163.

75. Nietzsche, *On the Genealogy of Morality*, 35.

76. Foucault, *The Will to Knowledge*, 136.

77. Ibid.

78. Ann Laura Stoler aptly observes of Foucault's rhetorical-historiographical method that "one could read [him] as a master at the art of crafting bold dichotomies that he recants as quickly as he sets them up"; see *Race and the Education of Desire: Foucault's "History of Sexuality" and the Colonial Order of Things* (Durham, NC: Duke University Press, 1995), 38. Admittedly, there are ample grounds in Foucault's work for the view that he sees various historical eras as being defined by certain technologies of power and that each era succeeds the previous one at the expense of its (now defunct) definitive technology. See, for one example, Foucault, *The Will to Knowledge*, 147–48. But as Stoler notes, these dichotomous historical contrasts are then just as frequently recanted (as he does with the example just given; see ibid., 149). Hence the more nuanced interpretation is that new modalities of power do not replace earlier ones entirely, but rather "complement," "penetrate," and "permeate" them (Foucault, *"Society Must Be Defended,"* 241) in order to create a more complex arrangement. In this vein, Foucault famously insists that discipline does not supersede sovereignty and that discipline is in its turn not superseded by governmentality, but rather that the different modalities subsist in a "triangulated" relationship. See Foucault, *Security, Territory, Population*, 107.

79. Foucault, *Discipline and Punish*, 220.

80. Ibid., 170.

81. Michel Foucault, *Abnormal: Lectures at the Collège de France 1974–1975*, trans. Graham Burchell (London: Verso, 2003), 87.

82. Foucault, *Discipline and Punish*, 194.

83. Ibid., 217.

84. Foucault consistently maintained a conceptual distinction between a disciplinary *norm* and a legal *rule*. Whereas a law divides a possible range of acts or behaviors into the binary categories of the permitted and the forbidden, a norm distributes individuals along a continuum, such that one embodies a norm errantly or imperfectly, rather than, strictly speaking, failing to observe or transgressing it. For Foucault, norms are not imposed externally upon a social group but arise immanently from their social practices. They are formulated through the local observation of different groups and their various aptitudes and capacities, and this knowledge is then fed back, so to speak, into the management of those groups and used as a tool to inculcate and propagate cer-

tain behaviors. It is in this sense that, for him, norms are more formative of subjectivity than are juridical rules. For discussion, see François Ewald, "Norms, Discipline, and the Law," trans. Marjorie Beale, in *Law and the Order of Culture*, ed. Robert Post (Berkeley: University of California Press, 1991). This distinction between norms and legal rules is part of a wider debate about the relationship of law to disciplinary power in Foucault's thought. See Hunt and Wickham, *Foucault and Law*; and Ben Golder and Peter Fitzpatrick, *Foucault's Law* (Abingdon, UK: Routledge, 2009).

85. Foucault, *Discipline and Punish*, 222.

86. Ibid., 223.

87. See, for example, Michel Foucault, "About the Concept of the 'Dangerous Individual' in Nineteenth-Century Legal Psychiatry," in *Essential Works of Foucault*, vol. 3, *Power*, for a historical discussion of this trend in French criminal law.

88. While the first contemporary usage of the term is generally attributed to Foucault, biopolitics, ironically, is nowhere in his work given a full articulation. It is discussed in a fairly schematic and cursory way in *The Will to Knowledge* and *"Society Must Be Defended"* compared to the historical and conceptual detail in which subjects such as disciplinary power or governmentality are described. Subsequent to Foucault's usage of the term in the late 1970s, however, the thematic of biopolitics has become a productive one in much critical theory and continental philosophy, and has given rise to a range of very different analyses by thinkers such as Giorgio Agamben, Michael Hardt and Antonio Negri, and Roberto Esposito, to name only the most prominent. For a helpful recent discussion of the critical post-Foucauldian afterlives of the concept, see Thomas Lemke, *Biopolitics: An Advanced Introduction* (New York: NYU Press, 2011). See also Paul Rabinow and Nikolas Rose, "Biopower Today," *BioSocieties* 1, no. 2 (2006).

89. See Foucault, *Security, Territory, Population*, 100–101. See also Ian Hacking, "How Should We Do the History of Statistics?," in *The Foucault Effect*. I am in agreement with Colin Koopman about the contingent, and not necessary, relationship between statistics and biopolitics (see his "Michel Foucault's Critical Empiricism Today: Concepts and Analytics in the Critique of Biopower and Infopower," in *Foucault Now: Critical Perspectives in Foucault Studies*, ed. James Faubion [Cambridge, UK: Polity, 2014], 99–100).

90. Foucault, *"Society Must Be Defended,"* 246. It must be remembered that the population is not conceived of as a unitary phenomenon. Foucault's brief analysis of racism in the last of his 1976 lectures indicates that biopolitics envisages the splitting of the population—which for Foucault represents the very principle of racism—such that some must be killed in order for others to live (see *"Society Must Be Defended,"* 254–63). On this, see also Giorgio Agamben, *Remnants of Auschwitz: The Witness and the Archive*, trans. Daniel Heller-Roazen (New York: Zone Books, 2002), 82–86. The idea of internally dividing the population recurs in *Security, Territory, Population*, although it is not figured in explicitly racial terms there; rather, the split is between the "pertinent" and the "instrumental" levels of the population (see *Security, Territory, Population*, 42).

91. Foucault, *The Will to Knowledge*, 103.

92. Foucault, *"Society Must Be Defended,"* 246.

93. Foucault, *Security, Territory, Population*, 107.

94. Foucault, *The Will to Knowledge*, 139.

95. See references in the Introduction, nn. 24–25.

96. See Foucault, *The Will to Knowledge*, 15–49.

97. Ibid., 83.

98. Ibid., 85 (emphasis in original).

99. Foucault, *"Society Must Be Defended,"* 26.

100. Foucault, *The Will to Knowledge*, 86.

101. Judith Butler, "Sexual Inversions," in *Foucault and the Critique of Institutions*, ed. John Caputo and Mark Yount (University Park: Pennsylvania State University Press, 1993), 86–87 (emphasis in original).

102. Foucault, *The Will to Knowledge*, 94.

103. Foucault, *The Archaeology of Knowledge*, 15.

104. Ibid., 22.

105. Ibid., 25. Foucault's contemporary, Maurice Blanchot, appreciates the point: "And were not his own principles more complex than his official discourse, with its striking formulations, led one to think? For example, it is accepted as a certainty that Foucault, adhering in this to a certain conception of literary production, got rid of, purely and simply, the notion of the subject: no more oeuvre, no more author, no more creative unity. But things are not that simple. The subject does not disappear; rather its excessively determined unity is put in question" (Maurice Blanchot, "Michel Foucault as I Imagine Him," in *Foucault/Blanchot*, trans. Jeffrey Mehlman [New York: Zone Books, 1990], 76).

106. For example, see Davidson, "In Praise," 26; Thomas Lemke, "Foucault, Governmenality, and Critique," *Rethinking Marxism* 14, no. 3 (2002): 50.

107. Indeed, Davidson argues that "without access to these courses, it was extremely difficult to understand Foucault's reorientation from an analysis of the strategies and tactics of power immanent in the modern discourse on sexuality to an analysis of the ancient forms and modalities of relation to oneself by which one constituted oneself as a moral subject of sexual conduct" ("In Praise," 26).

108. Michel Foucault, "Technologies of the Self," in *Essential Works of Foucault*, vol. 1, *Ethics*, 225.

109. The work of scholars such as Nikolas Rose and Peter Miller, as well as some of the pioneering translation and interpretive work of Colin Gordon and Graham Burchell, has been central to the reception, popularization, and application of Foucault's work on governmentality (often featured in the pages of the journal *Economy & Society*). Two edited collections in English are of particular note: *The Foucault Effect* and *Foucault and Political Reason: Liberalism, Neo-Liberalism and Rationalities of Government*, ed. Andrew Barry, Thomas Osborne, and Nikolas Rose (London: Routledge, 1996). For some of the seminal early scholarship of Rose and Miller, see Nikolas Rose, "The Death of the Social?: Re-Figuring the Territory of Government," *Economy & Society* 25, no. 3 (1996); Peter Miller and Nikolas Rose, "Governing Economic Life," *Economy & Society* 19, no. 1 (1990); and Nikolas Rose and Peter Miller, "Political Power Beyond the State: Problematics of Government," *British Journal of Sociology* 43, no. 2 (1992). For a compre-

hensive summary of Foucault's ideas and their subsequent development in the context of "governmentality studies," see Mitchell Dean, *Governmentality: Power and Rule in Modern Society*, 2nd ed. (London: SAGE, 2010).

110. First published in English in the journal *Ideology & Consciousness* in 1979, the lecture was reprinted and revised as Michel Foucault, "Governmentality," trans. Colin Gordon, in *The Foucault Effect*.

111. Michel Foucault, "Two Lectures," in *Power/Knowledge*. Foucault's wish, expressed in a letter sent a year before he died and interpreted as his literary will, was that there should be no "posthumous publication" of his work. Nevertheless, the publication and translation of his lecture courses into English has proceeded on the assumption that his work of this period was, if not published in written form, nevertheless "in the public domain" (they were given as public lectures, and recorded on audio cassettes). For a discussion of the theoretical issues surrounding the use of the lecture courses for Foucault scholarship, see Brad Elliott Stone, "Defending Society from the Abnormal: The Archaeology of Bio-Power," *Foucault Studies* 1 (2004): 77–79.

112. Foucault, *Security, Territory, Population*, 215.

113. Such critics obviously included proponents of materialist state theory and those Marxists who felt that Foucault had failed to take proper account of the repressive role of the state in his analysis of modern power relations. See, for example, Nicos Poulantzas, *State, Power, Socialism*, trans. Patrick Camiller (London: Verso, 2000), 77. In a number of interviews at this time Foucault stresses that he had not failed to account for the state apparatus, but that his analytic focus simply lay elsewhere (that is to say, on governmental practice): "I don't claim at all that the State apparatus is unimportant" and "I don't want to say that the State isn't important; what I want to say is that relations of power, and hence the analysis that must be made of them, necessarily extend beyond the limits of the State" (Michel Foucault, "Body/Power," in *Power/Knowledge*, 60; Foucault, "Truth and Power," 122). However, the 1978 lecture course constitutes a fuller and more theoretically robust response than these brief remarks.

114. Gordon, "Governmental Rationality," 4.

115. Foucault, *Security, Territory, Population*, 247–48.

116. See generally Paul Veyne, "Foucault Revolutionizes History," trans. Catherine Porter, in *Foucault and His Interlocutors*, ed. Arnold I. Davidson (Chicago: University of Chicago Press, 1997).

117. Foucault, *Security, Territory, Population*, 248.

118. Foucault, *"Society Must Be Defended,"* 27.

119. Foucault, *Security, Territory, Population*, 106.

120. Foucault, "The Subject and Power," 341.

121. Foucault, *Security, Territory, Population*, 193.

122. Davidson, "In Praise," 26–27.

123. Michel Foucault, "Power and Strategies," in *Power/Knowledge*, 138.

124. For more on the lecture course as a whole and its relation to Foucault's work at the time, see Ben Golder, "Foucault and the Genealogy of Pastoral Power," *Radical Philosophy Review* 10, no. 2 (2007).

125. Much of the material on the historical development of the Christian pastorate, on *raison d'État*, and on the statist doctrine of *police*, was also delivered in the form of public lectures in the United States (for example, see Michel Foucault, "The Political Technology of Individuals," and "'*Omnes et Singulatim*': Toward a Critique of Political Reason," both in *Essential Works of Foucault*, vol. 3, *Power*).

126. Foucault, *Security, Territory, Population*, 223.

127. Ibid., 223, 247.

128. Ibid., 173–79. In the seventh of the 1978 lectures (22 February 1978), Foucault discusses the Christian pastorate in more detail. In addition to the general aspects of pastoral power just discussed, the pastorate is characterized by the following further elements: first, the principle of "analytical responsibility," according to which the pastor must account for "every act of each of his sheep, for everything that may have happened between them, and everything good and evil they may have done at any time" (229); second, the principle of "exhaustive and instantaneous transfer," according to which the merits and demerits of each individual sheep are imputed to the pastor (229–30); third, the principle of "sacrificial reversal," under which the pastor must be prepared to sacrifice himself in order to save his sheep (230–31); and finally, the principle of "alternate correspondence," according to which the merits of the sheep, and their prospects of salvation, are increased in inverse proportion to the failings of their pastor, and vice versa, the pastor rises in the eyes of the Lord, and will assure his own salvation, if he has struggled with a recalcitrant flock (231–32).

129. Ibid., 242.

130. Ibid., 245.

131. Ibid.

132. Ibid., 194.

133. Ibid., 204.

134. Ibid., 205.

135. Ibid.

136. Ibid., 208.

137. Ibid., 207.

138. Ibid.

139. Foucault, *The Will to Knowledge*, 95 (emphasis added).

140. Ibid., 96.

141. For a helpful summary of some of these critical readings of Foucault on resistance, see John Muckelbauer, "On Reading Differently: Through Foucault's Resistance," *College English* 63, no. 1 (2000).

142. Some of these differing views are discussed and critiqued in Hoffman, *Foucault and Power*, 1.

143. Michel Foucault, quoted in Rex Martin, "Truth, Power, Self: An Interview with Michel Foucault," in *Technologies of the Self: A Seminar with Michel Foucault*, ed. Luther H. Martin, Huck Gutman, and Patrick H. Hutton (Amherst: University of Massachusetts Press, 1988), 10.

144. Foucault, *Security, Territory, Population*, 214–15.

145. Foucault begins the lecture on counter-conducts by acknowledging the "external blockages" presented to the pastorate by those resistant to its expansion in the Middle Ages and into the sixteenth century (ibid., 194) and concludes it by observing, in a portion of the written manuscript not read aloud, that his emphasis upon "these tactical elements that gave precise and recurrent forms to pastoral insubordinations . . . is not in any way so as to suggest that it is a matter of internal struggles, endogenous contradictions, pastoral power devouring itself or encountering the limits and barriers of its operations" but rather to "identify the 'points of entry' (*"les entrées"*) through which processes, conflicts and transformations [external to the pastorate] . . . can enter into the field of exercise of the pastorate" (ibid., 216).

146. Foucault, *"Society Must Be Defended,"* 40.

147. Pickett, *Use and Abuse,* 77–99; Mourad, "After Foucault," 452–53.

Chapter 2

The epigraph to this chapter is from Wendy Brown, "Suffering Rights as Paradoxes," *Constellations* 7, no. 2 (2000): 240.

1. The thinkers I engage with most closely toward the end of this chapter and in the following one are Judith Butler, Jacques Rancière, and Wendy Brown. This by no means exhausts the range of those who theorize rights as groundless. For a further postfoundationalist discussion of human rights, see the account given by the neopragmatist Richard Rorty in his "Human Rights, Rationality, and Sentimentality," in *On Human Rights.*

2. See Foucault, *Discipline and Punish,* 3–6; and *The Order of Things,* xv. For more on Foucault's genealogical uses of rhetoric, see William E. Connolly, "Taylor, Foucault, and Otherness," *Political Theory* 13, no. 3 (1985): 368; and Bernstein, "Critique as a Philosophical Ethos," 222–26.

3. The common and perhaps deliberate misunderstanding of the first passage cited is that Foucault is advocating some broad anti-humanist thesis that celebrates the dissolution of the human or else is somehow opposed to creative or agentive human action. Rather, here and elsewhere in *The Order of Things* Foucault is making a much more specific critique of a figure of "man" (referable to Kant), in which the human becomes simultaneously both the (finite) object of knowledge and the (transcendental) condition of possibility of knowledge (in his terms, an "empirico-transcendental doublet"). Here he is stressing the paradoxes and contingencies of such a figure, which he does not equate with human possibility or with the human as such. Instead, such a conception of "man" is a discursive product of the modern episteme that in his view is coming to a close. As a result, it will be replaced by other conceptions of human possibility, self-understanding, and relationality. For the quotation above, see Foucault, *The Order of Things,* 318. On Foucault and anti-humanism more broadly, see nn. 77–81 below, and text accompanying.

4. Foucault, *The Order of Things,* 387; Foucault, "Confronting Governments: Human Rights," 475.

5. Wolin, "Foucault the Neohumanist?," 106.

6. See Foucault, "On Power," 100.

7. Dosse, *History of Structuralism*, 2:336–38.

8. Ibid., 336. Dosse is right to discern a contemporary political motivation for Foucault's particular return to Greece. It is important to stress that for Foucault, as for Nietzsche before him, classical studies could have no meaning if they were not *untimely*—in the sense, as the latter elegantly puts it, of "acting counter to our time and thereby acting on our time and, let us hope, for the benefit of a time to come" ("On the Uses and Disadvantages of History for Life," in *Untimely Meditations*, trans. R. J. Hollingdale, ed. Daniel Breazeale [Cambridge: Cambridge University Press, 1997], 60). Historical study is directly political for both thinkers, but it does not follow that Foucault seeks to exhume the Greeks as some kind of normative political model for the present (and future). What his study of ancient antiquity is intended to provide is a new way of thinking about subjectivity and not some kind of ready-made, directly transposable historical solution for the problems of the present; not a renaissance, that is, but rather a problematization of the present through the past. See his comments in Michel Foucault, "On the Genealogy of Ethics: An Overview of Work in Progress," in Dreyfus and Rabinow, *Beyond Structuralism*, 231–32, 234. What is the political motivation for Foucault's return to ancient Greece? He understands that the political technologies of modernity (such as discipline and biopolitics) function at least in part by subjects internalizing and acting upon a "true" understanding of themselves (a form of political "hermeneutics of the subject" that in a late lecture he calls "the government of individuals by their own verity" [Foucault, "*Omnes et Singulatim*," 312]. Hence the motivation for the late investigation of ethics is to derive a model of relation to self that disrupts these relations between subjectivity and truth, and delinks the subject from a true core or essence (insisting instead on the subject as unfinished). We might call this a critical politics of *de*subjectification (see Foucault, "What Is Critique?," 386). The Greeks, Foucault insists, present a more promising avenue (through their notions of ascesis and aesthetics) for the contemporary realization of this project of inventing and creating a subject anew, as opposed to discovering it or attesting to its truth. I discuss the concept of ethics as an "aesthetics of existence" in n. 27 below, and take it up further in the context of the right to die in Chapter 4.

9. Dosse, *History of Structuralism*, 2:336.

10. Paras, *Foucault 2.0*, 4.

11. Ibid., 12.

12. Ibid., 14.

13. Ibid., 101.

14. Ibid., 156.

15. Ibid., 12.

16. Ibid., 155. The media phenomenon of the *nouveaux philosophes* is excellently discussed by Julian Bourg in *From Revolution to Ethics*, 225–333, whose treatment commences with Maurice Clavel and concludes with the better-known protagonists Bernard-Henri Lévy and André Glucksmann. It is largely due to Foucault's glowing three-page book review and endorsement of the latter's *Les maîtres penseurs* in 1977 in the pages of *Le nouvel observateur* that many have asserted a fundamental kinship be-

tween Foucault and the *nouveaux philosophes*. In his *Foucault 2.0* Paras emphasizes that Foucault was "closely aligned" (78) with them, while Michael Scott Christofferson, in his otherwise helpful *French Intellectuals Against the Left*, at one point uses the phrase "Glucksmann's Foucauldian politics" (187). While there is no denying Foucault's endorsement of Glucksmann's book, and indeed their shared critique of a certain Marxism and opposition to communism, Paras and Christofferson are far too quick to assimilate Foucault's genealogical and critical politics to the moralistic, Manichaean, state-phobic liberalism of the *nouveaux philosophes*. Bourg puts it nicely: for Foucault, after the publication of *Discipline and Punish*, "New Philosophy was . . . [merely a] passing engagement" (240).

17. Paras, *Foucault 2.0*, 21.

18. Ibid., 45.

19. The best-known contemporary example of such a politics of performative resignification is doubtless Judith Butler's work in gender studies and queer theory, commencing with *Gender Trouble: Feminism and the Subversion of Identity* (New York: Routledge, 1990) and thematized most directly in *Excitable Speech: A Politics of the Performative* (New York: Routledge, 1997). Butler draws (not uncritically) on Foucault's genealogical approach (as well as on Hegel and Lacanian psychoanalysis) in order to "trouble" the putatively naturalized parameters of gender identity. The name of the body of work, as well as the political movement, with which Butler is most frequently associated is itself a good example of the unstable historicity of given names and identity categories. Originally (and still in part) a term of homophobic abuse, "queer" has subsequently been reappropriated as the basis of a political movement that itself not only affirms what was previously reviled in the name but also contests and aims to transcend the heteronormative binary of "gay" and "straight" itself.

20. Foucault, *The Use of Pleasure*; Michel Foucault, *The Care of the Self*, vol. 3 of *The History of Sexuality*, trans. Robert Hurley (Harmondsworth, UK: Penguin Books, 1990). In *The Use of Pleasure* Foucault addresses the problematization of sexual conduct in classical Greece, whereas in *The Care of the Self* he focuses on these practices in Hellenistic, or late, antiquity. In that latter work, focusing on Stoic texts, he discerns "a certain strengthening of austerity themes" (235) that separates late antiquity from classical Greece with respect to the problematization of sexual pleasure, but he nevertheless does not read this heightened austerity as a simple historical precursor of Christian ethics (the topic of what was to be volume 4 of *The History of Sexuality*). For him, there remains a great divide between ancient and Christian modes of subjectification (see Foucault, *The Care of the Self*, 235–40).

21. These are, in chronological order, Michel Foucault, *Du gouvernement des vivants: Cours au Collège de France, 1979–1980* (Paris: Seuil, 2012); Michel Foucault, *Subjectivité et vérité: Cours au Collège de France, 1980–1981* (Paris: Seuil, 2014); Michel Foucault, *The Hermeneutics of the Subject: Lectures at the Collège de France, 1981–1982*, trans. Graham Burchell (New York: Picador, 2005); Michel Foucault, *The Government of Self and Others: Lectures at the Collège de France, 1982–1983*, trans. Graham Burchell (Basingstoke, UK: Palgrave Macmillan, 2010); and Michel Foucault, *The Courage of Truth:*

Lectures at the Collège de France, trans. Graham Burchell (Basingstoke, UK: Palgrave Macmillan, 2011).

22. Foucault, "On the Genealogy of Ethics," 237–38.

23. Ibid., 238–43, 238, 239.

24. See Michel Foucault, "Friendship as a Way of Life," in *Essential Works of Foucault 1954–1984*, vol. 1, *Ethics*, 137.

25. It is important to stress the masculine pronoun here, for one of the patently objectionable elements of this ethical project as it was practiced in ancient Greece (and an issue for its contemporary actualization and generalization) was its constitutive sexism and exclusivity. For a feminist viewpoint on the late work, see *Feminism and the Final Foucault*, ed. Diana Taylor and Karen Vintges (Urbana: University of Illinois Press, 2004).

26. See generally Foucault, "Technologies of the Self."

27. The ancient *technē tou biou*, or "aesthetics of existence" as Foucault has it, has proved consistently vexing for readers of the late work. In the interview with Dreyfus and Rabinow cited above, he reminds his interlocutors that "the principal aim, the principal target of this kind of ethics, was an aesthetic one" (Foucault, "On the Genealogy of Ethics," 230). By this he meant that the Greeks acted to "give to their life certain values (reproduce certain examples, leave behind them an exalted reputation, give the maximum possible brilliance to their lives). It was a question of making one's life into an object for a sort of knowledge, for a *techne*—for an art" (245; emphasis in original). In summary, ethics was fundamentally concerned with the "elaboration of one's own life as a personal work of art" (Michel Foucault, "An Aesthetics of Existence," in *Politics, Philosophy, Culture*, 49). And yet Foucault does not simply describe the ethical project in aesthetic terms, but commends it as a possible critical resource in the present (especially in the context of his interventions into gay politics and debates about gay subjectivity, which I discuss in detail in Chapter 3). "The idea of the *bios* as a material for an aesthetic piece of art is something which fascinates me," he writes. "Why should the lamp or the house be an art object, but not our life?" (Foucault, "On the Genealogy of Ethics," 235, 236; emphasis in original). What does he mean by describing (and commending) ethics in these terms? Two main lines of criticism have been leveled at him in this regard. The first, informed by a Habermasian desire to keep the aesthetic lifeworld in its proper cognitive place, is concerned with the "pan-aestheticism" of Foucault's proposal, which amounts at best to a ludic, dandyish, and unserious form of ethico-political action in the world and at worst tends potentially toward fascism (see Richard Wolin, "Foucault's Aesthetic Decisionism," in *Michel Foucault: Critical Assessments*, vol. 3, ed. Barry Smart [London: Routledge, 1994]). The other, informed by the Marxist concern that such aestheticization of the ethical constitutes a retreat from properly political action, is worried about the reinforcement of social atomization and the failure to engage with late capitalist modes of production that this model of action implies (see Dews, "The Return of the Subject," 40; and Alex Callinicos, *Against Postmodernism* [Cambridge, UK: Polity, 1989], 91). These currents are of course neither mutually exclusive (see Terry Eagleton, *The Ideology of the Aesthetic* [Oxford, UK: Blackwell, 1990], 366–418) nor exhaustive of

the criticisms made of the late ethical project, but they do rest on misreadings of Foucault's texts. These misreadings are best addressed in O'Leary, *Foucault and the Art of Ethics*, 121–38, where it is argued that Foucault's understanding of the "aesthetic" should be understood in the sense of *travail* and not *oeuvre*, that is, that the project of ethically working upon oneself does not represent the attempt to perfect oneself and to render oneself a beautiful whole, but is intended to capture through metaphor the experience of the ongoing and always-incomplete task of self-critique and desubjectification entailed in escaping from disciplinary and biopolitical logics and modes of subjectification.

28. Paras, *Foucault 2.0*, 14.

29. Foucault, *The Birth of Biopolitics*, 20.

30. Paras, *Foucault 2.0*, 104. In a provocative and powerful rereading of the late Foucault, Michael C. Behrent argues that while Foucault turns approvingly to liberalism at this time, it is precisely because the economic liberalism of the neoliberals (who are the subject of the 1979 Collège lectures) dispenses with the anthropological presuppositions of political liberalism that he can "strategically endorse" the latter ("Liberalism Without Humanism," 567). Behrent thus argues that Foucault makes a turn to liberalism, but this argument reaches what looks like a similar conclusion to that of Paras (namely, that the late Foucault is a liberal) by taking a very different argumentative route. Behrent proceeds by separating the doctrines of political and economic liberalism, by conceding that Foucault continues his critique of subjectivity into the late work (*contra* Paras) but that (now *contra* me) this by no means prevents him from becoming (an economic) liberal (546). For Behrent, it is precisely because the economic liberalism of the neoliberal thinkers does not rest upon any anthropological assumptions about human nature or essence that their theories are acceptable to Foucault, whose critique of humanist subjectivity continues unabated into the late work. If this is what renders economic liberalism acceptable to him, Behrent argues that what attracts Foucault to the neoliberals is a shared theoretical and normative (political) opposition to the state (545). Behrent's novel and provocative reading is both helpful and, in my view, flawed. It is helpful because it forces us to attend to the political limits of an anti-essentialist critique of subjectivity. Such a critique, Behrent teaches us, need not necessarily lead one to oppose forms of economic inequality and exploitation (or always and uniformly be useful for such a project). But Behrent's attribution to Foucault of an endorsement—even a "strategic" one—of neoliberalism is too strong, in my view. I think Behrent's reading mistakes the genealogical tone of the 1979 lectures for fascination and normative approval, but more seriously, I think he overplays what he perceives as Foucault's normative opposition to the state and state power (when in fact Foucault's theoretical work tries to problematize but not evacuate or reject the state, and his political work with rights shows his continued yet critical engagement with the mechanisms of state power). But if I could suggest my own critique of Behrent's operative distinction between an economic liberalism denuded of humanism and a political liberalism dependent upon it, I think it is just as arguable that when neoliberal thinking (which surely encompasses both the political and the economic) "configure[s the human being] exhaustively as *homo oeconomicus*," it is reliant upon a form of, if not quite "political metaphysics," then at least a strong-

form claim about the human *qua* rational agent that is equally as susceptible to genealogical problematization as the traditional humanist entailments of political liberalism. For the last two quotations, see Wendy Brown, *Edgework: Critical Essays on Knowledge and Power* (Princeton, NJ: Princeton University Press, 2005), 40; and Andrew Zimmerman, "Foucault in Berkeley and Magnitogorsk: Totalitarianism and the Limits of Liberal Critique," *Contemporary European History* 23, no. 2 (2014): 236. For Behrent's related and fascinating treatment of François Ewald's intellectual trajectory, see "Accidents Happen: François Ewald, the 'Antirevolutionary' Foucault, and the Intellectual Politics of the French Welfare State," *Journal of Modern History* 82, no. 3 (2010).

31. Paras, *Foucault 2.0*, 122 (emphasis in original).

32. Nietzsche, *On the Genealogy of Morality*, 25.

33. Paras, *Foucault 2.0*, 122–23 (emphasis in original).

34. Foucault, "Technologies of the Self," 225.

35. Jon Simons glosses such readings when he writes that in places Foucault has become "a prophet of entrapment who induces despair by indicating that there is no way out of our subjection" (Jon Simons, *Foucault & the Political* [London: Routledge, 1995], 3).

36. Paras, *Foucault 2.0*, 4.

37. Foucault, *Discipline and Punish*, 202–3.

38. See Peter Fitzpatrick, "Foucault's Case: Subject and Subjection in Law," in *Michel Foucault: Critical Assessments*, vol. 7, ed. Barry Smart (London: Routledge, 1995), 225.

39. Michel Foucault, "The Ethics of the Concern for Self as a Practice of Freedom," in *Essential Works of Foucault*, vol. 1, *Ethics*, 291.

40. Ibid., 290.

41. Judith Butler, "What Is Critique?: An Essay on Foucault's Virtue," in *The Judith Butler Reader*, ed. Sara Salih (with Judith Butler) (Oxford, UK: Blackwell, 2004), 320.

42. Ibid., 321.

43. See the texts cited in the Introduction, n. 62.

44. "Let us recall first of all that the term 'agent,'" writes Perry Anderson, "recalls a curious ambiguity in ordinary usage, possessing two opposite connotations. It signifies at once active initiator and passive instrument" (*Arguments Within English Marxism* [London: New Left Books, 1980], 18). It is this constitutive ambivalence of the notion of "agency" that will lead a poststructuralist theorist such as Judith Butler, thinking with Foucault, to prefer the term "agency" to "autonomy" or "sovereignty" whenever describing the subject's capacity to answer back, to resist, or to reframe the norms by which she is constituted. Agency in this sense is not the property of a subject (something it either does or does not have), but rather references the condition of subjectivity. As she writes in *Giving an Account of Oneself*, her most serious attempt to articulate poststructuralist notions of agency and responsibility:

> The norm does not produce the subject as its necessary effect, nor is the subject fully free to disregard the norm that inaugurates its reflexivity; one invariably struggles with conditions of one's own life that one could not have chosen. If there is an operation of agency or, indeed, freedom in this struggle, it takes place in the context

of an enabling and limiting field of constraint. This ethical agency is neither fully determined nor radically free. Its struggle or primary dilemma is to be produced by a world, even as one must produce oneself in some way. This struggle with the un-chosen conditions of one's life, a struggle—an agency—is also made possible, para-doxically, by the persistence of this primary condition of unfreedom. Whereas many critics have claimed that the view of the subject proffered by Foucault—and other poststructuralists—undermines the capacity to conduct ethical deliberations and to ground human agency, Foucault turns both to agency and to deliberation in new ways in his so-called ethical writings and offers a reformulation of each that deserves serious consideration. (*Giving an Account of Oneself* [New York: Fordham University Press, 2004], 19)

I shall revisit these issues at length in Chapter 3, space limitations preventing a fuller discussion of Butler's argument in this context. However, her reason for why the "norm does not produce the subject as its necessary effect" is the citational and temporal struc-ture of normalization. Norms are reiterated through time, cited again and anew, as in-deed they must be if they are to "work" as norms. But in this "working" they are also serially "unworked," for they necessarily differ in each iteration, and this slippage opens the possibility of their overturning or displacement. What we might call the agential possibilities disclosed by the temporality of normalization is a theme in Butler's early work (from at least *Gender Trouble* onward), but for an explicit discussion of the issue, which brings Foucault into dialogue with Derrida, see *Bodies That Matter: On the Dis-cursive Limits of "Sex"* (New York: Routledge, 1993), 244–46n8.

45. This problematic of "rights inflation" is one that recurs in engagements with rights from both the political right (Mary Ann Glendon, *Rights Talk: The Impoverish-ment of Political Discourse* [New York: Free Press, 1991]) and the political left (Douzinas, *The End of Human Rights*).

46. Johannes Morsink, *Inherent Human Rights: Philosophical Roots of the Universal Declaration* (Philadelphia: University of Pennsylvania Press, 2009), 1.

47. Patton, "Foucault, Critique and Rights," 269.

48. See Donnelly, *Universal Human Rights*, 1.

49. Francis Fukuyama, *Our Posthuman Future: Consequences of the Biotechnology Revolution* (London: Penguin, 2002), 101.

50. Foucault, "Vérité, pouvoir et soi," 1598.

51. Reynolds, "'Pragmatic Humanism,'" 971.

52. For a useful historical account of the Iranian revolution that not only provides context for Foucault's journalistic interventions but also translates into English some previously untranslated articles, see Afary and Anderson, *Foucault and the Iranian Rev-olution*. The authors are highly critical of Foucault's interpretation of the events he cov-ered for *Corriere della sera* and seek to relate this critique to trends in his own philoso-phy. This latter aspect of their reading is fundamentally misguided—relying as it does upon the false imputation to Foucault of a valorization of pre-modern, mystical, and Oriental social forms (as against Western secularism and rationalism) and a misreading of what he understood by "limit experiences." In this latter respect it draws upon the

canonical misreading of Foucault proffered by James Miller in his *The Passion of Michel Foucault* (Cambridge, MA: Harvard University Press, 1993). For a much more nuanced reading of Foucault's work on Iran, see Bonnie Honig, "What Foucault Saw at the Revolution: On the Use and Abuse of Theology for Politics," *Political Theory* 36, no. 2 (2008).

53. Foucault, "Open Letter," 439.

54. Ibid., 439–40.

55. Ibid., 440.

56. Ibid., 441.

57. David Macey, *The Lives of Michel Foucault: A Biography* (New York: Vintage Books, 1993), 445.

58. Foucault, "Moral and Social Experience," 469.

59. Ibid., 471.

60. Eribon, *Michel Foucault*, 279.

61. Foucault, "Confronting Governments."

62. The best-known discussion of this short text is by Thomas Keenan and Paul Patton. See Keenan, "The 'Paradox' of Knowledge and Power"; and Paul Patton, "Power and Right in Nietzsche and Foucault," *International Studies in Philosophy* 36, no. 3 (2004) (and see also Patton, "Foucault, Critique and Rights"). Patton's work on Foucault, Nietzsche, and rights is part of a broader argument about a "naturalist" conception of rights (which understands rights as grounded in elements of the social and historical world). However, in "Power and Right in Nietzsche and Foucault," he takes issue with Keenan's reading of Foucault's "Confonting Governments" text. Keenan provides a Derridean reading of the text, emphasizing its performative character as a declaration of rights. For Patton, however illuminating it might otherwise be, such an emphasis "nevertheless ignores the conditions which make possible the emergence of this right" (55). These conditions include shifts in global politics and the rise of transnational civil society groups such as Amnesty International. For me, the salient question is not whether either is correct in his emphasis, but whether rights—irreducibly dependent upon the matrix of power relations from which they emerge (per Patton)— can nevertheless work a change in those relations and thereby bring new relations and new worlds into being (per Keenan). Put differently, this is of course the question of whether forms of counter-conduct can ever seriously break with the political logic of the forms of government to which they are indebted and out of which they emerge. See also on these issues Cadman, "How (Not) to Be Governed"; Whyte, "Confronting Governments: Human Rights?"; and David Campbell, "Why Fight: Humanitarianism, Principles, and Post-Structuralism," *Millennium: Journal of International Studies* 27, no. 3 (1998).

63. Foucault's use of concepts such as "the rights of the governed" and "human rights" is fundamentally indebted to the ways in which these forms of power are instantiated in particular historical locations and are actually deployed in practice. These are not hermetically sealed categories; rather, they take on variable meanings in practice. Sometimes they might be opposed, at other times converge or overlap. Foucault notably discusses the relationship between the two terms in *The Birth of Biopolitics*. There

he opposes two approaches, both of which aim to limit the practice of government. In the first, which he calls the French revolutionary tradition, juridical limits are imposed upon government based on the respect for original rights. In the second, which Foucault calls the English radical tradition, limits to government are imposed from the perspective of the utility or non-utility of a governmental practice itself. Each tradition works with a different conception of freedom: for the revolutionary tradition, it is conceived as the originary freedom of the subject, but for the radical tradition as the independence of the governed in respect of government. He writes:

> We have therefore two absolutely heterogeneous conceptions of freedom, one based on the rights of man, and the other starting from the independence of the governed. I am not saying that the two systems of the rights of man and of the independence of the governed do not intertwine, but they have different historical origins and I think they are essentially heterogeneous or disparate. With regard to the problem of what are currently called human rights, we would only need to look at where, in what countries, how, and in what form these rights are claimed to see that at times the question is actually the juridical question of rights, and at others it is a question of this assertion or claim of the independence of the governed vis-à-vis governmentality. (*The Birth of Biopolitics*, 42)

64. Foucault, "Confronting Governments," 474–75.

65. Foucault, "The Ethics of the Concern for Self," 290.

66. Michel Foucault, "Useless to Revolt?," in *Essential Works of Foucault*, vol. 3, *Power*, 449.

67. Foucault, "Confronting Governments," 474.

68. Foucault, "Truth and Power," 126.

69. Foucault, "Confronting Governments," 474.

70. Keenan, "The 'Paradox' of Knowledge and Power," 160.

71. Michel Foucault, "Space, Knowledge, and Power," in *Essential Works of Foucault*, vol. 3, *Power*, 354–55 (emphasis in original).

72. For more on the performativity of rights claiming, see generally Zivi, *Making Rights Claims*.

73. Michel Foucault, "Le vrai sexe," in *Dits et écrits II, 1976–1988*, quoted in Philippe Chevallier, "Michel Foucault and the Question of Right," in *Re-Reading Foucault*, 177.

74. Chevallier, "Michel Foucault and the Question of Right," 177.

75. Foucault, "Moral and Social Experience," 465. See also Judith Butler and Gayatri Chakravorty Spivak, *Who Sings the Nation State? Language, Politics, Belonging* (Oxford, UK: Seagull Books, 2007), 64.

76. Anthony C. Alessandrini, "The Humanism Effect: Fanon, Foucault, and Ethics Without Subjects," *Foucault Studies* 7 (2009): 78.

77. Gilles Deleuze, *Foucault*, trans. Seán Hand (London: Continuum, 1999), 77.

78. James Bernauer, "Michel Foucault's Philosophy of Religion: An Introduction to the Non-Fascist Life," in *Michel Foucault and Theology: The Politics of Religious Experience*, ed. James Bernauer and Jeremy Carrette (Aldershot, UK: Ashgate, 2004), 87–88. On Foucault's affirmation of certain human values while critiquing humanism,

see Alexander E. Hooke, "The Order of Others: Is Foucault's Antihumanism Against Human Action?," *Political Theory* 15, no. 1 (1987).

79. Foucault's relationship to humanism is clearly a complex matter that is arguably not amply captured by phrases such as "anti-humanism" (cf. my "What Is an Anti-Humanist Human Rights?," *Social Identities* 16, no. 5 [2010]). As Derrida reminds us:

> To be suspicious about the limits of man is not to be anti-humanist, on the contrary, it's a way of respecting what remains "to come," under the name and the face of what we call "man." You have to be more and more human, and it's not obvious what it means. We are not human enough, we are never human enough, so from that point of view unconditional hospitality is not restricted by what one knows under the name of man or what is proper to man. We have to be hospitable to what is coming, and to a new figure, a new shape of what one calls humanity. (Jacques Derrida, "A Discussion with Jacques Derrida," *Theory & Event* 5, no. 1 [2001]: para. [44])

Irrespective of how one labels Foucault's stance with regard to humanism (and Michael Hardt and Antonio Negri have even referred to it as an "antihumanist (or posthuman) humanism"), the important point is that Foucault operates within humanism and deploys its resources but with an intention to critically refashion and reimagine the meaning of the human. For the quotation, see Michael Hardt and Antonio Negri, *Empire* (Cambridge, MA: Harvard University Press, 2000), 91.

80. Charles E. Scott, "Foucault and the Question of Humanism," in *The Question of Humanism: Challenges and Possibilities*, ed. David Goicoechea, John Luik, and Tim Madigan (Buffalo, NY: Prometheus, 1991), 213.

81. Michel Foucault, quoted in Martin, "Truth, Power, Self," 15.

82. Rancière, "Who Is the Subject of the Rights of Man?," 303 (emphasis in original).

83. See n. 27 above.

84. Butler, "Beside Oneself," 36–37.

85. Ibid., 35.

86. Ibid., 33.

87. Foucault, "What Is Enlightenment?," 319.

88. Sundhya Pahuja, "Rights as Regulation: The Intersection of Development and Human Rights," in *The Intersection of Rights and Regulation: New Directions in Socio-Legal Scholarship*, ed. Bronwen Morgan (Aldershot, UK: Ashgate, 2007), 169.

89. See, for example, Morsink, *Inherent Human Rights*. This, as Colin Koopman argues persuasively, need not commit Foucault to an outright rejection of universalism but simply (actually, more complexly) to a reconceptualization of universalism as compatible with contingency. See *Genealogy as Critique*, 228–41.

90. Michel Foucault, "Va-t-on extrader Klaus Croissant?," in *Dits et écrits II, 1976–1988*, quoted in Chevallier, "Michel Foucault and the Question of Right," 178.

91. Michel Foucault, "Interview with Michel Foucault," in *Essential Works of Foucault*, vol. 3, *Power*, 274.

92. Ibid., 275.

93. Samuel Chambers argues that, for both Butler and Rancière, the exposure of

contingency is not an answer but rather something that "demands responsible action." See *The Lessons of Rancière*, 163.

94. Susan Marks, "False Contingency," *Current Legal Problems* 62, no. 1 (2009): 1. For the quotation, see Karl Marx, *The Eighteenth Brumaire of Louis Bonaparte*, 3rd ed. (London: Lawrence and Wishart, 1954), 6, cited in Marks, "False Contingency," 1.

95. Marks, "False Contingency," 2.

96. Foucault, quoted in Martin, "Truth, Power, Self: An Interview," 15.

97. Ibid.

98. For a discussion of the "emptiness" of the signifier "human" in human rights, see the discussion at the beginning of the next chapter in nn. 1–7 and text accompanying.

99. The problematic of juridical form (as homologous to the commodity form) has been explored most extensively in the Marxist legal tradition, but in the next chapter I want to add to these powerful insights by bringing Foucault to the question of form (and more specifically the disciplinary dimensions of the juridical form). For the Marxist references, see Evgeny Pashukanis, "The General Theory of Law and Marxism," in *Pashukanis: Selected Writings on Marxism and Law*, trans. Peter B. Maggs, ed. Piers Beirne and Robert Sharlet (London: Academic Press, 1980); and for a more contemporary engagement with Pashukanis's theory in the context of international law, see China Miéville, *Between Equal Rights: A Marxist Theory of International Law* (Chicago: Haymarket, 2006).

Chapter 3

The epigraph to this chapter is from Judith Butler and Athena Athanasiou, *Dispossession: The Performative in the Political* (Cambridge, UK: Polity, 2013), 85–86.

1. For the purposes of the present argument about the (subject of the) politics of rights I am drawing a limited comparison between the writings of Foucault and Rancière. For a further examination of the similarities between the two thinkers (yet obviously attentive to their differences) from the perspective of the latter, see Chambers, *The Lessons of Rancière*, 42, 70, 98–104.

2. Foucault, quoted in Martin, "Truth, Power, Self," 15.

3. On the thematic of staging, see the analysis of the democratic state provided by Claude Lefort as constituting a "theatre of contestation" for new and expanding rights (Lefort, "Politics and Human Rights," 258). On the thematic of haunting, especially as it pertains to rights, see Samuel A. Chambers, "Ghostly Rights," *Cultural Critique* 54 (Spring 2003). It is no doubt possible to read a tacit, teleological, and utopian progressivism into Foucault's formulation that the human can never be defined. On such a reading, while the human always exceeds our efforts to codify it in law, nevertheless the result of our incomplete attempts at definition is to expand and progressively make more inclusive our legal notions of who is a human and who is not. Such a view is implied, for example, in Jack Donnelly's understanding of the ever-expanding liberal franchise of human rights law in which first nonpropertied men, then women, and finally a succession of racial and ethnic others came to insist upon their equal humanity as rights holders (see his "Human Rights and Asian Values: A Defence of 'Western' Universal-

ism," in *The East Asian Challenge for Human Rights*, ed. Joanne R. Bauer and Daniel A. Bell [Cambridge: Cambridge University Press, 1999], 63–64). Bonnie Honig helpfully explores the way in which such a chrono-logic of rights evacuates the contingency of political struggle in the present over who or what is rightful (see her *Paradox, Law, Democracy: Emergency Politics* [Princeton, NJ: Princeton University Press, 2009], 46–47). Indeed, this is a common trait of much of the recent historiography of human rights, admirably captured by the historian and legal thinker Samuel Moyn with the epithet "teleology, tunnel vision, and triumphalism" (see *The Last Utopia*, 311). For reasons explored more fully in Chapter 1, Foucault's genealogical approach to history dispenses equally with dialectics and teleology. There is neither an immanent logic nor a final destination to the human (who could just as easily "go backwards," were we to continue to think in these temporal terms). The "promise" of the human in Foucault's account amounts to the contingency of its being (and hence its always possibly being otherwise), and thus what explains its semantic expansion (or contraction) is political struggle alone.

4. Rancière, "Who Is the Subject of the Rights of Man?," 302.

5. Ibid., 304.

6. Ayten Gündoğdu, "A Revolution in Rights: Reflections on the Democratic Invention of the Rights of Man," *Law, Culture and the Humanities* 10, no. 3 (2014); Joe Hoover, "Towards a Politics for Human Rights: Ambiguous Humanity and Democratizing Rights," *Philosophy & Social Criticism* 39, no. 3 (2013); James D. Ingram, "What Is a 'Right to Have Rights'?: Three Images of the Politics of Human Rights," *American Political Science Review* 102, no. 4 (2008).

7. This shift from the critique of abstraction (as masking a particular bourgeois interest) to the celebration of its political possibilities is perhaps most evident in the Marxist and post-Marxist tradition. Compare, for example, Karl Marx, "On the Jewish Question," trans. T. B. Bottomore, in *The Marx-Engels Reader*, ed. Robert C. Tucker (New York: W. W. Norton, 1972), 40–44, with Lefort, "Politics and Human Rights," 257–58. We see it obviously in the work of Rancière, discussed above in the text. And finally, the post-Marxist, radical democratic work of Ernesto Laclau and Chantal Mouffe on hegemonic struggles and the rearticulation of the universal as an "empty signifier" has been especially influential in recent political and legal theory on rights. See, for example, Chambers, "Giving Up (on) Rights?"; and the work of the international legal theorist Martti Koskenniemi, discussed in n. 37 below.

8. Foucault, "Critical Theory/Intellectual History," 39.

9. See Jürgen Habermas, "Paradigms of Law," *Cardozo Law Review* 17, nos. 4–5 (1995–96).

10. The political theorist Duncan Ivison has recently discussed rights in similar terms. For him, rights can be understood "as *conduits*, that is, as modes for distributing capabilities and forms of power and influence and thus shaping behaviour as much as constraining it. The key idea here is that rights are often implicated in various relations of power as much as they are a means of criticizing them . . . [and indeed] can represent a distinctive relation of power [themselves]." See Ivison, *Rights* (Stocksfield, UK: Acumen, 2008), 180 (emphasis in original).

11. However, I by no means want to confine the point about rights functioning as a means of governmental control to the disciplinary or the identity-producing context which is my particular focus in this chapter. As has already been discussed in previous chapters, in later work Foucault supplements his account of disciplinary subject formation with an account of liberal governmentality and apparatuses of security (on the articulation of law, discipline, and apparatuses of security, see Foucault, *Security, Territory, Population*, 29–49). These latter modalities of power work in large part through enabling the circulation of people, capital, and commodities within a population to be governed. The focus in such modalities is hence neither (per law) on the abstract subject, nor (per discipline) on the material body of the individual-to-be-corrected, but rather on optimizing observable regularities within a population. What is governmentally "pertinent" for such technologies of power is not the individual per se but the aggregate spatio-temporal regularities observable at the level of the population and how they might be preserved and optimized (ibid., 45). And yet rights attaching to the individual are still enormously important in this context, for they enable not simply the freedom of the individual but also the freedom (conceived as "circulation") needed to sustain and govern the population as an entity (ibid., 48–49). It is in this dual sense that we can understand Foucault's assertion toward the end of *Security, Territory, Population* that "the right of individuals . . . is an element that has become indispensable to governmentality itself. Henceforth, a condition of governing well is that freedom, or certain forms of freedom, are really respected" (353). While the individual exercises his rights, in so exercising them that individual simultaneously enables a circulation which is functional to his government as a member of the population. In this sense, via rights, individuals can indeed be "governed through their freedom." See Rose and Miller, "Political Power Beyond the State," 201. For further reflections on the regulatory capacities of rights regimes indebted to Foucault's understanding of governmentality, see Bal Sokhi-Bulley, "Governing (Through) Rights: Statistics as Technologies of Governmentality," *Social & Legal Studies* 20, no. 2 (2011); Sokhi-Bulley, "Government(ality) by Experts: Human Rights as Governance," *Law & Critique* 22, no. 3 (2011).

12. Not all rights are strictly rights of privacy, and, it may be argued, many classical civil and political rights actually aim to enable intersubjective and associational life (by means of protecting speech or association, for example). Indeed, even the value of the right to privacy could be conceived in social terms (as enabling self-formation in the private sphere, which then becomes a prerequisite for robust engagement in the public sphere or in civil society). My claim is simply that the form such rights adopt in order to enable this social connection nevertheless presupposes an individualist liberal ontology of the subject.

13. From the critique of the "repressive hypothesis" in *The Will to Knowledge*, we know that Foucault is skeptical of notions of emancipation and liberation that presuppose "a human nature or base that, as a consequence of certain historical, economic, and social processes, has been concealed, alienated, or imprisoned in and by mechanisms of repression," but this is not to argue that "liberation as such, or this or that form of liberation, does not exist" (see Foucault, "The Ethics of the Concern for Self," 291).

14. Foucault, *Discipline and Punish*, 222.

15. McClure, "Taking Liberties in Foucault's Triangle," 171.

16. Hunt and Wickham, *Foucault and Law*, 63, 64.

17. Fraser, "Foucault's Body-Language," 65.

18. Foucault, "Two Lectures," 94.

19. Foucault, *"Society Must Be Defended,"* 26.

20. Ibid., 43.

21. Ibid., 46.

22. Ibid., 47. Foucault's account of the emergence of the historico-political discourse is hence a genealogy of a genealogy in the sense that he is himself providing a genealogy of a particular kind of political discourse which itself (*qua* genealogy, as Foucault and Nietzsche conceive the practice) mobilizes the use of historical knowledge in order to undo sovereign claims to truth and universality.

23. Ibid., 49.

24. Ibid., 49–50.

25. Ibid., 50.

26. Ibid. See R.d. Crano, "Genealogy, Virtuality, War," *Foucault Studies* 11 (2011).

27. Foucault, *"Society Must Be Defended,"* 48.

28. Ibid., 51.

29. Ibid., 52.

30. Ibid., 53.

31. Ibid., 52.

32. Ibid.

33. Ibid. For a related discussion of the question of rights in the context of the "historico-political discourse," see Duncan Ivison, *The Self at Liberty: Political Argument and the Arts of Government* (Ithaca, NY: Cornell University Press, 1997), 45–47.

34. Foucault, *"Society Must Be Defended,"* 53–54.

35. Ibid., 25–26.

36. Ibid., 57–58.

37. This difference has been captured by the international legal theorist Martti Koskenniemi in the conceptual opposition between "kitsch," on the one hand, and a "culture of formalism," on the other—the latter accommodating a more poststructuralist, mobile, and contingent articulation of "the universal." See Koskenniemi, "International Law in Europe: Between Tradition and Renewal," *European Journal of International Law* 16, no. 1 (2005): 122–23; and *The Gentle Civilizer of Nations: The Rise and Fall of International Law, 1870–1960* (Cambridge: Cambridge University Press, 2002), 507. The latter formulation draws upon the work of Ernesto Laclau (and others) on contingent universals and hegemonic struggles. For a sample of these debates, see *Contingency, Hegemony, Universality: Contemporary Dialogues on the Left*, ed. Judith Butler, Ernesto Laclau, and Slavoj Žižek (London: Verso, 2000).

38. No claim of right can successfully characterize itself as purely particular, as it is in the very nature of rights discourse to generalize or universalize beyond the instant claim (see Chambers, "Giving Up (on) Rights?," 195–96), and indeed Foucault's own

other articulations, especially of human rights, acknowledge this point. For further discussion, see Chapter 2, n. 89.

39. Foucault, "*Society Must Be Defended*," 50.

40. Hoffman, *Foucault and Power*, 76–77.

41. Foucault, "*Society Must Be Defended*," 30.

42. Foucault, "Preface to *Anti-Oedipus*," 109.

43. I am using the work of Wendy Brown to illustrate the Foucauldian point about the regulatory, disciplinary function of rights for two main reasons. The first is that while Foucault discusses how disciplinary power subjectifies individuals, he does not extend this insight as explicitly as he might to the scene of rights—rather, it is largely presupposed (although for an example of where he *does* explicitly state the point, see "*Society Must Be Defended*," 27). It is hence in Brown's work of the 1990s and early 2000s that we find a much more developed account of the disciplinary, subjectifying logics of rights. Interestingly, Brown herself vacillates between attributing the insight to Foucault that rights subjectify and advancing the claim as a corrective to Foucault's failing to perceive this same fact (cf. "Suffering Rights as Paradoxes," 231–32; and *States of Injury*, 99), just as she speaks in places of the "convergence" of juridical and disciplinary modalities of power (*States of Injury*, 133) and in others speaks directly of the disciplinary function of rights. My interpretation is that Brown develops a point about the disciplinary dimensions of rights discourse which is often largely implicit in Foucault's work and that her development of it is entirely consistent with Foucault's understanding of disciplinarity. (That is to leave to one side the creative dialogues which Brown sets up between Foucault and Marx, for example, but also between Foucault and Freud, Weber, and critical theory.) The second reason why I have chosen to use Brown as an exemplar of this point about the disciplinarity of rights is that her work on rights has spurred a great deal of debate on the politics of rights in political and legal theory, and hence this work of hers presents an opportunity to bring Foucault into dialogue with some of those contemporary debates.

44. See her "Wounded Attachments," *Political Theory* 21, no. 3 (1993); the chapter is reprinted in amended form in her book *States of Injury*, 52–76.

45. Brown, *States of Injury*, 121.

46. Patricia J. Williams, *The Alchemy of Race and Rights* (Cambridge, MA: Harvard University Press, 1991), 164. Williams's book is a contribution to a debate between scholars of critical legal studies (CLS) and critical race theory (CRT) on the value of rights for political struggles. Many of the original CLS critiques of rights (revolving around the indeterminacy, abstraction, and individualism of rights) are to be found in a special issue of the *Texas Law Review* (no. 8 of 1984). For responses from proponents of CRT to the CLS critique of rights, see, for example, Richard Delgado, "The Ethereal Scholar: Does Critical Legal Studies Have What Minorities Want?," *Harvard Civil Rights–Civil Liberties Law Review* 22, no. 2 (1987); and Robert A. Williams, Jr., "Taking Rights Aggressively: The Perils and Promise of Critical Legal Theory for Peoples of Color," *Law & Inequality* 5, no. 1 (1987–88).

47. Williams, *The Alchemy of Race and Rights*, 165.

48. Brown, *States of Injury*, 130 (emphasis in original).

49. There is a discernible shift in this regard in MacKinnon's work from her *Feminism Unmodified: Discourses on Life and Law* (Cambridge, MA: Harvard University Press, 1987), in which she stakes out a critical position on the masculinity of the formal rule of law and its rights guarantees, to the companion text two years later, *Towards a Feminist Theory of the State* (Cambridge, MA: Harvard University Press, 1989), which offers a rapprochement with the masculine state form and its law, now seen as amenable to feminist intervention. These interventions are conceived by MacKinnon as processes of concretization, materialization, and substantialization whereby the reality of women's lives (and their substantive inequality with men) are somehow introduced into legal discourse. The opening for such processes is the notion of equality as juridified in law (see n. 50 below). The tension between the former and latter positions is revealingly condensed in the two parts of Catherine MacKinnon, "Reflections on Sex Equality Under Law," *Yale Law Journal* 100, no. 5 (1991).

50. MacKinnon, *Towards a Feminist Theory of the State*, 242. What seems to occasion MacKinnon's shift in tone and outlook, from the more critical "dominance theory" enunciated in *Feminism Unmodified* to the more affirmative "feminist theory of the state" articulated in the latter text, is precisely the notion of equality. This is methodologically interesting on several levels. While MacKinnon, as Drucilla Cornell notes, "transposes the Marxist critique of liberalism into her analysis of imposed sexuality as the basis of female gender identity," she nevertheless parts company with Marx's analysis of rights and of the state in some crucial respects (Drucilla Cornell, *Transformations: Recollective Imagination and Sexual Difference* [New York: Routledge, 1993], 119). Whereas Marx dismisses the formal right to equality in "On the Jewish Question" as having "no political significance whatsoever" (in the sense of its not envisioning substantive, real equality but merely reproducing a formal equality of abstract rights-holding subjects before the law, hence in fact conducing to a material inequality under capitalist relations of production), for MacKinnon it is the right to equality and what it suggests that provides the "peculiar jurisprudential opportunity" for feminists to introduce legal reforms occasioning real equality (see Marx, "On the Jewish Question," 40; MacKinnon, *Towards a Feminist Theory of the State*, 242). What makes this opportunity unique and peculiar is because, as she goes on to write, "law does not usually guarantee rights to things that do not exist." While MacKinnon here grasps (in a way Marx refused to do in the text cited above) the performative possibilities of equality jurisprudence, she curiously does not extend this insight to other types of rights protection (that is, she fails to see how in fact law, through rights, cannot help but promise things which do not yet exist). On the other hand, Marx was markedly more "positive" toward rights than most of his detractors acknowledge—but his selective mobilization of rights was always in the service not (per MacKinnon) of a refashioning of the state form but of its revolutionary overcoming via immanent critique. All of which decidedly complicates MacKinnon's polemical claim to be "methodologically postmarxist" (*Feminism Unmodified*, 60).

51. For more on this tendency in contemporary critical engagements with human rights, see Ben Golder, "Beyond Redemption: Problematizing the Critique of Human

Rights in Contemporary International Legal Thought," *London Review of International Law* 2, no. 1 (2014).

52. Brown, *States of Injury*, 133.

53. Ibid.

54. Brown, "Suffering Rights as Paradoxes," 232 (emphasis in original).

55. Wendy Brown, "Revaluing Critique: A Response to Kenneth Baynes," *Political Theory* 28, no. 4 (2000): 472. See also Butler, "Sexual Inversions," 87.

56. Brown, "Suffering Rights as Paradoxes," 231–32 (emphasis in original).

57. Richard T. Ford, "Beyond 'Difference': A Reluctant Critique of Legal Identity Politics," in *Left Legalism/Left Critique*, 56. This dynamic is reproduced not simply in legal fora where litigants assert their rights, but also where, for example, "culture" is adduced by way of "defense" to or in mitigation of an alleged crime. See Leti Volpp, "(Mis)Identifying Culture: Asian Women and the 'Cultural Defense,'" *Harvard Women's Law Journal* 17 (1994).

58. Ford, "Beyond 'Difference,'" 46 (emphasis added).

59. Ibid. (emphasis added).

60. See, for example, Judith Butler, "Is Kinship Always Already Heterosexual?," in *Undoing Gender*.

61. Michael Warner, *The Trouble with Normal: Sex, Politics, and the Ethics of Queer Life* (Cambridge, MA: Harvard University Press, 1999), 96.

62. Chambers, "Ghostly Rights," 167.

63. This is of course Foucault's insight about the dispersed social and institutional operation of punishment beyond the juridical scene of the criminal law. "The judges of normality are everywhere," he writes. "We are in the society of the teacher-judge, the doctor-judge, the educator-judge, the 'social worker'-judge." Foucault, *Discipline and Punish*, 304.

64. Foucault, *"Society Must Be Defended,"* 27.

65. Brown, *States of Injury*, 121n41.

66. Just as I was concerned above not to delimit the broader argument about the regulatory capacity of rights to their disciplinary or identity-producing function (see n. 11), so too has Brown extended her argument about the disciplinary dimensions of rights beyond the example of identity-based rights claims to contemporary discourses of human rights, which latter, she argues, "produce[] a certain type of subject in need of a certain kind of protection" (see "'The Most We Can Hope For'?: Human Rights and the Politics of Fatalism," *South Atlantic Quarterly* 103, nos. 2–3 [2004]: 460).

67. For an analysis of the subjectifying dimensions of a type of legal protection which is preeminently a site of recognition (refugee law and the claim to refugee status), see some of the work of Cynthia Hardy and Roger Zetter. For Hardy, "the refugee subject is a product of the processes of determination that lead to his or her classification as well as the broader discourses that impinge on and overlap with refugee discourse. There is, then, no autonomous subject [who enunciates a prior experience]: a refugee only exists insofar as he or she is named and recognized by others" ("Refugee Determination: Power and Resistance in Systems of Foucauldian Power," *Administration &*

Society 35, no. 4 [2003]: 476–77). Bluntly, then, we might simply say with Roger Zetter that the refugee is "one who conforms to institutional requirements" ("Labelling Refugees: Forming and Transforming a Bureaucratic Identity," *Journal of Refugee Studies* 4, no. 1 [1991]: 51).

68. Foucault, *"Society Must Be Defended,"* 27.

69. Foucault, "On the Genealogy of Ethics," 256.

70. The Tanner Lectures appear as Michel Foucault, "'*Omnes et Singulatim*,'" and the book is Dreyfus and Rabinow, *Beyond Structuralism*.

71. Macey, *The Lives of Michel Foucault*, 430. And on the phenomenon of "French theory" in America, see François Cusset, *French Theory: How Foucault, Derrida, Deleuze, & Co. Transformed the Intellectual Life of the United States*, trans. Jeff Fort (Minneapolis: University of Minnesota Press, 2008).

72. Macey, *The Lives of Michel Foucault*, 430.

73. The infamous example remains Miller, *The Passion of Michel Foucault*.

74. Michel Foucault, "Sex, Power, and the Politics of Identity," in *Essential Works of Foucault*, vol. 1, *Ethics*, 164.

75. Michel Foucault, "Sexual Choice, Sexual Act," in *Essential Works of Foucault*, vol. 1, *Ethics*, 143.

76. Foucault, "Social Triumph," 157.

77. Ibid., 158.

78. Foucault, "Sex, Power, and the Politics of Identity," 166.

79. Ibid., 164.

80. Ibid., 163.

81. Ibid., 166.

82. Foucault, "Friendship as a Way of Life," 136. Foucault's remarks here should be read in the light of his late understanding of aesthetics, asceticism, and the care of the self (discussed in Chapter 2, nn. 20–27 and text accompanying).

83. The ending of the friendship between Foucault and Deleuze is often attributed by many commentators to their divergent political positions on the "Croissant Affair" of 1977 (see Introduction, n. 43 and accompanying text). Foucault's proceduralist and rights-based insistence on the importance of legal counsel as opposed to Deleuze's more radical, political critique of the West German state and seeming endorsement of the Baader-Meinhof group is seen to be key to this rupture (see John Marks, *Gilles Deleuze: Vitalism and Multiplicity* [London: Pluto Press, 1998], 109–10; but cf. François Dosse, *Gilles Deleuze and Félix Guattari: Intersecting Lives*, trans. Deborah Glassman [New York: Columbia University Press, 2010], 306–30, which discusses their friendship and lists a range of political and philosophical differences). Certainly Deleuze's oft-expressed and virulent rejection of what he took to be "human rights" (as a universalist, meaningless, lifeless abstraction) lends support to the view that, at least on the question of rights and human rights, their split was based upon a real difference of philosophical and political opinion. However, as Paul Patton has helpfully pointed out to me, the two are actually much closer on the question of rights than such a view admits. The interpretation of Foucault's human rights politics that I advanced in the preceding

chapter and the account of a rights-based becoming-gay politics of friendship offered in the present one can be read alongside Deleuze's endorsement of what the latter calls "jurisprudence" (as a case-based, situational, mobile, open-ended, and jurisgenerative form of lawmaking). See Paul Patton, "Deleuze and Democracy," *Contemporary Political Theory* 4, no. 4 (2005): 403–6; and Alexandre Lefebvre, *The Image of Law: Deleuze, Bergson, Spinoza* (Stanford, CA: Stanford University Press, 2008), 53–59.

84. Foucault, "Social Triumph," 158.

85. See Martha Minow and Mary Lyndon Shanley, "Relational Rights and Responsibilities: Revisioning the Family in Liberal Political Theory and Law," *Hypatia* 11, no. 1 (1996): 23.

86. Foucault, "Social Triumph," 162.

87. Ibid., 158.

88. Ibid.

89. Ibid., 160 (emphasis in original).

90. Zivi, *Making Rights Claims*, 82.

91. Paul Rabinow, "Introduction: The History of Systems of Thought," in *Essential Works of Foucault*, vol. 1, *Ethics*, xxxix.

92. Foucault, *The Hermeneutics of the Subject*, 192–202.

93. Foucault, "On the Genealogy of Ethics," 231–32, 234.

94. Steven Garlick, "The Beauty of Friendship: Foucault, Masculinity and the Work of Art," *Philosophy & Social Criticism* 28, no. 5 (2002): 559, 561.

95. Tom Roach, *Friendship as a Way of Life: Foucault, AIDS, and the Politics of Shared Estrangement* (Albany, NY: SUNY Press, 2012), 8.

96. Foucault, "Friendship as a Way of Life," 136.

97. Ibid.

98. An interpretation developed in Roach, *Friendship as a Way of Life*.

99. Foucault, "Friendship as a Way of Life," 138.

100. Mark Kingston, "Subversive Friendships: Foucault on Homosexuality and Social Experimentation," *Foucault Studies* 7 (2009): 9.

101. Foucault, "Sex, Power, and the Politics of Identity," 166–67 (emphasis in original).

102. Ibid., 167. Hence I cannot agree with the conclusion of Frédéric Gros, in his "Course Context" essay for Foucault's *The Hermeneutics of the Subject*, when he writes that "Foucault opposes what he calls 'modes of life,' 'choices of existence,' 'styles of life,' and 'cultural forms' to both the demands of community and individual rights together" (544). In fact, Foucault attempts to mobilize individual rights in the service of "modes of life" and so forth.

103. Foucault, "Sex, Power, and the Politics of Identity," 166.

104. Foucault, *The Birth of Biopolitics*, 65.

105. Foucault, "Space, Knowledge, and Power," 354.

106. Johanna Oksala, *Foucault on Freedom* (Cambridge: Cambridge University Press, 2005), 188.

107. Foucault, "Power and Strategies," 142.

108. Foucault, "The Ethics of the Concern for Self," 284.

109. Foucault, "The Subject and Power," 342.

110. Oksala, *Foucault on Freedom*, 188.

111. Prozorov, *Foucault, Freedom and Sovereignty*, 29.

112. For discussion, see ibid., 25–36.

113. Foucault, "The Subject and Power," 342; Foucault, "The Ethics of the Concern for Self," 283.

114. Foucault, *The Will to Knowledge*, 95.

115. Brown, *States of Injury*, 115.

116. Butler, "What Is Critique?," 320.

117. Friedrich Nietzsche, *"The Twilight of the Idols" and "The Anti-Christ,"* trans. R. J. Hollingdale (Harmondsworth, UK: Penguin, 1990), 103.

118. Foucault, "Space, Knowledge, and Power," 355.

119. Foucault, "The Subject and Power," 342.

120. Judith Butler, "Competing Universalities," in *Contingency, Hegemony, Universality*, 177.

Chapter 4

The epigraph to this chapter is from Michel Foucault, "Des supplices aux cellules," *Le monde*, 21 February 1975, quoted in Didier Eribon, *Michel Foucault*, trans. Betsy Wing (Cambridge, MA: Harvard University Press), 237.

1. Foucault, "Polemics, Politics and Problematizations," 111.

2. Ibid., 111–12.

3. Ibid., 111.

4. Although, as Paul Patton helpfully points out to me, the metaphor of the game is not an entirely apt one with which to theorize rights in a liberal democratic society: while dialogical participants in the game share an overriding goal (namely, truth), the same cannot be said for rights holders in such societies, who pursue diverse interests and agendas.

5. Foucault, "Polemics, Politics and Problematizations," 112.

6. Ibid. In his lecture course for 1982 at the Collège de France, Foucault had schematized two understandings of the relationship between the subject and truth in Western philosophy. The first, originally classical and spiritual, involves a subject who in seeking to gain access to the truth brought about a transformation or a transfiguration of her being (that is, no access to the truth without a change brought about to the subject); the second, modern and nominally post-Cartesian, holds that knowledge alone constitutes a sufficient condition for access to the truth. See Foucault, *The Hermeneutics of the Subject*, 1–19.

7. We might conclude, for example, that while the purpose of a polemic is to refuse the terms of a debate, it also and more importantly seeks to inaugurate a new debate on different terms and hence does not represent a simple refusal of dialogue but rather a critical displacement of it onto a different terrain (and potentially a pluralization of the debate itself). Indeed, Foucault's own intellectual practice might be characterized as just

such a polemic. See Chapter 1, n. 11 and text accompanying; and for a consideration of Rancière as a "polemicist," see chapter 4 of Chambers, *The Lessons of Rancière*. See also Chambers's comparison of Rancière with Foucault at 175n23. In the interview I have been discussing, Foucault goes on to link the figure of the polemicist with the repression of dissenting views in the Soviet Union and the elimination of the other (at 112–13). These comments of his come at the end of a long arc (arguably starting with the provocative remarks about state racism and socialist struggle in the concluding moments of the "'Society Must Be Defended'" lecture course in 1976), where Foucault moves from the Nietzschean "war hypothesis" toward more refined models of understanding power relations. On the debate surrounding the "war model" in Foucault's thought, see n. 22 below. For the references to racism and socialism, see Foucault, *"Society Must Be Defended,"* 261–63.

8. For further discussion of these issues, see Ben Golder, "Human Rights *Contra* Critique: Preliminary Notes on the Politics of Interpretation," *Australian Journal of Human Rights* 17, no. 2 (2011); and Golder, "Beyond Redemption."

9. Foucault, *Security, Territory, Population*, 99. See also Dean Spade, "Laws as Tactics," *Columbia Journal of Gender and Law* 21, no. 2 (2011).

10. Foucault clarifies what he means by the notion of a "game" in a late interview: "When I say 'game,' I mean a set of rules by which truth is produced. It is not a game in the sense of an amusement; it is a set of procedures that lead to a certain result, which, on the basis of its principles and rules of procedure, may be considered valid or invalid, winning or losing." See Foucault, "The Ethics of the Concern for Self," 297. It is common to refer to rights, as Foucault does in the interview cited above in the text, by invoking the metaphor of the game. The most famous description of rights along these lines is probably the notion of rights as trumps, popularized by the liberal legal theorist Ronald Dworkin (see, for example, his "Rights as Trumps," in *Theories of Rights*, ed. Jeremy Waldron [New York: Oxford University Press, 1984]). For a recent and very useful reflection on the notion of rights as trumps, see Zivi, *Making Rights Claims*, 24–42. On a "gaming" approach to state law, see also Simon Halliday and Bronwen Morgan, "I Fought the Law and the Law Won?: Legal Consciousness and the Critical Imagination," *Current Legal Problems* 66, no. 1 (2013).

11. The anxiety surrounding an instrumentalist theory of or orientation toward law and rights is as pervasive in liberal legal theory as it is entrenched in everyday legal practice. From a landmark text such as Dworkin's *Taking Rights Seriously* to Brian Tamanaha's more recent survey of instrumentalist legal theories in the American academy, practice, and courts, the worry has always been that such an open endorsement of a juridical *bellum omnium contra omnes* leaches law of substantive moral content and normative obligation and weakens the rule of law. See Ronald Dworkin, *Taking Rights Seriously* (Cambridge, MA: Harvard University Press, 1978); and Brian Z. Tamanaha, *Law as a Means to an End: Threat to the Rule of Law* (Cambridge: Cambridge University Press, 2006).

12. Foucault, *The Hermeneutics of the Subject*, 403.

13. Robert Knox, "Strategy and Tactics," *Finnish Yearbook of International Law* 21 (2010): 197.

14. I call it a "debate" (in quotation marks) because the encounter between, first, Foucault and Marx(ism and -ists) and then, second, between Foucault's followers or interpreters and those working in a rival Marxist tradition (say, for example, between proponents of a governmentality analysis and adherents of Marxist state theory) has been overly marked by caricature on both sides. On Foucault's own reduction of Marx, see Brown, *States of Injury*, 12–14. For an early and sympathetic account of Foucault from within the Marxist tradition, see Barry Smart, *Foucault, Marxism and Critique* (Abingdon, UK: Routledge, 2010). Lately, some of the work of the sociologist Thomas Lemke has been useful in bringing contemporary work informed by Foucault and Marx into greater dialogue. See Lemke, "Foucault, Governmentality, and Critique"; and "An Indigestible Meal?: Foucault, Governmentality and State Theory," *Distinktion: Scandinavian Journal of Social Theory* 8, no. 2 (2007).

15. Alan Hunt, "Getting Marx and Foucault into Bed Together!," *Journal of Law and Society* 31, no. 4 (2004). However, were one to do so, I think a profitable way to begin this rapprochement might be to refuse the reifying figures of "Foucault" and "Marx" and adopt toward Marxism (as a movement and a way of thinking) the stance that is frequently (if sometimes problematically) adopted toward Foucault: namely, that of using Marx's critical "tools" and reading Marxism as a toolbox or a critical repertoire. Frequently the assumption about Marxism, often repeated by Foucauldians, is that if one purports to "use" Marx, one is necessarily wedded, for example, to a metaphysics of species being or a teleologic of history. I think this assumption unhelpfully marginalizes the work that other Marxist analytics might do in the service of a critique and history of the present. This is not, I hasten to say, to dispute the profound differences between the two ways of thinking; but it is to insist that that difference cannot be allowed to prevent dialogue and indeed to suggest that the tension between Marxist and Foucauldian perspectives can itself be theoretically generative.

16. Foucault, *"Society Must Be Defended,"* 15. For considerations of the relationship between Foucault and Clausewitz, see Roger Deacon, "Foucault and Clausewitz: War and Power," *Scientia Militaria* 31, no. 1 (2003); and Julian Reid, "Foucault on Clausewitz: Conceptualizing the Relationship Between War and Power," *Alternatives* 28, no. 1 (2003).

17. Karl von Clausewitz, *War, Politics and Power* (Chicago: Gateway Press, 1965), 171, quoted in Knox, "Strategy and Tactics," 197.

18. Knox, "Strategy and Tactics," 197.

19. Antonio Gramsci, *Selections from the Prison Notebooks* (London: Lawrence and Wishart, 2003), 177–78, quoted in Knox, "Strategy and Tactics," 199.

20. Knox, "Strategy and Tactics," 199.

21. Ibid., 200.

22. There is an ongoing debate within Foucault scholarship over whether Foucault jettisons the "war model," developed in the mid-1970s, and replaces it with the notion of conduct, governmentality, or an aesthetics of existence in the late work. For example, Kevin Thompson argues that Foucault develops two distinct models of power (the strategic and the governmental), that each model entails different forms of resistance (tactical reversal and an aesthetics of existence), and that he moves from the strategic to

the governmental in the late work. Meanwhile, Marcelo Hoffman argues convincingly that while Foucault does—in work subsequent to "'Society Must Be Defended'"—retreat from the (Nietzschean) hypothesis that societal power relations can be thought entirely through the prism of a violent and warlike struggle, he does not go so far as to jettison the related notions of strategy and struggle (which continue to inform the governmental model of power into the late work). See Kevin Thompson, "Forms of Resistance: Foucault on Tactical Reversal and Self-Formation," *Continental Philosophy Review* 36, no. 2 (2003); and Hoffman, *Foucault and Power*, 47–91. My own view, in line with Hoffman's, is that it is important to emphasize the continuing relevance of struggle and strategy to Foucault's conception of power relations well into the late work, and in so doing to delink the question of strategy from the question of violent warlike relations per se. Struggle and strategy need not imply direct violence. In an interview given in late January 1984, for example, Foucault remarks that "power relations . . . [are] the strategies by which individuals try to direct and control the conduct of others," and that "power is games of strategy." See Foucault, "The Ethics of the Concern for Self," 298.

23. Foucault, *The Will to Knowledge*, 92.

24. Ibid., 102.

25. Amy Allen, *The Politics of Ourselves: Power, Autonomy, and Gender in Contemporary Critical Theory* (New York: Columbia University Press, 2008), 50.

26. Foucault, *The Will to Knowledge*, 102. As he says in the "Interview with *Actes*," "strategic relations . . . are necessarily unstable and subject to change" (see Michel Foucault, "Interview with *Actes*," in *Essential Works of Foucault*, vol. 3, *Power*, 397). Regarding this conception of power relations as being mobile, contingent, and reversible, Foucault introduces a distinction in the late work between power relations (understood to have these malleable characteristics) and states of domination (understood as asymmetrical relations of power that have hardened and cannot be reversed, such that one side of the relation is always permitted to dominate the other). See Foucault, "The Ethics of the Concern for Self," 299 (and see also his "The Subject and Power," 340–42).

27. Part of the problem is that many theorists—I suspect Foucault on occasion as well—use the terms "strategy" and "tactics" interchangeably and sometimes lacking the precision they deserve. On this point generally, see Knox, "Strategy and Tactics." On Foucault specifically, I follow Amy Allen in interpreting him as adopting two main understandings of strategy (see Allen, *The Politics of Ourselves*, 192n27). The first is a broad meaning that aligns with his model of power relations being defined by instrumentalism, confrontation, and reversibility. The second is a more specific meaning that aligns more closely with the military and Marxist renditions of strategy (which I discuss in the text, above). To complete the picture, we could say that Foucault also maintains the broad understanding of tactical, meaning instrumentalist, that I discussed in the first section of this chapter. For the purposes of my analysis in this chapter I want to hold on to the more specific meanings that bring Foucault into political dialogue with the Marxist tradition.

28. Foucault, "Power and Strategies," 142.

29. Ibid.

30. Ibid.

31. Foucault, *The Will to Knowledge*, 99.

32. Ibid., 100.

33. Ibid., 94.

34. Ibid., 95.

35. Hunt and Wickham, *Foucault and Law*, 30.

36. Foucault, *The Will to Knowledge*, 95.

37. We might list Foucault's late engagement with Kant and the French Revolution, his reporting on the Iranian revolution, and his reflections on the Marxist revolutionary tradition as important reference points in this regard. For a helpful discussion, see Jessica Whyte, "Is Revolution Desirable?: Michel Foucault on Revolution, Neoliberalism and Rights," in *Re-Reading Foucault*. I think Foucault had a more ambivalent position on revolution than is frequently acknowledged. He often critiqued and problematized revolution; but this stance, in the way I have understood critique in this book, leaves open the possibility of resignifying and reimagining revolution, and he is thus far from being an anti-revolutionary thinker.

38. Foucault, "What Is Enlightenment?," 316.

39. Foucault, "Power and Strategies," 144.

40. Ibid.

41. Ibid., 145. Hence Foucault will insist upon constructing "an ascending analysis of power" (see *"Society Must Be Defended,"* 30).

42. "For Foucault, resistance can only be random and sporadic," runs this familiar refrain (David Ward, *A Poetics of Resistance: Narrative and the Writings of Pier Paolo Pasolini* [Cranbury, NJ: Associated University Press, 1995], 169).

43. Posed at the broadest level (namely, as a question about the relation of law to radical or transformative political agendas) this is a perennial and very productive question to which no definitive answer can ever really be given. In the American legal academy, for example, one could read the history of successive critical movements as attempts to generate different responses to this question, from the emergence of the Law and Society movement to the rise in the late 1970s of the Critical Legal Studies (CLS) movement, and then more recently to the emergence of groups such as LatCrits in the 1990s and ClassCrits in the 2000s. (Much has been written on this particular and evolving history, but for a recent and valuable account, see Adam Gearey, "'Change Is Gonna Come': Critical Legal Studies and the Legacies of the New Left," *Law & Critique* 24, no. 3 [2013]). While many of these groups were, and are, understandably framed in pedagogic terms—indeed, the problematic of the reproduction of legal knowledge has been the predominant form in which critical (academic) movements in law have been articulated, from the legal realist challenge to formalism to Duncan Kennedy's seminal CLS pamphlet on legal education as training for hierarchy—they essentially revolve around the question of law and the political. (For the reference, see Duncan Kennedy, "Legal Education and the Reproduction of Hierarchy," *Journal of Legal Education* 32, no. 4 [1982]). In the United Kingdom, for example, there are different genealogies and trajectories, obviously. For a recent and quite personal

discussion of these, see the account given in Bill Bowring, "What Is Radical in 'Radical International Law'?," *Finnish Yearbook of International Law* 22 (2011). As the title of this article aptly indicates, it is in the field of international law that the particular and narrower question of a politico-legal strategy has recently been reflected upon most explicitly. In addition to Knox's "Strategy and Tactics," see also his "Marxism, International Law, and Political Strategy," *Leiden Journal of International Law* 22, no. 3 (2009). Much of his and others' scholarship is written in response to Miéville, *Between Equal Rights*, which revives the commodity exchange theory of the Soviet-era Marxist jurist Evgeny Pashukanis.

44. Christodoulidis, "Strategies of Rupture," 9 (emphasis in original).

45. Ibid., 6.

46. Ibid., 9–15.

47. Brenna Bhandar, "Strategies of Legal Rupture: The Politics of Judgment," *Windsor Yearbook of Access to Justice* 30 (2012); Richard Bailey, "Strategy, Rupture, Rights: Reflections on Law and Resistance in Immigration Detention," *Australian Feminist Law Journal* 31, no. 1 (2009).

48. The most comprehensive English-language discussion of Vergès and his judicial strategy is contained in Jonathan Widell, "Jacques Vergès, Devil's Advocate: A Psychohistory of Vergès' Judicial Strategy" (PhD diss., McGill University, 2012), from which I have benefited greatly.

49. Jacques Derrida, "Ethics and Politics Today," in *Negotiations: Interventions and Interviews, 1971–2001*, trans. and ed. Elizabeth Rottenberg (Stanford, CA: Stanford University Press, 2002), 308 (emphasis in original).

50. The following brief description of the case and the defense tactics and strategy draws upon Guyora Binder, "Representing Nazism: Advocacy and Identity at the Trial of Klaus Barbie," *Yale Law Journal* 98, no. 7 (1989); and Martti Koskenniemi, "Between Impunity and Show Trials," *Max Planck Yearbook of United Nations Law* 6 (2002).

51. Christodoulidis, "Strategies of Rupture," 5.

52. Quoted in ibid., 6. Izieu is a town east of Lyon from where, in 1944, Barbie deported forty-four children to the extermination camps.

53. Bhandar, "Strategies of Legal Rupture," 60; and see generally Christodoulidis, "Strategies of Rupture."

54. The phrase "legal left" names a particular, if not exactly seamless, grouping. In the United States, for example, it can be taken to refer to left-wing law students and law professors working largely in the field of what was and is referred to as CLS. At Harvard University, there is a student-run journal called *Unbound: Harvard Journal of the Legal Left* (see www.legalleft.org), and much of the intellectual work of the journal and its affiliated students is catalyzed by the CLS scholarship of Duncan Kennedy (on whose work a retrospective was recently organized at the School of Oriental and African Studies in London on 22 May 2014, titled "The Past and Future of the Legal Left: Celebrating the Scholarship of Duncan Kennedy"). For a critique of the work of *Unbound* that problematizes the conjunction of "legal" and "left," written from a Marxist perspective by a former editor of the journal, see Tor Krever, "A Journal of the Legal Left?," *Unbound:*

Harvard Journal of the Legal Left 9, no. 1 (2015). See also Knox, "Marxism, International Law, and Political Strategy," 433–34.

55. Foucault, "Préface à la deuxième edition," in *Dits et écrits II, 1976–1988.*

56. Ibid., 952.

57. Ibid.

58. Ibid.

59. For a brief discussion, see Widell, "Devil's Advocate," 15–16.

60. Foucault, *"Society Must Be Defended,"* 239–64.

61. Foucault, *The Will to Knowlege,* 138.

62. Emile Durkheim, *Suicide: A Study in Sociology,* trans. John A. Spaulding and George Simpson (New York: Free Press, 1979). See also Thomas F. Tierney, "The Governmentality of Suicide: Peuchet, Marx, Durkheim, and Foucault," *Journal of Classical Sociology* 10, no. 4 (2010).

63. Foucault, *The Will to Knowledge,* 138–39.

64. Ibid., 138. For related discussions of the political mobilization of death under the label of, respectively, "necropolitics" and "thanatopolitics," see Achille Mbembe, "Necropolitics," trans. Libby Meintjes, *Public Culture* 15, no. 1 (2003); and Stuart J. Murray, "Thanatopolitics: On the Use of Death for Mobilising Political Life," *Polygraph* 18 (2006).

65. Foucault, "The Risks of Security," 380.

66. Ibid.

67. Ibid.

68. Thomas F. Tierney, "Suicidal Thoughts: Hobbes, Foucault and the Right to Die," *Philosophy & Social Criticism* 32, no. 5 (2006): 602.

69. Ibid., 614, 615–16 (see also Michel Foucault, "The Social Extension of the Norm," in *Foucault Live,* 197). Tierney is here discussing biopolitics largely as a phenomenon of the social power of medicine and medical authorities, which of course is an important element of what Foucault understood by the concept (though by no means the only element). For example, see the set of lectures he gave in Rio de Janeiro in late 1974 devoted to the topic of "social medicine." These have been published as "The Crisis of Medicine or the Crisis of Antimedicine?," trans. Edgar C. Knowlton, Jr., William King, and Clare O'Farrell, *Foucault Studies* 1 (2004); "The Birth of Social Medicine," in *Essential Works of Foucault,* vol. 3, *Power;* and "The Incorporation of the Hospital into Modern Technology," trans. Edgar Knowlton, Jr., William J. King, and Stuart Elden, in *Space, Knowledge and Power: Foucault and Geography,* ed. Jeremy W. Crampton and Stuart Elden (Aldershot, UK: Ashgate, 2007). Tierney is likewise discussing biopolitics here in its contemporary neoliberal iteration, wherein subjects are governed at a distance by being encouraged to take charge of the conduct of their own health. For a similar analysis, see Kevin Thompson, "The Spiritual Disciplines of Biopower," *Radical Philosophy Review* 7, no. 1 (2004). Medicine, while not of course the only vector of biopolitics, is a privileged instance for Foucault because it "is a power-knowledge that can be applied to both the body and the population, both the organism and biological processes, and it will therefore have both disciplinary effects and regulatory effects." See Foucault, *"Society Must Be Defended,"* 252.

70. Currently three US states have death-with-dignity acts: Washington, Vermont, and Oregon.

71. Tierney, "Suicidal Thoughts," 632.

72. *Washington v Glucksberg* 521 US 702 (1997).

73. Ronald Dworkin et al., "Assisted Suicide: The Philosophers' Brief," *New York Review of Books*, 27 March 1997, available online at http://www.nybooks.com/articles/archives/1997/mar/27/assisted-suicide-the-philosophers-brief/.

74. Tierney, "Suicidal Thoughts," 631.

75. For a powerful feminist critique of the interaction between the discourses of law and medicine, especially over the issue of the control of women's bodies and the construction and contouring of autonomy, see Carol Smart, *Feminism and the Power of Law* (London: Routledge, 1989). Consider also in this context Foucault's advocacy of access to abortions in France and his opposition to a draft bill that would strengthen the power of medicine to determine the conditions of the procedure: "Who will make the decision? Two doctors. So there will be a strengthening of a medical power that is already great, too great, but that becomes intolerable when it is coupled with a 'psychological' power that has earned a reputation for incompetence and abuse in its application to internments, medico-legal evaluations, 'children at risk,' and 'predelinquent' young people." See "Summoned to Court," in *Essential Works of Foucault*, vol. 3, *Power*, 424–25.

76. In the conclusion the authors relate, for example, how "Jane Doe['s] . . . cancer made even the most basic bodily functions such as swallowing, coughing, and yawning extremely painful," how "George A. Kingsley, in advanced stages of AIDS which included . . . the attachment of a tube to an artery in his chest which made even routine functions burdensome," how "Jane Roe . . . had been almost completely bedridden [with cancer] . . . and experienced constant pain that could not be alleviated by medication," and how these, and other sufferings, cumulatively compelled the following proposition: "A state may not deny the liberty claimed by the patient-plaintiffs in these cases without providing them an opportunity to demonstrate, in whatever way the state might reasonably think wise and necessary, that the conviction they expressed for an early death is competent, rational, informed, stable, and uncoerced" (see Dworkin et al., "Assisted Suicide," unpaginated).

77. For more on the (anti-)political implications of the subject of suffering, see the different critiques made, for example, of Judith Butler's recent turn to the ontology of vulnerability and what Bonnie Honig (discussing Butler and others) terms the new "mortalist humanism": Julian Reid, "The Vulnerable Subject of Liberal War," *South Atlantic Quarterly* 110, no. 3 (2011); and Bonnie Honig, "Antigone's Two Laws: Greek Tragedy and the Politics of Humanism," *New Literary History* 41, no. 1 (2010). See also, specifically in reference to the types of subjectivity the discourse of human rights presupposes and reproduces, Brown, "'The Most We Can Hope For'?," 460.

78. For a critical discussion of the metaphor of "balancing," see Jeremy Waldron, "Security and Liberty: The Image of Balance," *Journal of Political Philosophy* 11, no. 2 (2003).

79. 521 US 702, 728 (citing *Cruzan* 497 US 261, 282 [per Rehnquist CJ]).

80. Foucault, "'*Omnes et Singulatim*,'" 325.

81. Tierney, "Suicidal Thoughts," 605, 604.

82. For a recent exception which reads human rights not from a Foucauldian but a Bergsonian perspective, as a form of self-care, see Alexandre Lefebvre, *Human Rights as a Way of Life: On Bergson's Political Philosophy* (Stanford, CA: Stanford University Press, 2013).

83. Foucault, "The Simplest of Pleasures," 295.

84. Ibid.

85. Ibid., 295–96.

86. Ibid., 296.

87. Ibid., 297. On Foucault's concept of "heterotopias," see Michel Foucault, "Of Other Spaces," trans. Jay Miskowiec, *Diacritics* 16, no. 1 (1986).

88. Foucault, "The Simplest of Pleasures," 297.

89. Hence in my opinion it is somewhat beside the point that, as Tierney frames it, Foucault's suggestions are "facetious" and "extreme," and that he may not even have been "serious" about actualizing them. It is much more relevant to consider the effect that their invocation produces (which Tierney goes on to recognize). See Tierney, "Suicidal Thoughts," 626.

90. Foucault, "The Simplest of Pleasures," 296.

91. Ibid.

92. Foucault, *The Hermeneutics of the Subject*, 357–58.

93. Ibid., 478.

94. Ibid., 108.

95. Ibid., 479.

96. Ibid., 497.

97. Ibid., 478.

98. Ibid. (and see also ibid., 504).

99. Foucault, "The Simplest of Pleasures," 296 (and for the classic reference to a philosophy that tries to "dictate to others, to tell them where their truth is and how to find it" as being "ludicrous," see Foucault, *The Use of Pleasure*, 9).

100. Quoted in Gros, "Course Context," in Foucault, *The Hermeneutics of the Subject*, 521.

101. Foucault, "On the Genealogy of Ethics," 233.

102. Ibid., 231.

103. Ibid., 230.

104. Ibid., 235.

105. Zivi, *Making Rights Claims*, 7.

106. Foucault, "The Simplest of Pleasures," 296.

107. Foucault, *The Hermeneutics of the Subject*, 252.

108. See Sonu Bedi, *Rejecting Rights* (New York: Cambridge University Press, 2009).

109. Foucault, *Discipline and Punish*, 1–7.

110. On the former point, see my discussion in n. 78 of Chapter 1. On the specific question of the historiography of the death penalty in Foucault's work, see Michael

Meranze, "Michel Foucault, the Death Penalty and the Crisis of Historical Understanding," *Historical Reflections/Réflexions Historiques* 29, no. 2 (2003).

111. Importantly, it is not simply the rationale and purpose of capital punishment that have been altered, but the practice as well—from more to less spectacular, from gruesome to medicalized, from "noose" to "needle." For a discussion of some of these shifts, see Timothy V. Kaufman-Osborn, *From Noose to Needle: Capital Punishment and the Late Liberal State* (Ann Arbor: University of Michigan Press, 2002), esp. chaps. 2 and 7; and his "A Critique of Contemporary Death Penalty Abolitionism," *Punishment & Society* 8, no. 3 (2006).

112. Foucault, *"Society Must Be Defended,"* 254.

113. Ibid.

114. Ibid., 255.

115. Ibid.

116. Foucault, *The Will to Knowledge*, 138.

117. Adam Thurschwell, "Ethical Exception: Capital Punishment in the Figure of Sovereignty," *South Atlantic Quarterly* 107, no. 3 (2008): 578.

118. Michel Foucault, "Pompidou's Two Deaths," in *Essential Works of Foucault*, vol. 3, *Power*, 418.

119. Ibid., 419.

120. Ibid.

121. Ibid.

122. Ibid.

123. See generally Foucault, "About the Concept of the 'Dangerous Individual.'"

124. Michel Foucault, "The Proper Use of Criminals," in *Essential Works of Foucault*, vol. 3, *Power*, 433.

125. For a discussion of this historical moment and a comparison to a previous (unsuccessful) attempt at abolition, see Robert Nye, "Two Capital Punishment Debates in France: 1908 and 1981," *Historical Reflections/Réflexions Historiques* 29, no. 2 (2003).

126. Michel Foucault, "Against Replacement Penalties," in *Essential Works of Foucault*, vol. 3, *Power*, 459.

127. Ibid., 460.

128. Ibid. Of course, Foucault's subsequent account of neoliberal forms of penality, which are based not upon an anthropology of the criminal subject but rather upon the rational-choice logic of an interest-maximizing subject, demonstrates that the former disciplinary logic does not exhaust the penal repertoire. Again, I assume that both forms operate simultaneously, sometimes reinforcing and sometimes opposing the other. See Foucault, *The Birth of Biopolitics*, esp. lectures 9 and 10. For an excellent discussion, see Pat O'Malley, "The Birth of Biopolitical Justice," in *Re-Reading Foucault*. And finally, for an account of how these shifts in neoliberal penality play out in the particular political context of American capital punishment, see Andrew Dilts, "Death Penalty 'Abolition' in Neoliberal Times: The SAFE California Act and the Nexus of Savings and Security," in *Death and Other Penalties*, ed. Geoffrey Adelsberg, Lisa Guenther, and Scott Zeman (New York: Fordham University Press, 2015).

129. Foucault, "Pompidou's Two Deaths," 419.

130. Foucault, "About the Concept of the 'Dangerous Individual,'" 178.

131. Quoted in Nye, "Two Capital Punishment Debates in France," 223.

132. Foucault, "Against Replacement Penalties," 460.

133. Michel Foucault, "The Anxiety of Judging," in *Foucault Live*, 254.

134. Article 6 of the International Covenant on Civil and Political Rights (ICCPR) reads: "Every human being has the inherent right to life. This right shall be protected by law. No one shall be arbitrarily deprived of his life." Article 7 of the European Convention on Human Rights reads, in relevant part: "No one shall be subjected to torture or to cruel, inhuman or degrading treatment or punishment." Article 6 of the ICCPR reflects the tension between the universalist language of inherency and the pragmatic accommodation to state practice which, as critical observers of international law have long maintained, structures the operation of the discourse (for the classic reference, see Martti Koskenniemi, *From Apology to Utopia: The Structure of International Legal Argument* [Cambridge: Cambridge University Press, 2005]). While the opening language of Article 6 that I have just quoted might lead one to assume international human rights law forbids the death penalty outright, subsequent references to those condemned to die having "the right to seek pardon or commutation of the sentence," for example, make clear that human rights law stops short of outlawing capital punishment per se (only its "arbitrary forms"). It provides a regulatory framework for, rather than a normative critique of, the death penalty. Articles 2 and 3 of the European Convention on Human Rights are cast in similar terms. For an appreciation of the role that international human rights law has played in domestic struggles for abolition of the death penalty, see William A. Schabas, "International Law, Politics, Diplomacy and the Abolition of the Death Penalty," *William & Mary Bill of Rights Journal* 13, no. 2 (2004).

135. According to Amnesty International the death penalty represents a contravention of both rights. See Amnesty International, "The Death Penalty in International Law," http://www.amnesty.org/en/death-penalty/international-law.

136. Foucault, "Against Replacement Penalties," 460 (and see Foucault, "The Anxiety of Judging," 254).

137. Foucault, *The Will to Knowledge*, 144.

138. Ibid., 145.

139. For an account of an "affirmative" biopolitics of rights developed not through Foucault but via Arendt and Agamben, see chapter 7 of Miguel Vatter, *The Republic of the Living: Biopolitics and the Critique of Civil Society* (New York: Fordham University Press, 2014).

140. In the context of American death penalty abolitionism Andrew Dilts demonstrates very clearly the political dangers of simply opposing the death penalty through the invocation of "life" in his analysis of the campaign to support "life imprisonment without the possibility of parole" (LWOP) as a replacement for or alternative punishment to the death penalty. See Dilts, "Death Penalty 'Abolition' in Neoliberal Times."

141. For a discussion of Foucault's involvement in protesting Franco's execution of

militants from ETA (the Basque separatist group) and FRAP (a Maoist group) in 1975, see Macey, *The Lives of Michel Foucault*, 341–50.

142. *Furman v Georgia* 408 US 238 was the Supreme Court case in 1972 that produced a nationwide de facto moratorium on the death penalty through holding that as currently practiced by the states the punishment violated the US Constitution's 8th Amendment guarantee against "cruel and unusual punishment" because of the arbitrary and capricious way in which it was administered (but not because it was, per se, cruel). In a subsequent decision in 1976, *Gregg v Georgia* 428 US 153, the Supreme Court constitutionally vindicated the post-*Furman* capital procedures of five separate states (Georgia, Florida, Texas, North Carolina, and Louisiana), opening the way to the retention and procedural amelioration of the death penalty. On the paradoxical position in which the reformist "path to abolition" has placed abolitionists, see Timothy V. Kaufman-Osborn, "Perfect Execution: Abolitionism and the Paradox of Lethal Injection," in *The Road to Abolition?: The Future of Capital Punishment in the United States*, ed. Charles J. Ogletree, Jr., and Austin Sarat (New York: NYU Press, 2009).

143. See his dissenting opinion in *Callins v Collins* 510 US 1141.

144. For the most penetrating account available of the interconnection of Foucault's political work on prisons and his theorization of disciplinary power, see Hoffman, *Foucault and Power*, 15–45.

Conclusion

The epigraphs to this chapter, respectively, are from Samuel Moyn, *The Last Utopia: Human Rights in History* (Cambridge, MA: Belknap Press of Harvard University Press, 2010), 4; Wendy Brown, *Politics Out of History* (Princeton, NJ: Princeton University Press, 2001), 102; and Frédéric Mégret, "Where Does the Critique of International Human Rights Stand?: An Exploration in 18 Vignettes," in *New Approaches to International Law: The European and the American Experiences*, ed. José Maria Beneyto and David Kennedy (The Hague: JMC Asser Press, 2012), 32.

1. Michel Foucault, "What Is Called 'Punishing'?," in *Essential Works of Foucault*, vol. 3, *Power*, 384.

2. Quoted in "Dialogue Between Michel Foucault and Baqir Parham," reproduced as an appendix in Afary and Anderson, *Foucault and the Iranian Revolution*, 185.

3. See Mark Kelly, "Against Utopia and Prophecy: Foucault and the Future," *Thesis Eleven* 120, no. 1 (2014); and Foucault, "What Is Enlightenment?," 316.

4. The "short twentieth century" (1914–1991) is a creation of the historian Eric Hobsbawm (see his masterful *The Age of Extremes: The Short Twentieth Century, 1914–1991* [London: Abacus, 1994]). For a passing comment of his on the rise of human rights in the age of anti-communism which aligns with Moyn's thesis, see Eric Hobsbawm, *How to Change the World: Marx and Marxism, 1840–2011* (London: Little, Brown, 2011), 397–98.

5. Moyn, *The Last Utopia*.

6. It has not conclusively silenced it, however. To the contrary, Moyn's book has in fact generated a significant critical literature which I cannot survey in its entirety here.

For a recent discussion of the book, see the contributions of Jason Frank, Pheng Cheah, Antony Anghie, and Seyla Benhabib in a special issue of the journal *Qui Parle* (vol. 22, no. 1 [Fall/Winter 2013]) titled "Human Rights Between Past and Future." For Moyn's own response to some of these debates, see his *Human Rights and the Use of History* (London: Verso, 2014).

7. For example, see Ishay, *The History of Human Rights*.

8. For example, see Hunt, *Inventing Human Rights*.

9. For example, see Ignatieff, *Human Rights as Politics and Idolatry*.

10. Moyn, *The Last Utopia*, 155.

11. On human rights and poverty, see Susan Marks, "Human Rights and the Bottom Billion," *European Human Rights Law Review* 1 (2009).

12. For the minimalist claim, see Ignatieff, *Human Rights as Politics and Idolatry*. For a parsing and critique of this claim from two different traditions in political philosophy, see Brown, "'The Most We Can Hope For'?"; and Joshua Cohen, "Minimalism About Human Rights: The Most We Can Hope For?," *Journal of Political Philosophy* 12, no. 2 (2004).

13. Moyn, *The Last Utopia*, 4.

14. On anti-politics, see Brown, "'The Most We Can Hope For'?"

15. Moyn, *The Last Utopia*, 213.

16. For one such attempt, see Martin Krygier, "The Rule of Law After the Short Twentieth Century: A Global Career," in *Law, Society and Community: Essays in Honour of Roger Cotterrell*, ed. Richard Nobles and David Schiff (Aldershot, UK: Ashgate, 2014).

17. Wolin, "From the 'Death of Man' to Human Rights," 177–78.

18. As discussed in Chapter 2.

19. Wolin, "From the 'Death of Man' to Human Rights," 180.

20. Ibid., 181.

21. Ibid., 181–82.

22. See, for example, Michael Walzer, "The Politics of Michel Foucault," in *Foucault: A Critical Reader*, 66–67.

23. Foucault, "On the Genealogy of Ethics," 256.

24. Cf. Beaulieu, "Towards a Liberal Utopia."

25. For a fuller consideration of "human rights pragmatism," see my "Theorising Human Rights," in *The Oxford Handbook of International Legal Theory*, ed. Florian Hoffmann and Anne Orford (Oxford: Oxford University Press, forthcoming 2015). Of course, the characterization of Foucault as "a certain pragmatist" begs a range of philosophical questions that this study is ill equipped and now out of time to answer. Thankfully, that territory has been masterfully mapped by Colin Koopman. His *Genealogy as Critique* (a book primarily about Foucault) makes the argument in its closing chapters for supplementing Foucault with the intellectual and reconstructive resources of pragmatism, while his *Pragmatism as Transition: Historicity and Hope in James, Dewey, and Rorty* (New York: Columbia University Press, 2009) makes, in its closing chapter, the argument for the connection between Foucault and pragmatism from the other side: pragmatism. Koopman's project is hence not to assimilate Foucault to pragmatism (or

vice versa) but to generate a dialogue between the two philosophical traditions and approaches.

26. Patricia Williams, cited in Brown, *States of Injury*, 121n41.

27. Patton, "Foucault, Critique and Rights," 284.

28. *Pace* Pickett, *Use and Abuse*, 97n19.

29. Michel Foucault, "The End of the Monarchy of Sex," in *Foucault Live*, 225.

30. Todd May, "Foucault Now?," *Foucault Studies* 3 (2005): 76.

31. Ibid., 72.

32. Ibid.

33. For a helpful methodological reflection on the deployment of Foucault's analytics (or "methods"), as against the turning of his concepts into global categories, see Colin Koopman and Tomas Matza, "Putting Foucault to Work: Analytic and Concept in Foucaultian Inquiry," *Critical Inquiry* 39, no. 4 (2013). The Foucauldian politics of rights that I have argued for in this book is of course not exactly a method—in the same way, for example, as are genealogy and archaeology—but is instead an orientation that plays out differently in different political contexts. The same lesson that Koopman and Matza draw from their parsing of Foucault, though, broadly applies to my project—namely, an attention to context and the way in which certain aspects of his work travel while others call for further problematizing and rethinking.

34. Brown, "Revaluing Critique," 471.

35. Douzinas, *The End of Human Rights*, 1.

36. For example, see Brown, "'The Most We Can Hope For'?"; and David Kennedy, *The Dark Sides of Virtue: Reassessing International Humanitarianism* (Princeton, NJ: Princeton University Press, 2004).

37. Zachary Manfredi, "Recent Histories and Uncertain Futures: Contemporary Critiques of International Human Rights and Humanitarianism," *Qui Parle* 22, no. 1 (2013): 7.

38. I analyze this tendency more fully in Golder, "Beyond Redemption?"

39. For the classic references, see *Nonsense on Stilts: Bentham, Burke and Marx on the Rights of Man*, ed. Jeremy Waldron (London: Methuen, 1987).

40. Frédéric Mégret, "Where Does the Critique of International Human Rights Stand?: An Exploration in 18 Vignettes," in *New Approaches to International Law: The European and the American Experiences*, ed. José Maria Beneyto and David Kennedy (The Hague: JMC Asser Press, 2012), 5.

41. In political theory, see also Zivi, *Making Rights Claims*; and in the field of postcolonial legal studies, Ratna Kapur, "In the Aftermath of Critique We Are Not in Epistemic Free Fall: Human Rights, the Subaltern Subject, and the Non-Liberal Search for Freedom and Happiness," *Law & Critique* 25, no. 1 (2014). The point is broader than the particular reliance by theorists upon Foucault; rather, it is about the almost axiomatic acceptance of certain key Foucauldian premises about the genealogical counterdeployment and resignification of rights.

42. Manfredi, "Recent Histories and Uncertain Futures," 7. The point, though, is surely that there are hardly any on the left today who have done or continue to do so.

For some uncompromising exceptions to the general rule, see Alain Badiou, *Ethics: An Essay on the Understanding of Evil*, trans. Peter Hallward (London: Verso, 2002); and Giorgio Agamben, "Beyond Human Rights," in *Means Without End: Notes on Politics*, trans. Vincenzo Binetti and Cesare Casarino (Minneapolis: University of Minnesota Press, 2000).

43. Butler, "Competing Universalities," 177.

44. This is the question that Brown, "'The Most We Can Hope For'?," poses.

45. Foucault, "What Is Enlightenment?," 313.

BIBLIOGRAPHY

Afary, Janet, and Kevin B. Anderson. *Foucault and the Iranian Revolution: Gender and the Seductions of Islamism*. Chicago: University of Chicago Press, 2005.

Agamben, Giorgio. "Beyond Human Rights." In *Means Without End: Notes on Politics*, translated by Vincenzo Binetti and Cesare Casarino, 14–26. Minneapolis: University of Minnesota Press, 2000.

———. *Remnants of Auschwitz: The Witness and the Archive*. Translated by Daniel Heller-Roazen. New York: Zone Books, 2002.

Alessandrini, Anthony C. "The Humanism Effect: Fanon, Foucault, and Ethics Without Subjects." *Foucault Studies* 7 (2009): 64–80.

Allen, Amy. *The Politics of Ourselves: Power, Autonomy, and Gender in Contemporary Critical Theory*. New York: Columbia University Press, 2008.

Alston, Philip. "Does the Past Matter?: On the Origins of Human Rights." *Harvard Law Review* 126, no. 7 (2013): 2043–81.

Anderson, Perry. *Arguments Within English Marxism*. London: New Left Books, 1980.

Badiou, Alain. *Ethics: An Essay on the Understanding of Evil*. Translated by Peter Hallward. London: Verso, 2002.

Bailey, Richard. "Strategy, Rupture, Rights: Reflections on Law and Resistance in Immigration Detention." *Australian Feminist Law Journal* 31, no. 1 (2009): 33–56.

Balibar, Étienne. "'Rights of Man' and 'Rights of the Citizen': The Modern Dialectic of Equality and Freedom." In *Masses, Classes, Ideas: Studies on Politics and Philosophy Before and After Marx*, translated by James Swenson, 39–60. New York: Routledge, 1994.

Ball, Carlos A. "Sexual Ethics and Postmodernism in Gay Rights Philosophy." *North Carolina Law Review* 80, no. 2 (2002): 367–464.

Barry, Andrew, Thomas Osborne, and Nikolas Rose, eds. *Foucault and Political Reason: Liberalism, Neo-Liberalism and Rationalities of Government*. London: Routledge, 1996.

Beaulieu, Alain. "Towards a Liberal Utopia: The Connection Between Foucault's Reporting on the Iranian Revolution and the Ethical Turn." *Philosophy & Social Criticism* 36, no. 7 (2010): 801–18.

Bedi, Sonu. *Rejecting Rights*. New York: Cambridge University Press, 2009.

Behrent, Michael C. "Accidents Happen: François Ewald, the 'Antirevolutionary' Foucault, and the Intellectual Politics of the French Welfare State." *Journal of Modern History* 82, no. 3 (2010): 585–624.

———. "Liberalism Without Humanism: Michel Foucault and the Free-Market Creed, 1976–1979." *Modern Intellectual History* 6, no. 3 (2009): 539–68.

Bernauer, James. "Michel Foucault's Philosophy of Religion: An Introduction to the Non-Fascist Life." In *Michel Foucault and Theology: The Politics of Religious Experience*, edited by James Bernauer and Jeremy Carrette, 77–98. Aldershot, UK: Ashgate, 2004.

Bernstein, Richard J. "Foucault: Critique as a Philosophical Ethos." In *Critique and Power: Recasting the Foucault/Habermas Debate*, edited by Michael Kelly, 211–41. Cambridge, MA: MIT Press, 1994.

Bhandar, Brenna. "Strategies of Legal Rupture: The Politics of Judgment." *Windsor Yearbook of Access to Justice* 30 (2012): 59–78.

Biebricher, Thomas. "Foucault and the Politics of Rights." *Journal of Political Power* 5, no. 2 (2012): 301–18.

———. "Habermas, Foucault and Nietzsche: A Double Misunderstanding." *Foucault Studies* 3 (2005): 1–26.

———. "The Practices of Theorists: Habermas and Foucault as Public Intellectuals." *Philosophy & Social Criticism* 37, no. 6 (2011): 709–34.

Binder, Guyora. "Representing Nazism: Advocacy and Identity at the Trial of Klaus Barbie." *Yale Law Journal* 98, no. 7 (1989): 1321–83.

Blanchot, Maurice. "Michel Foucault as I Imagine Him." In *Foucault/Blanchot*, translated by Jeffrey Mehlman, 61–109. New York: Zone Books, 1990.

Bourg, Julian. *From Revolution to Ethics: May 1968 and Contemporary French Thought*. Montreal: McGill-Queens University Press, 2007.

Bowring, Bill. "What Is Radical in 'Radical International Law'?" *Finnish Yearbook of International Law* 22 (2011): 3–29.

Brich, Cecile. "The Groupe d'Information sur les Prisons: The Voice of Prisoners? Or Foucault's?" *Foucault Studies* 5 (2008): 26–47.

Brown, Wendy. *Edgework: Critical Essays on Knowledge and Power*. Princeton, NJ: Princeton University Press, 2005.

———. "Genealogical Politics." In *The Later Foucault*, edited by Jeremy Moss, 33–49. London: SAGE, 1998.

———. "'The Most We Can Hope For'?: Human Rights and the Politics of Fatalism." *South Atlantic Quarterly* 103, nos. 2 and 3 (2004): 451–63.

———. *Politics Out of History*. Princeton, NJ: Princeton University Press, 2001.

———. "Revaluing Critique: A Response to Kenneth Baynes." *Political Theory* 28, no. 4 (2000): 469–79.

———. *States of Injury: Power and Freedom in Late Modernity.* Princeton, NJ: Princeton University Press, 1995.

———. "Suffering Rights as Paradoxes." *Constellations* 7, no. 2 (2000): 229–41.

———. "Wounded Attachments." *Political Theory* 21, no. 3 (1993): 390–410.

Brown, Wendy, and Janet Halley, eds. *Left Legalism/Left Critique.* Durham, NC: Duke University Press, 2002.

Brusseau, James. *Decadence of the French Nietzsche.* Plymouth, UK: Lexington, 2005.

Burchell, Graham, Colin Gordon, and Peter Miller, eds. *The Foucault Effect: Studies in Governmentality.* Chicago: University of Chicago Press, 1991.

Butler, Judith. "Beside Oneself: On the Limits of Sexual Autonomy." In *Undoing Gender,* 17–39. New York: Routledge, 2004.

———. *Bodies That Matter: On the Discursive Limits of "Sex."* New York: Routledge, 1993.

———. "Competing Universalities." In *Contingency, Hegemony, Universality: Contemporary Dialogues on the Left,* edited by Judith Butler, Ernesto Laclau, and Slavoj Žižek, 136–81.

———. "Contingent Foundations: Feminism and the Question of 'Postmodernism.'" In *Feminists Theorize the Political,* edited by Judith Butler and Joan W. Scott, 3–21. New York: Routledge, 1992.

———. *Excitable Speech: A Politics of the Performative.* New York: Routledge, 1997.

———. *Gender Trouble: Feminism and the Subversion of Identity.* New York: Routledge, 1990.

———. *Giving an Account of Oneself.* New York: Fordham University Press, 2004.

———. "Is Kinship Always Already Heterosexual?" In *Undoing Gender,* 102–30. New York: Routledge, 2004.

———. "The Sensibility of Critique: Reply to Asad and Mahmood." In *Is Critique Secular?: Blasphemy, Injury and Free Speech,* edited by Talal Asad, Wendy Brown, Judith Butler, and Saba Mahmood, 101–36. Berkeley, CA: Townsend Center for the Humanities, 2009.

———. "Sexual Inversions." In *Foucault and the Critique of Institutions,* edited by John Caputo and Mark Yount, 81–98. University Park: Pennsylvania State University Press, 1993.

———. "What Is Critique?: An Essay on Foucault's Virtue." In *The Judith Butler Reader,* edited by Sara Salih (with Judith Butler), 301–22. Oxford, UK: Blackwell, 2004.

Butler, Judith, and Athena Athanasiou. *Dispossession: The Performative in the Political.* Cambridge, UK: Polity, 2013.

Butler, Judith, Ernesto Laclau, and Slavoj Žižek, eds. *Contingency, Hegemony, Universality: Contemporary Dialogues on the Left.* London: Verso, 2000.

Butler, Judith, and Gayatri Chakravorty Spivak. *Who Sings the Nation State?: Language, Politics, Belonging.* Oxford, UK: Seagull Books, 2007.

Cadman, Louisa. "How (Not) to Be Governed: Foucault, Critique, and the Political." *Environment and Planning D: Society and Space* 28, no. 3 (2010): 539–56.

Cahill, Ann J. "Foucault, Rape, and the Construction of the Feminine Body." *Hypatia* 15, no. 1 (2000): 43–63.

Callinicos, Alex. *Against Postmodernism*. Cambridge, UK: Polity, 1989.

Campbell, David. "Why Fight: Humanitarianism, Principles, and Post-Structuralism." *Millennium: Journal of International Studies* 27, no. 3 (1998): 497–521.

Chambers, Samuel A. "Ghostly Rights." *Cultural Critique* 54 (Spring 2003): 148–77.

———. "Giving Up (on) Rights?: The Future of Rights and the Project of Radical Democracy." *American Journal of Political Science* 48, no. 2 (2004): 185–200.

———. *The Lessons of Rancière*. New York: Oxford University Press, 2013.

Chevallier, Philippe. "Michel Foucault and the Question of Right." In *Re-Reading Foucault: On Law, Power and Rights*, edited by Ben Golder, 171–87. Abingdon, UK: Routledge, 2012.

Christodoulidis, Emilios. "Strategies of Rupture," *Law & Critique* 20, no. 1 (2009): 3–26.

Christofferson, Michael Scott. *French Intellectuals Against the Left: The Antitotalitarian Moment of the 1970s*. New York: Berghahn Books, 2004.

Cohen, Joshua. "Minimalism About Human Rights: The Most We Can Hope For?" *Journal of Political Philosophy* 12, no. 2 (2004): 190–213.

Connolly, William E. "Taylor, Foucault, and Otherness." *Political Theory* 13, no. 3 (1985): 365–76.

Cornell, Drucilla. *Transformations: Recollective Imagination and Sexual Difference*. New York: Routledge, 1993.

Crano, R.d. "Genealogy, Virtuality, War." *Foucault Studies* 11 (2011): 156–78.

Cusset, François. *French Theory: How Foucault, Derrida, Deleuze, & Co. Transformed the Intellectual Life of the United States*. Translated by Jeff Fort. Minneapolis: University of Minnesota Press, 2008.

Davidson, Arnold I. "In Praise of Counter-Conduct." *History of the Human Sciences* 24, no. 4 (2011): 25–41.

Deacon, Roger. "Foucault and Clausewitz: War and Power." *Scientia Militaria* 31, no. 1 (2003): 37–48.

Dean, Mitchell. *Governmentality: Power and Rule in Modern Society*. 2nd ed. London: SAGE, 2010.

Deleuze, Gilles. *Foucault*. Translated by Seán Hand. London: Continuum, 1999.

Delgado, Richard. "The Ethereal Scholar: Does Critical Legal Studies Have What Minorities Want?" *Harvard Civil Rights–Civil Liberties Law Review* 22, no. 2 (1987): 301–22.

Derrida, Jacques. "A Discussion with Jacques Derrida." *Theory & Event* 5, no. 1 (2001): paras. [1]–[49].

———. "Ethics and Politics Today." In *Negotiations: Interventions and Interviews, 1971–2001*, translated and edited by Elizabeth Rottenberg, 295–314. Stanford, CA: Stanford University Press, 2002.

Dews, Peter. *Logics of Disintegration: Post-Structuralist Thought and the Claims of Critical Theory*. London: Verso, 1987.

———. "The Return of the Subject in Late Foucault." *Radical Philosophy* 51 (Spring 1989): 37–41.

Dilts, Andrew. "Death Penalty 'Abolition' in Neoliberal Times: The SAFE California Act and the Nexus of Savings and Security." In *Death and Other Penalties*, edited by

Geoffrey Adelsberg, Lisa Guenther, and Scott Zeman, 106–29. New York: Fordham University Press, 2015.

Donnelly, Jack. "Human Rights and Asian Values: A Defence of 'Western' Universalism." In *The East Asian Challenge for Human Rights*, edited by Joanne R. Bauer and Daniel A. Bell, 60–87. Cambridge: Cambridge University Press, 1999.

———. *Universal Human Rights in Theory and Practice*, 2nd ed. Ithaca, NY: Cornell University Press, 2003.

Dosse, François. *Gilles Deleuze and Félix Guattari: Intersecting Lives*. Translated by Deborah Glassman. New York: Columbia University Press, 2010.

———. *History of Structuralism*. Vol. 2, *The Sign Sets, 1967–Present*. Translated by Deborah Glassman. Minneapolis: University of Minnesota Press, 1997.

Douzinas, Costas. "*Adikia*: On Communism and Rights." In *The Idea of Communism*, edited by Costas Douzinas and Slavoj Žižek, 81–100. London: Verso, 2010.

———. *The End of Human Rights: Critical Legal Thought at the Turn of the Century*. Oxford, UK: Hart, 2000.

———. *Human Rights and Empire: The Political Philosophy of Cosmopolitanism*. Abingdon, UK: Routledge, 2007.

———. "Oubliez Critique." *Law & Critique* 16, no. 1 (2005): 47–69.

Dreyfus, Hubert, and Paul Rabinow. *Michel Foucault: Beyond Structuralism and Hermeneutics*. 2nd ed. Chicago: University of Chicago Press, 1983.

Durkheim, Emile. *Suicide: A Study in Sociology*. Translated by John A. Spaulding and George Simpson. New York: Free Press, 1979.

Dworkin, Ronald. "Rights as Trumps." In *Theories of Rights*, edited by Jeremy Waldron, 153–67. New York: Oxford University Press, 1984.

———. *Taking Rights Seriously*. Cambridge, MA: Harvard University Press, 1978.

Dworkin, Ronald, et al. "Assisted Suicide: The Philosophers' Brief." *New York Review of Books*, 27 March 1997, available online at: http://www.nybooks.com/articles/archives/1997/mar/27/assisted-suicide-the-philosophers-brief.

Eagleton, Terry. *The Ideology of the Aesthetic*. Oxford, UK: Blackwell, 1990.

Eribon, Didier. *Michel Foucault*. Translated by Betsy Wing. Cambridge, MA: Harvard University Press, 1991.

Ewald, François. "Norms, Discipline, and the Law." Translated by Marjorie Beale. In *Law and the Order of Culture*, edited by Robert Post, 138–61. Berkeley: University of California Press, 1991.

Fitzpatrick, Peter. "Foucault's Case: Subject and Subjection in Law." In *Michel Foucault: Critical Assessments*, vol. 7, edited by Barry Smart, 222–35. London: Routledge, 1995.

———. "Foucault's Other Law." In *Re-Reading Foucault: On Law, Power and Rights*, edited by Ben Golder, 39–63. Abingdon, UK: Routledge, 2012.

Ford, Richard T. "Beyond 'Difference': A Reluctant Critique of Legal Identity Politics." In *Left Legalism/Left Critique*, edited by Wendy Brown and Janet Halley, 38–79. Durham, NC: Duke University Press, 2002.

Foucault, Michel. *Abnormal: Lectures at the Collège de France 1974–1975*. Translated by Graham Burchell. London: Verso, 2003.

———. "About the Concept of the 'Dangerous Individual' in Nineteenth-Century Legal Psychiatry." In *Essential Works of Foucault 1954–1984*, vol. 3, *Power*, translated by Robert Hurley et al. and edited by James D. Faubion, 176–200. New York: New Press, 2000.

———. "An Aesthetics of Existence." In *Politics, Philosophy, Culture: Interviews and Other Writings, 1977–1984*, translated by Alan Sheridan et al. and edited by Lawrence D. Kritzman, 47–53. London: Routledge, 1988.

———. "Against Replacement Penalties." In *Essential Works of Foucault 1954–1984*, vol. 3, *Power*, translated by Robert Hurley et al. and edited by James D. Faubion, 459–61. New York: New Press, 2000.

———. "Alternatives to the Prison: Dissemination or Decline of Social Control?" *Theory, Culture & Society* 26, no. 6 (2009): 12–24.

———. "The Anxiety of Judging." In *Foucault Live: Collected Interviews, 1961–1984*, translated by Lysa Hochroth and John Johnston and edited by Sylvère Lotringer, 241–54. New York: Semiotext(e), 1996.

———. *The Archaeology of Knowledge.* Translated by A. M. Sheridan Smith. London: Routledge, 1972.

———. *The Birth of Biopolitics: Lectures at the Collège de France 1978–79.* Translated by Graham Burchell. Basingstoke, UK: Palgrave Macmillan, 2008.

———. "The Birth of Social Medicine." Translated by Edgar Knowlton, Jr., William J. King, and Stuart Elden. In *Essential Works of Foucault 1954–1984*, vol. 3, *Power*, edited by James D. Faubion, 134–56. New York: New Press, 2000.

———. "Body/Power." In *Power/Knowledge: Selected Interviews and Other Writings 1972–1977*, translated by Colin Gordon et al. and edited by Colin Gordon, 55–62. Brighton, UK: Harvester Press, 1980.

———. *The Care of the Self.* Vol. 3 of *The History of Sexuality.* Translated by Robert Hurley. Harmondsworth, UK: Penguin Books, 1990.

———. "Confronting Governments: Human Rights." In *Essential Works of Foucault 1954–1984*, vol. 3, *Power*, translated by Robert Hurley et al. and edited by James D. Faubion, 474–75. New York: New Press, 2000.

———. *The Courage of Truth: Lectures at the Collège de France.* Translated by Graham Burchell. Basingstoke, UK: Palgrave Macmillan, 2011.

———. "The Crisis of Medicine or the Crisis of Antimedicine?" Translated by Edgar C. Knowlton, Jr., William King, and Clare O'Farrell. *Foucault Studies* 1 (2004): 5–19.

———. "Critical Theory/Intellectual History." In *Politics, Philosophy, Culture: Interviews and Other Writings, 1977–1984*, translated by Alan Sheridan et al. and edited by Lawrence D. Kritzman, 17–46. London: Routledge, 1988.

———. *Discipline and Punish: The Birth of the Prison.* Translated by Alan Sheridan. Harmondsworth, UK: Penguin, 1991.

———. *Du gouvernement des vivants: Cours au Collège de France, 1979–1980.* Paris: Seuil, 2012.

———. "The End of the Monarchy of Sex." In *Foucault Live: Collected Interviews, 1961–1984*, translated by Lysa Hochroth and John Johnston and edited by Sylvère Lotringer, 214–25. New York: Semiotext(e), 1996.

———. "The Ethics of the Concern for Self as a Practice of Freedom." In *Essential Works of Foucault 1954–1984*, vol. 1, *Ethics, Subjectivity and Truth*, translated by Robert Hurley et al. and edited by Paul Rabinow, 281–301. Harmondsworth, UK: Allen Lane/Penguin, 1997.

———. "Friendship as a Way of Life." In *Essential Works of Foucault 1954–1984*, vol. 1, *Ethics, Subjectivity and Truth*, translated by Robert Hurley et al. and edited by Paul Rabinow, 135–40. Harmondsworth, UK: Allen Lane/Penguin, 1997.

———. "Governmentality." Translated by Colin Gordon. In *The Foucault Effect: Studies in Governmentality*, edited by Graham Burchell, Colin Gordon, and Peter Miller, 87–104. Chicago: University of Chicago Press, 1991.

———. *The Government of Self and Others: Lectures at the Collège de France, 1982–1983*. Translated by Graham Burchell. Basingstoke, UK: Palgrave Macmillan, 2010.

———. *The Hermeneutics of the Subject: Lectures at the Collège de France, 1981–1982*. Translated by Graham Burchell. New York: Picador, 2005.

———. *History of Madness*. Translated by Jonathan Murphy and Jean Khalfa. Abingdon, UK: Routledge, 2006.

———. "The Incorporation of the Hospital into Modern Technology." Translated by Edgar Knowlton, Jr., William J. King, and Stuart Elden. In *Space, Knowledge and Power: Foucault and Geography*, edited by Jeremy W. Crampton and Stuart Elden, 141–52. Aldershot, UK: Ashgate, 2007.

———. "Interview with *Actes*." In *Essential Works of Foucault 1954–1984*, vol. 3, *Power*, translated by Robert Hurley et al. and edited by James D. Faubion, 394–402. New York: New Press, 2000.

———. "Interview with Michel Foucault." In *Essential Works of Foucault 1954–1984*, vol. 3, *Power*, translated by Robert Hurley et al. and edited by James D. Faubion, 239–97. New York: New Press, 2000.

———. "Letter to Certain Leaders of the Left." In *Essential Works of Foucault 1954–1984*, vol. 3, *Power*, translated by Robert Hurley et al. and edited by James D. Faubion, 426–28. New York: New Press, 2000.

———. "The Masked Philosopher." Translated by Alan Sheridan. In *Politics, Philosophy, Culture: Interviews and Other Writings, 1977–1984*, edited by Lawrence D. Kritzman, 323–30. London: Routledge, 1988.

———. "The Moral and Social Experience of the Poles Can No Longer Be Obliterated." In *Essential Works of Foucault 1954–1984*, vol. 3, *Power*, translated by Robert Hurley et al. and edited by James D. Faubion, 465–73. New York: New Press, 2000.

———. "Nietzsche, Genealogy, History." In *Language, Counter-Memory, Practice: Selected Essays and Interviews*, translated by Donald F. Bouchard and Sherry Simon and edited by Donald F. Bouchard, 139–64. Ithaca, NY: Cornell University Press, 1977.

———. "Of Other Spaces." Translated by Jay Miskowiec. *Diacritics* 16, no. 1 (1986): 22–27.

———. "'Omnes et Singulatim': Toward a Critique of Political Reason." In *Essential Works of Foucault 1954–1984*, vol. 3, *Power*, translated by Robert Hurley et al. and edited by James D. Faubion, 298–325. New York: New Press, 2000.

———. "On Power." In *Politics, Philosophy, Culture: Interviews and Other Writings, 1977–1984*, translated by Alan Sheridan et al. and edited by Lawrence D. Kritzman, 96–109. London: Routledge, 1988.

———. "On the Genealogy of Ethics: An Overview of Work in Progress." In *Michel Foucault: Beyond Structuralism and Hermeneutics*, 2nd ed., written and edited by Hubert Dreyfus and Paul Rabinow, 229–52. Chicago: University of Chicago Press, 1983.

———. "Open Letter to Mehdi Bazargan." In *Essential Works of Foucault 1954–1984*, vol. 3, *Power*, translated by Robert Hurley et al. and edited by James D. Faubion, 439–42. New York: New Press, 2000.

———. *The Order of Things: An Archaeology of the Human Sciences*. Translated by Alan Sheridan. New York: Vintage Books, 1994.

———. "Orders of Discourse." Translated by Rupert Swyer. *Social Science Information* 10, no. 2 (1971): 7–30.

———. "Polemics, Politics and Problematizations: An Interview with Michel Foucault." In *Essential Works of Foucault 1954–1984*, vol. 1, *Ethics, Subjectivity and Truth*, translated by Robert Hurley et al. and edited by Paul Rabinow, 111–19. Harmondsworth, UK: Allen Lane/Penguin, 1997.

———. "The Political Technology of Individuals." In *Essential Works of Foucault 1954–1984*, vol. 3, *Power*, translated by Robert Hurley et al. and edited by James D. Faubion, 403–17. New York: New Press, 2000.

———. "Politics and the Study of Discourse." Translated by Colin Gordon. In *The Foucault Effect: Studies in Governmentality*, edited by Graham Burchell, Colin Gordon, and Peter Miller, 53–72. Chicago: University of Chicago Press, 1991.

———. "Pompidou's Two Deaths." In *Essential Works of Foucault 1954–1984*, vol. 3, *Power*, translated by Robert Hurley et al. and edited by James D. Faubion, 418–22. New York: New Press, 2000.

———. "Power and Strategies." In *Power/Knowledge: Selected Interviews and Other Writings 1972–1977*, translated by Colin Gordon et al. and edited by Colin Gordon, 134–45. Brighton, UK: Harvester Press, 1980.

———. "Préface à la deuxième edition." In *Dits et écrits II, 1976–1988*, edited by Daniel Defert and François Ewald, 949–53. Paris: Gallimard, 2001.

———. "Preface to *Anti-Oedipus*." In *Essential Works of Foucault 1954–1984*, vol. 3, *Power*, translated by Robert Hurley et al. and edited by James D. Faubion, 106–10. New York: New Press, 2000.

———. "Preface to *The History of Sexuality*, Volume Two." In *Essential Works of Foucault 1954–1984*, vol. 1, *Ethics, Subjectivity and Truth*, translated by Robert Hurley et al. and edited by Paul Rabinow, 199–205. Harmondsworth, UK: Allen Lane/Penguin, 1997.

———. "A Preface to Transgression." In *Language, Counter-Memory, Practice: Selected Essays and Interviews*, translated by Donald F. Bouchard and Sherry Simon and edited by Donald F. Bouchard, 29–52. Ithaca, NY: Cornell University Press, 1977.

———. "The Proper Use of Criminals." In *Essential Works of Foucault 1954–1984*, vol. 3, *Power*, translated by Robert Hurley et al. and edited by James D. Faubion, 429–34. New York: New Press, 2000.

———. "Questions of Method." Translated by Colin Gordon. In *The Foucault Effect: Studies in Governmentality*, edited by Graham Burchell, Colin Gordon, and Peter Miller, 73–86. Chicago: University of Chicago Press, 1991.

———. "The Risks of Security." In *Essential Works of Foucault 1954–1984*, vol. 3, *Power*, translated by Robert Hurley et al. and edited by James D. Faubion, 365–81. New York: New Press, 2000.

———. *Security, Territory, Population: Lectures at the Collège de France 1977–78*. Translated by Graham Burchell. Basingstoke, UK: Palgrave Macmillan, 2007.

———. "Sex, Power, and the Politics of Identity." In *Essential Works of Foucault 1954–1984*, vol. 1, *Ethics, Subjectivity and Truth*, translated by Robert Hurley et al. and edited by Paul Rabinow, 163–73. Harmondsworth, UK: Allen Lane/Penguin, 1997.

———. "Sexual Choice, Sexual Act." In *Essential Works of Foucault 1954–1984*, vol. 1, *Ethics, Subjectivity and Truth*, translated by Robert Hurley et al. and edited by Paul Rabinow, 141–56. Harmondsworth, UK: Allen Lane/Penguin, 1997.

———. "The Simplest of Pleasures." In *Foucault Live: Collected Interviews, 1961–1984*, translated by Lysa Hochroth and John Johnston and edited by Sylvère Lotringer, 295–97. New York: Semiotext(e), 1996.

———. "The Social Extension of the Norm." In *Foucault Live: Collected Interviews, 1961–1984*, translated by Lysa Hochroth and John Johnston and edited by Sylvère Lotringer, 196–99. New York: Semiotext(e), 1996.

———. "The Social Triumph of the Sexual Will." In *Essential Works of Foucault 1954–1984*, vol. 1, *Ethics, Subjectivity and Truth*, translated by Robert Hurley et al. and edited by Paul Rabinow, 157–62. Harmondsworth, UK: Allen Lane/Penguin, 1997.

———. *"Society Must Be Defended": Lectures at the Collège de France, 1975–76*. Translated by David Macey. London: Allen Lane, 2003.

———. "Space, Knowledge, and Power." In *Essential Works of Foucault 1954–1984*, vol. 3, *Power*, translated by Robert Hurley et al. and edited by James D. Faubion, 349–64. New York: New Press, 2000.

———. "The Subject and Power." In *Essential Works of Foucault 1954–1984*, vol. 3, *Power*, translated by Robert Hurley et al. and edited by James D. Faubion, 326–48. New York: New Press, 2000.

———. *Subjectivité et vérité: Cours au Collège de France, 1980–1981*. Paris: Seuil, 2014.

———. "Summoned to Court." In *Essential Works of Foucault 1954–1984*, vol. 3, *Power*, translated by Robert Hurley et al. and edited by James D. Faubion, 423–25. New York: New Press, 2000.

———. "Technologies of the Self." In *Essential Works of Foucault 1954–1984*, vol. 1, *Ethics, Subjectivity and Truth*, translated by Robert Hurley et al. and edited by Paul Rabinow, 223–51. Harmondsworth, UK: Allen Lane/Penguin, 1997.

———. "Truth and Power." In *Power/Knowledge: Selected Interviews and Other Writings 1972–1977*, translated by Colin Gordon et al. and edited by Colin Gordon, 109–33. Brighton, UK: Harvester Press, 1980.

———. "Two Lectures." In *Power/Knowledge: Selected Interviews and Other Writings*

1972–1977, translated by Colin Gordon et al. and edited by Colin Gordon, 78–108. Brighton, UK: Harvester Press, 1980.

———. "Useless to Revolt?" In *Essential Works of Foucault 1954–1984*, vol. 3, *Power*, translated by Robert Hurley et al. and edited by James D. Faubion, 449–53. New York: New Press, 2000.

———. *The Use of Pleasure*. Vol. 2 of *The History of Sexuality*. Translated by Robert Hurley. Harmondsworth, UK: Penguin, 1992.

———. "Vérité, pouvoir et soi." In *Dits et écrits II, 1976–1988*, edited by Daniel Defert and François Ewald, 1596–1602. Paris: Gallimard, 2001.

———. "What Is an Author?" Translated by Joseph V. Harari. In *Modern Criticism and Theory: A Reader*, edited by David Lodge, 197–210. London: Longman, 1988.

———. "What Is Called 'Punishing'?" In *Essential Works of Foucault 1954–1984*, vol. 3, *Power*, translated by Robert Hurley et al. and edited by James D. Faubion, 382–93. New York: New Press, 2000.

———. "What Is Critique?" Translated by Kevin Paul Geiman. In *What Is Enlightenment?: Eighteenth-Century Answers and Twentieth-Century Questions*, edited by James Schmidt, 382–98. Berkeley: University of California Press, 1996.

———. "What Is Enlightenment?" In *Essential Works of Foucault 1954–1984*, vol. 1, *Ethics, Subjectivity and Truth*, translated by Robert Hurley et al. and edited by Paul Rabinow, 303–19. Harmondsworth, UK: Allen Lane/Penguin, 1997.

———. *The Will to Knowledge*. Vol. 1 of *The History of Sexuality*. Translated by Robert Hurley. Harmondsworth, UK: Penguin, 1979.

———. *Wrong-Doing, Truth-Telling: The Function of Avowal in Justice*. Translated by Stephen W. Sawyer. Chicago: University of Chicago Press, 2014.

Fraser, Nancy. "Foucault on Modern Power: Empirical Insights and Normative Confusions." In *Unruly Practices: Power, Discourse, and Gender in Contemporary Social Theory*, 17–34. Minneapolis: University of Minnesota Press, 1989.

———. "Foucault's Body-Language: A Post-Humanist Political Rhetoric?" *Salmagundi* 61 (Fall 1983): 55–70.

———. "Michel Foucault: A 'Young Conservative'?" *Ethics* 96, no. 1 (1985): 165–84.

Fukuyama, Francis. *Our Posthuman Future: Consequences of the Biotechnology Revolution*. London: Penguin, 2002.

Garlick, Steven. "The Beauty of Friendship: Foucault, Masculinity and the Work of Art." *Philosophy & Social Criticism* 28, no. 5 (2002): 558–77.

Gearey, Adam. "'Change Is Gonna Come': Critical Legal Studies and the Legacies of the New Left." *Law & Critique* 24, no. 3 (2013): 211–28.

Geertz, Clifford. "Stir Crazy." *New York Review of Books*, 26 January 1978, 3–6.

Gemes, Ken. "Post-Modernism's Use and Abuse of Nietzsche." *Philosophy and Phenomenological Research* 62, no. 2 (2001): 337–60.

Glendon, Mary Ann. *Rights Talk: The Impoverishment of Political Discourse*. New York: Free Press, 1991.

Golder, Ben. "Beyond Redemption: Problematizing the Critique of Human Rights in

Contemporary International Legal Thought." *London Review of International Law* 2, no. 1 (2014): 77–114.

———. "Foucault and the Genealogy of Pastoral Power." *Radical Philosophy Review* 10, no. 2 (2007): 157–76.

———. "Foucault and the Unfinished Human of Rights." *Law, Culture and the Humanities* 6, no. 3 (2010): 354–74.

———. "Human Rights *Contra* Critique: Preliminary Notes on the Politics of Interpretation." *Australian Journal of Human Rights* 17, no. 2 (2011): 185–214.

———. "Theorising Human Rights." In *The Oxford Handbook of International Legal Theory*, edited by Florian Hoffmann and Anne Orford. Oxford: Oxford University Press, 2015 (forthcoming).

———. "What Is an Anti-Humanist Human Rights?" *Social Identities* 16, no. 5 (2010): 651–68.

Golder, Ben, and Peter Fitzpatrick. *Foucault's Law*. Abingdon, UK: Routledge, 2009.

Gordon, Colin. "Governmental Rationality: An Introduction." In *The Foucault Effect: Studies in Governmentality*, edited by Graham Burchell, Colin Gordon, and Peter Miller, 1–52. Chicago: University of Chicago Press, 1991.

Gros, Frédéric. "Course Context." In *The Hermeneutics of the Subject: Lectures at the Collège de France, 1981–1982*, 507–46. New York: Picador, 2005.

Gruber, David F. "Foucault's Critique of the Liberal Individual." *Journal of Philosophy* 86, no. 11 (1989): 615–21.

Gündoğdu, Ayten. "A Revolution in Rights: Reflections on the Democratic Invention of the Rights of Man." *Law, Culture and the Humanities* 10, no. 3 (2014): 367–79.

Gutting, Gary. *Michel Foucault's Archaeology of Scientific Reason*. Cambridge: Cambridge University Press, 1989.

Habermas, Jürgen. "Modernity Versus Postmodernity." *New German Critique* 22 (Winter 1981): 3–14.

———. "Paradigms of Law." *Cardozo Law Review* 17, nos. 4–5 (1995–96): 771–84.

———. "Some Questions Concerning the Theory of Power: Foucault Again." In *The Philosophical Discourse of Modernity: Twelve Lectures*, translated by Frederick G. Lawrence, 266–93. Cambridge, UK: Polity, 1997.

Hacking, Ian. "How Should We Do the History of Statistics?" In *The Foucault Effect: Studies in Governmentality*, translated by Colin Gordon and edited by Graham Burchell, Colin Gordon, and Peter Miller, 181–95. Chicago: University of Chicago Press, 1991.

———. "Self Improvement." In *Foucault: A Critical Reader*, edited by David Couzens Hoy, 221–40. Oxford, UK: Blackwell, 1986.

Halliday, Simon, and Bronwen Morgan. "I Fought the Law and the Law Won?: Legal Consciousness and the Critical Imagination." *Current Legal Problems* 66, no. 1 (2013): 1–32.

Han [Han-Pile], Béatrice. *Foucault's Critical Project: Between the Transcendental and the Historical*. Translated by Edward Pile. Stanford, CA: Stanford University Press, 2002.

——. "The 'Death of Man': Foucault and Anti-Humanism." In *Foucault and Philosophy*, edited by Timothy O'Leary and Christopher Falzon, 118–43. Oxford, UK: Wiley-Blackwell, 2010.

Hardt, Michael, and Antonio Negri. *Empire*. Cambridge, MA: Harvard University Press, 2000.

Hardy, Cynthia. "Refugee Determination: Power and Resistance in Systems of Foucauldian Power." *Administration & Society* 35, no. 4 (2003): 462–88.

Henkin, Louis. *The Age of Rights*. New York: Columbia University Press, 1990.

Hobsbawm, Eric. *The Age of Extremes: The Short Twentieth Century, 1914–1991*. London: Abacus, 1994.

——. *How to Change the World: Marx and Marxism, 1840–2011*. London: Little, Brown, 2011.

Hoffman, Marcelo. *Foucault and Power: The Influence of Political Engagement on Theories of Power*. New York: Bloomsbury, 2014.

Honig, Bonnie. "Antigone's Two Laws: Greek Tragedy and the Politics of Humanism." *New Literary History* 41, no. 1 (2010): 1–33.

——. *Paradox, Law, Democracy: Emergency Politics*. Princeton, NJ: Princeton University Press, 2009.

——. "What Foucault Saw at the Revolution: On the Use and Abuse of Theology for Politics." *Political Theory* 36, no. 2 (2008): 301–12.

Hooke, Alexander E. "The Order of Others: Is Foucault's Antihumanism Against Human Action?" *Political Theory* 15, no. 1 (1987): 38–60.

Hoover, Joe. "Towards a Politics for Human Rights: Ambiguous Humanity and Democratizing Rights." *Philosophy & Social Criticism* 39, no. 3 (2013): 935–61.

Hörnqvist, Magnus. *Risk, Power and the State: After Foucault*. Abingdon, UK: Routledge, 2010.

Horvath, Robert. "'The Solzhenitsyn Effect': East European Dissidents and the Demise of the Revolutionary Privilege." *Human Rights Quarterly* 29, no. 4 (2007): 879–907.

Hoy, David Couzens. *Critical Resistance: From Poststructuralism to Post-Critique*. Cambridge, MA: MIT Press, 2004.

——. "Foucault and Critical Theory." In *The Later Foucault*, edited by Jeremy Moss, 18–32. London: SAGE, 1998.

Hunt, Alan. "Getting Marx and Foucault into Bed Together!" *Journal of Law and Society* 31, no. 4 (2004): 592–609.

Hunt, Alan, and Gary Wickham. *Foucault and Law: Towards a Sociology of Law as Governance*. London: Pluto, 1994.

Hunt, Lynn. *Inventing Human Rights: A History*. New York: Norton, 2007.

Ignatieff, Michael. *Human Rights as Politics and Idolatry*. Princeton, NJ: Princeton University Press, 2001.

Ingram, James D. "What Is a 'Right to Have Rights'?: Three Images of the Politics of Human Rights." *American Political Science Review* 102, no. 4 (2008): 401–16.

Ishay, Micheline R. *The History of Human Rights: From Ancient Times to the Globalization Era*. Berkeley: University of California Press, 2008.

Ivison, Duncan. *Rights*. Stocksfield, UK: Acumen, 2008.

———. *The Self at Liberty: Political Argument and the Arts of Government*. Ithaca, NY: Cornell University Press, 1997.

Kant, Immanuel. "An Answer to the Question: 'What Is Enlightenment?'" In *Political Writings*, translated by H. B. Nisbet and edited by H. S. Reiss, 54–60. Cambridge: Cambridge University Press, 1970.

Kapur, Ratna. "In the Aftermath of Critique We Are Not in Epistemic Free Fall: Human Rights, the Subaltern Subject, and the Non-Liberal Search for Freedom and Happiness." *Law & Critique* 25, no. 1 (2014): 25–45.

Karlsen, Mads Peter, and Kaspar Villadsen. "Foucault, Maoism, Genealogy: The Influence of Political Militancy in Michel Foucault's Thought." *New Political Science* 37, no. 1 (2015): 91–117.

Kaufman-Osborn, Timothy V. "A Critique of Contemporary Death Penalty Abolitionism." *Punishment & Society* 8, no. 3 (2006): 365–83.

———. *From Noose to Needle: Capital Punishment and the Late Liberal State*. Ann Arbor: University of Michigan Press, 2002.

———. "Perfect Execution: Abolitionism and the Paradox of Lethal Injection." In *The Road to Abolition?: The Future of Capital Punishment in the United States*, edited by Charles J. Ogletree, Jr., and Austin Sarat, 215–51. New York: NYU Press, 2009.

Keenan, Thomas. "The 'Paradox' of Knowledge and Power: Foucault on the Bias." In *Fables of Responsibility: Aberrations and Predicaments in Ethics and Politics*, 134–74. Stanford, CA: Stanford University Press, 1997.

Kelly, Mark. "Against Utopia and Prophecy: Foucault and the Future." *Thesis Eleven* 120, no. 1 (2014): 104–18.

Kennedy, David. *The Dark Sides of Virtue: Reassessing International Humanitarianism*. Princeton, NJ: Princeton University Press, 2004.

Kennedy, Duncan. "Legal Education and the Reproduction of Hierarchy." *Journal of Legal Education* 32, no. 4 (1982): 591–615.

———. "The Stakes of Law, or Hale and Foucault!" In *Sexy Dressing Etc.*, 83–125. Cambridge, MA: Harvard University Press, 1993.

Kingston, Mark. "Subversive Friendships: Foucault on Homosexuality and Social Experimentation." *Foucault Studies* 7 (2009): 7–17.

Knox, Robert. "Marxism, International Law, and Political Strategy." *Leiden Journal of International Law* 22, no. 3 (2009): 413–36.

———. "Strategy and Tactics." *Finnish Yearbook of International Law* 21 (2010): 193–229.

Koopman, Colin. *Genealogy as Critique: Foucault and the Problems of Modernity*. Bloomington: Indiana University Press, 2013.

———. "Michel Foucault's Critical Empiricism Today: Concepts and Analytics in the Critique of Biopower and Infopower." In *Foucault Now: Critical Perspectives in Foucault Studies*, edited by James Faubion, 88–111. Cambridge, UK: Polity, 2014.

———. *Pragmatism as Transition: Historicity and Hope in James, Dewey, and Rorty*. New York: Columbia University Press, 2009.

Koopman, Colin, and Tomas Matza. "Putting Foucault to Work: Analytic and Concept in Foucaultian Inquiry." *Critical Inquiry* 39, no. 4 (2013): 817–40.

Koskenniemi, Martti. "Between Impunity and Show Trials." *Max Planck Yearbook of United Nations Law* 6 (2002): 1–35.

———. *From Apology to Utopia: The Structure of International Legal Argument.* Cambridge: Cambridge University Press, 2005.

———. *The Gentle Civilizer of Nations: The Rise and Fall of International Law, 1870–1960.* Cambridge: Cambridge University Press, 2002.

———. "International Law in Europe: Between Tradition and Renewal." *European Journal of International Law* 16, no. 1 (2005): 113–24.

Krever, Tor. "A Journal of the Legal Left?" *Unbound: Harvard Journal of the Legal Left* 9, no. 1 (2015): 1–12.

Krygier, Martin. "The Rule of Law After the Short Twentieth Century: A Global Career." In *Law, Society and Community: Essays in Honour of Roger Cotterrell,* edited by Richard Nobles and David Schiff, 327–46. Aldershot, UK: Ashgate, 2014.

Lefebvre, Alexandre. *Human Rights as a Way of Life: On Bergson's Political Philosophy.* Stanford, CA: Stanford University Press, 2013.

———. *The Image of Law: Deleuze, Bergson, Spinoza.* Stanford, CA: Stanford University Press, 2008.

Lefort, Claude. "Politics and Human Rights." In *The Political Forms of Modern Society: Bureaucracy, Democracy, Totalitarianism,* edited by John B. Thompson, 239–72. Cambridge, MA: MIT Press, 1986.

Lemke, Thomas. *Biopolitics: An Advanced Introduction.* New York: NYU Press, 2011.

———. "Foucault, Governmenality, and Critique." *Rethinking Marxism* 14, no. 3 (2002): 49–64.

———. "An Indigestible Meal?: Foucault, Governmentality and State Theory." *Distinktion: Scandinavian Journal of Social Theory* 8, no. 2 (2007): 43–64.

Lyotard, Jean-François. "The Other's Rights." In *On Human Rights,* translated by Chris Miller and Robert Smith and edited by Stephen Shute and Susan L. Hurley, 135–47. New York: Basic Books, 1993.

Macey, David. *The Lives of Michel Foucault: A Biography.* New York: Vintage Books, 1993.

MacKinnon, Catherine. *Feminism Unmodified: Discourses on Life and Law.* Cambridge, MA: Harvard University Press, 1987.

———. "Reflections on Sex Equality Under Law." *Yale Law Journal* 100, no. 5 (1991): 1281–1328.

———. *Towards a Feminist Theory of the State.* Cambridge, MA: Harvard University Press, 1989.

Malpas, Jeff. "Governing Theory: Ontology, Methodology and the Critique of Metaphysics." In *Rethinking Law, Society and Governance: Foucault's Bequest,* edited by Gary Wickham and George Pavlich, 125–40. Oxford, UK: Hart, 2001.

Manfredi, Zachary. "Recent Histories and Uncertain Futures: Contemporary Critiques of International Human Rights and Humanitarianism." *Qui Parle* 22, no. 1 (2013): 3–32.

Marks, John. *Gilles Deleuze: Vitalism and Multiplicity.* London: Pluto Press, 1998.

Marks, Susan. "False Contingency." *Current Legal Problems* 62, no. 1 (2009): 1–29.

———. "Human Rights and the Bottom Billion." *European Human Rights Law Review* 1 (2009): 37–49.

Martin, Rex. "Truth, Power, Self: An Interview with Michel Foucault." In *Technologies of the Self: A Seminar with Michel Foucault*, edited by Luther H. Martin, Huck Gutman, and Patrick H. Hutton, 9–15. Amherst: University of Massachusetts Press, 1988.

Marx, Karl. "On the Jewish Question." In *The Marx-Engels Reader*, translated by T. B. Bottomore and edited by Robert C. Tucker, 24–51. New York: W. W. Norton, 1972.

Matsuda, Mari J. "When the First Quail Calls: Multiple Consciousness as Jurisprudential Method." *Women's Rights Law Reporter* 11, no. 1 (1989): 7–10.

May, Todd. "Foucault Now?" *Foucault Studies* 3 (2005): 65–76.

Mbembe, Achille. "Necropolitics." Translated by Libby Meintjes. *Public Culture* 15, no. 1 (2003): 11–40.

McClure, Kirstie. "Taking Liberties in Foucault's Triangle: Sovereignty, Discipline, Governmentality, and the Subject of Rights." In *Identities, Politics, and Rights*, edited by Austin Sarat and Thomas R. Kearns, 149–92. Ann Arbor: University of Michigan Press, 1995.

Mégret, Frédéric. "Where Does the Critique of International Human Rights Stand?: An Exploration in 18 Vignettes." In *New Approaches to International Law: The European and the American Experiences*, edited by José Maria Beneyto and David Kennedy, 3–40. The Hague: JMC Asser Press, 2012.

Meranze, Michael. "Michel Foucault, the Death Penalty and the Crisis of Historical Understanding." *Historical Reflections/Réflexions Historiques* 29, no. 2 (2003): 191–209.

Miéville, China. *Between Equal Rights: A Marxist Theory of International Law*. Chicago: Haymarket, 2006.

Miller, James. *The Passion of Michel Foucault*. Cambridge, MA: Harvard University Press, 1993.

Miller, Peter, and Nikolas Rose. "Governing Economic Life." *Economy & Society* 19, no. 1 (1990): 1–31.

Minow, Martha, and Mary Lyndon Shanley. "Relational Rights and Responsibilities: Revisioning the Family in Liberal Political Theory and Law." *Hypatia* 11, no. 1 (1996): 4–29.

Morsink, Johannes. *Inherent Human Rights: Philosophical Roots of the Universal Declaration*. Philadelphia: University of Pennsylvania Press, 2009.

Mourad, Roger. "After Foucault: A New Form of Right." *Philosophy & Social Criticism* 29, no. 4 (2003): 451–81.

Moyn, Samuel. *Human Rights and the Use of History*. London: Verso, 2014.

———. *The Last Utopia: Human Rights in History*. Cambridge, MA: Belknap Press of Harvard University Press, 2010.

———. "Substance, Scale, and Salience: The Recent Historiography of Human Rights." *Annual Review of Law and Social Science* 8 (2012): 123–40.

Muckelbauer, John. "On Reading Differently: Through Foucault's Resistance." *College English* 63, no. 1 (2000): 71–94.

Murray, Stuart J. "Thanatopolitics: On the Use of Death for Mobilising Political Life." *Polygraph* 18 (2006): 191–215.

Nancy, Jean-Luc. *The Inoperative Community*. Translated by Peter Connor et al. Minneapolis: University of Minnesota Press, 1991.

Nealon, Jeffrey T. *Foucault Beyond Foucault: Power and Its Intensifications Since 1984*. Stanford, CA: Stanford University Press, 2008.

Nedelsky, Jennifer. "Law, Boundaries, and the Bounded Self." *Representations* 30 (Spring 1990): 162–89.

Nietzsche, Friedrich. *On the Genealogy of Morality*. Translated by Maudemarie Clark and Alan J. Swensen. Indianapolis: Hackett, 1998.

———. "On the Uses and Disadvantages of History for Life." In *Untimely Meditations*, translated by R. J. Hollingdale and edited by Daniel Breazeale, 59–123. Cambridge: Cambridge University Press, 1997.

———. *"The Twilight of the Idols" and "The Anti-Christ."* Translated by R. J. Hollingdale. Harmondsworth, UK: Penguin, 1990.

———. *The Will to Power*. Translated by Walter Kauffmann and R. J. Hollingdale. New York: Random House, 1969.

Nye, Robert. "Two Capital Punishment Debates in France: 1908 and 1981." *Historical Reflections/Réflexions Historiques* 29, no. 2 (2003): 211–28.

Oksala, Johanna. *Foucault on Freedom*. Cambridge: Cambridge University Press, 2005.

O'Leary, Timothy. *Foucault and the Art of Ethics*. London: Continuum, 2002.

O'Malley, Pat. "The Birth of Biopolitical Justice." In *Re-Reading Foucault: On Law, Power and Rights*, edited by Ben Golder, 151–68. Abingdon, UK: Routledge, 2012.

Pahuja, Sundhya. "Rights as Regulation: The Intersection of Development and Human Rights." In *The Intersection of Rights and Regulation: New Directions in Socio-Legal Scholarship*, edited by Bronwen Morgan, 167–91. Aldershot, UK: Ashgate, 2007.

Paras, Eric. *Foucault 2.0: Beyond Power and Knowledge*. New York: Other Press, 2006.

Pashukanis, Evgeny. "The General Theory of Law and Marxism." In *Pashukanis: Selected Writings on Marxism and Law*, translated by Peter B. Maggs and edited by Piers Beirne and Robert Sharlet, 37–131. London: Academic Press, 1980.

Patton, Paul. "Deleuze and Democracy." *Contemporary Political Theory* 4, no. 4 (2005): 400–413.

———. "Foucault and Normative Political Philosophy." In *Foucault and Philosophy*, edited by Timothy O'Leary and Christopher Falzon, 204–21. Oxford, UK: Wiley-Blackwell, 2010.

———. "Foucault, Critique and Rights." *Critical Horizons* 6, no. 1 (2005): 267–87.

———. "From Resistance to Government: Foucault's Lectures 1976–1979." In *A Companion to Foucault*, edited by Christopher Falzon, Timothy O'Leary, and Jana Sawicki, 172–88. Oxford, UK: Blackwell, 2013.

———. "Historical Normativity and the Basis of Rights." In *Re-Reading Foucault: On Law, Power and Rights*, edited by Ben Golder, 188–206. Abingdon, UK: Routledge, 2012.

———. "Power and Right in Nietzsche and Foucault." *International Studies in Philosophy* 36, no. 3 (2004): 43–61.

Pavlich, George. "Experiencing Critique." *Law & Critique* 16, no. 1 (2005): 95–112.

Pickett, Brent. *On the Use and Abuse of Foucault for Politics.* Oxford, UK: Lexington, 2005.

Poulantzas, Nicos. *State, Power, Socialism.* Translated by Patrick Camiller. London: Verso, 2000.

Prozorov, Sergei. *Foucault, Freedom and Sovereignty.* Aldershot, UK: Ashgate, 2007.

Rabinow, Paul. "Introduction: The History of Systems of Thought." In *Essential Works of Foucault 1954–1984*, vol. 1, *Ethics, Subjectivity and Truth*, translated by Robert Hurley et al. and edited by Paul Rabinow, xi–xlii. Harmondsworth, UK: Allen Lane/Penguin, 1997.

Rabinow, Paul, and Nikolas Rose. "Biopower Today." *BioSocieties* 1, no. 2 (2006): 195–217.

Rancière, Jacques. "Who Is the Subject of the Rights of Man?" *South Atlantic Quarterly* 103, nos. 2–3 (2004): 297–310.

Reid, Julian. "Foucault on Clausewitz: Conceptualizing the Relationship Between War and Power." *Alternatives* 28, no. 1 (2003): 1–28.

———. "The Vulnerable Subject of Liberal War." *South Atlantic Quarterly* 110, no. 3 (2011): 770–79.

Reynolds, Joan M. "'Pragmatic Humanism' in Foucault's Later Work." *Canadian Journal of Political Science* 37, no. 4 (2004): 951–77.

Roach, Tom. *Friendship as a Way of Life: Foucault, AIDS, and the Politics of Shared Estrangement.* Albany, NY: SUNY Press, 2012.

Rorty, Richard. "Human Rights, Rationality, and Sentimentality." In *On Human Rights*, edited by Stephen Shute and Susan L. Hurley, 111–34. New York: Basic Books, 1993.

Rose, Nikolas. "The Death of the Social?: Re-Figuring the Territory of Government." *Economy & Society* 25, no. 3 (1996): 327–56.

Rose, Nikolas, and Peter Miller. "Political Power Beyond the State: Problematics of Government." *British Journal of Sociology* 43, no. 2 (1992): 173–205.

Schabas, William A. "International Law, Politics, Diplomacy and the Abolition of the Death Penalty." *William & Mary Bill of Rights Journal* 13, no. 2 (2004): 417–44.

Schmidt, James, and Thomas E. Wartenburg. "Foucault's Enlightenment: Critique, Revolution, and the Fashioning of the Self." In *Critique and Power: Recasting the Foucault/Habermas Debate*, edited by Michael Kelly, 283–314. Cambridge, MA: MIT Press, 1994.

Scott, Charles E. "Foucault and the Question of Humanism." In *The Question of Humanism: Challenges and Possibilities*, edited by David Goicoechea, John Luik, and Tim Madigan, 205–13. Buffalo, NY: Prometheus, 1991.

Simons, Jon. *Foucault & the Political.* London: Routledge, 1995.

Smart, Barry. *Foucault, Marxism and Critique.* Abingdon, UK: Routledge, 2010.

Smart, Carol. *Feminism and the Power of Law.* London: Routledge, 1989.

Sokhi-Bulley, Bal. "Governing (Through) Rights: Statistics as Technologies of Governmentality." *Social & Legal Studies* 20, no. 2 (2011): 139–55.

———. "Government(ality) by Experts: Human Rights as Governance." *Law & Critique* 22, no. 3 (2011): 251–71.

Spade, Dean. "Laws as Tactics." *Columbia Journal of Gender and Law* 21, no. 2 (2011): 40–71.

Stoler, Ann Laura. *Race and the Education of Desire: Foucault's "History of Sexuality" and the Colonial Order of Things.* Durham, NC: Duke University Press, 1995.

Stone, Brad Elliott. "Defending Society from the Abnormal: The Archaeology of Bio-Power." *Foucault Studies* 1 (2004): 77–91.

Tamanaha, Brian Z. *Law as a Means to an End: Threat to the Rule of Law.* Cambridge: Cambridge University Press, 2006.

Taylor, Diana, and Karen Vintges, eds. *Feminism and the Final Foucault.* Urbana: University of Illinois Press, 2004.

Thomas, Kendall. "Beyond the Privacy Principle." *Columbia Law Review* 92, no. 6 (1992): 1431–516.

Thompson, Kevin. "Forms of Resistance: Foucault on Tactical Reversal and Self-Formation." *Continental Philosophy Review* 36, no. 2 (2003): 113–38.

———. "The Spiritual Disciplines of Biopower." *Radical Philosophy Review* 7, no. 1 (2004): 59–76.

Thurschwell, Adam. "Ethical Exception: Capital Punishment in the Figure of Sovereignty." *South Atlantic Quarterly* 107, no. 3 (2008): 571–96.

Tierney, Thomas F. "The Governmentality of Suicide: Peuchet, Marx, Durkheim, and Foucault." *Journal of Classical Sociology* 10, no. 4 (2010): 357–89.

———. "Suicidal Thoughts: Hobbes, Foucault and the Right to Die." *Philosophy & Social Criticism* 32, no. 5 (2006): 601–38.

Vatter, Miguel. *The Republic of the Living: Biopolitics and the Critique of Civil Society.* New York: Fordham University Press, 2014.

Vergès, Jacques. *De la stratégie judiciaire.* Paris: Éditions de Minuit, 1968.

Veyne, Paul. "Foucault Revolutionizes History." Translated by Catherine Porter. In *Foucault and His Interlocutors*, edited by Arnold I. Davidson, 146–82. Chicago: University of Chicago Press, 1997.

Volpp, Leti. "(Mis)Identifying Culture: Asian Women and the 'Cultural Defense.'" *Harvard Women's Law Journal* 17 (1994): 57–101.

Waldron, Jeremy, ed. *Nonsense on Stilts: Bentham, Burke and Marx on the Rights of Man.* London: Methuen, 1987.

———. "Security and Liberty: The Image of Balance." *Journal of Political Philosophy* 11, no. 2 (2003): 191–210.

Walzer, Michael. "The Politics of Michel Foucault." In *Foucault: A Critical Reader*, edited by David Couzens Hoy, 51–68. Oxford, UK: Blackwell, 1986.

Ward, David. *A Poetics of Resistance: Narrative and the Writings of Pier Paolo Pasolini.* Cranbury, NJ: Associated University Press, 1995.

Warner, Michael. *The Trouble with Normal: Sex, Politics, and the Ethics of Queer Life.* Cambridge, MA: Harvard University Press, 1999.

White, Stephen K. "Foucault's Challenge to Critical Theory." *American Political Science Review* 80, no. 2 (1986): 419–32.

Whyte, Jessica. "Confronting Governments: Human Rights?" In *New Critical Legal*

Thinking: Law and the Political, edited by Matthew Stone, Illan rua Wall, and Costas Douzinas, 11–31. Abingdon, UK: Routledge, 2012.

———. "Is Revolution Desirable?: Michel Foucault on Revolution, Neoliberalism and Rights." In *Re-Reading Foucault: On Law, Power and Rights*, edited by Ben Golder, 207–28. Abingdon, UK: Routledge, 2012.

Widell, Jonathan. "Jacques Vergès, Devil's Advocate: A Psychohistory of Vergès' Judicial Strategy." PhD diss., McGill University, 2012.

Williams, Patricia J. *The Alchemy of Race and Rights*. Cambridge, MA: Harvard University Press, 1991.

Williams, Robert A., Jr. "Taking Rights Aggressively: The Perils and Promise of Critical Legal Theory for Peoples of Color." *Law & Inequality* 5, no. 1 (1987–88): 103–34.

Wolin, Richard. "Foucault's Aesthetic Decisionism." In *Michel Foucault: Critical Assessments*, vol. 3, edited by Barry Smart, 251–65. London: Routledge, 1994.

———. "Foucault the Neohumanist?" *Chronicle of Higher Education*, 1 September 2006, http://chronicle.com/article/Foucault-the-Neohumanist-/23118.

———. "From the 'Death of Man' to Human Rights: The Paradigm Change in French Intellectual Life, 1968–1986." In *The Frankfurt School Revisited, and Other Essays on Politics and Society*, 171–84. New York: Routledge, 2006.

Zetter, Roger. "Labelling Refugees: Forming and Transforming a Bureaucratic Identity." *Journal of Refugee Studies* 4, no. 1 (1991): 39–62.

Zimmerman, Andrew. "Foucault in Berkeley and Magnitogorsk: Totalitarianism and the Limits of Liberal Critique." *Contemporary European History* 23, no. 2 (2014): 225–36.

Zivi, Karen. *Making Rights Claims: A Practice of Democratic Citizenship*. New York: Oxford University Press, 2012.

Žižek, Slavoj. "Against Human Rights." *New Left Review* 35 (July–August 2005): 115–31.

INDEX